THE USE
OF THE BIBLE
IN CHRISTIAN ETHICS

A Constructive Essay

THE USE
OF THE BIBLE
IN CHRISTIAN ETHICS

THOMAS W. OGLETREE

FORTRESS PRESS   PHILADELPHIA

Library of Congress Cataloging in Publication Data

Ogletree, Thomas W.
    The use of the Bible in Christian ethics.

    Bibliography: p.
    Includes indexes.
    1. Christian ethics. 2. Ethics in the Bible.
    3. Bible—Criticism, interpretation, etc. I. Title.
    BJ1275.038 1983   241   83-5489
    ISBN 0-8006-0710-4

K123B83   Printed in the United States of America   1-710

For M. L.

CONTENTS

Preface   xi

1. The Interpretive Task   1

   In Quest of Moral Understanding
   Biblical Scholarship and Christian Ethics

2. Preunderstandings of the Moral Life   15

   Goal-Oriented Actions
       The Intentional Structure of Action
       Consequentialist Ethical Theory

   Human Interactions
       Intersubjectivity
       Deontology in Ethical Theory

   The Formation of the Self
       The Implication of the Self in Action
       Perfectionist Ethical Theory

   The Temporal Horizon of Experience
       The Historicity of Moral Understanding
       The Question of the Meaning of Being

3. Covenant and Commandment: Old Testament
   Understandings of the Moral Life   47

   The Covenantal Context of Moral Obligation

   The Content of Israel's Legal Traditions
       Apodictic Commands and Casuistic
         Regulations
       The Intermixture of Cultic and Social
         Regulations

CONTENTS

The Special Status of the Vulnerable
Exclusiveness

The Struggle for Covenant Fidelity
The Challenge of Canaanite Culture
The Rise of the Monarchy

Prophetic Judgment on Covenantal Infidelity
Israel's Covenant Failure
Structural Bases of Economic Injustice
Eschatological Hopes
The Anthropological Roots of Human Evil
The Universal Lordship of Yahweh

Postexilic Adaptations to the World Empires
A People of the Book
The Emergence of Perfectionist Themes

The Challenge to Moral Understanding in
Israel's Legacy

4. Synoptic Portrayals of Eschatological Existence   87

Discipleship and the Community of Disciples

Gathered Communities and the Legacy of Israel
Mark: The Primacy of the Moral Law
Luke: The Continuing Authority of the
Mosaic Law
Matthew: Law as the Perfection of Love

Social Motifs in Synoptic Thought
The Locus of Institutional Creativity
Matthew: Mercy and Forbearance as a
Basis of Community
Luke: Communal Uses of Possessions

The Challenge to Moral Understanding in the
Synoptic Gospels

5. Revisioning the Bases of Human Life: Paul's Account
of Christian Freedom   135

The Primacy of Promise
Promise as Justification by Faith
The Relation of Law and Promise

CONTENTS

Dying and Rising with Christ
    The Resource for Christian Freedom
    The Model for Christian Obedience

Cultural Pluralism and the Unity of Faith
    The Unity of Jew and Gentile
    Marriage and Household Relations
    The Equality of Women

The Pauline Challenge to Moral Understanding

6. Toward Common Grounds of Understanding   175

    The Eschatological Horizon of Moral
    Understanding
        Futurist and Dialectical Eschatologies
        Social Alienation and Communal
           Commitment
        The Possibility of a Social Witness

    The Modality of Moral Understanding
        Person and Community
        Law and Promise

Selected Bibliography   207

Indexes   213

    Subject Index
    Scripture Index

PREFACE

In recent American scholarship there has been a troublesome gap between biblical studies and Christian ethics. The gap is not an indication of a lack of interest in substantive exchanges between the two specialties. There are biblical scholars who devote considerable energy to ethical questions, and there are students of Christian ethics who are deeply concerned about the rootage of their basic convictions in biblical faith. The gap is a function of a growing complexity in the two fields, both in the range of materials treated and in the methodological refinements devised to deal with them. In fact, biblical studies and Christian ethics, rather than being two easily identifiable specialties, have themselves become loosely connected families of more or less discrete subspecialties. The proliferation of subspecialties considerably broadens and deepens the social stock of knowledge, but it makes the use of such knowledge in constructive interpretations all the more demanding. It is difficult enough for a specialist in the study of the Synoptic Gospels to maintain contact with the leading questions in pentateuchal criticism without also attempting to follow technical discussions in Christian ethics on the relation in policy analysis between normative discourse and the human sciences. Alternatively, persons in Christian ethics who focus on policy questions have scarcely been able to maintain a lively connection with inquiries into the theological foundations of ethics, let alone to assess the respective merits of tradition criticism, redaction criticism, and literary criticism in the study of biblical texts.

Despite the problems involved, the hunger for significant interaction remains. We know intuitively that biblical studies cannot retain their pertinence if they are unable to inform contemporary questions about the good life; we know as well that Christian ethics soon loses its distinctive power if it cuts itself off from its biblical foundations. This study is motivated by the desire to develop more fruitful connections between the two fields of inquiry. More specifically, it is an attempt to examine some of the ramifications of recent biblical scholarship for ethics, aided by the questions, categories, and modes of analysis of contemporary Christian ethics. The aim is not simply to advance a discourse between some scholarly disciplines; it is to enhance our grasp of the moral life by way of a critical engagement with the biblical texts.

In the past fifteen years, there have appeared in American Christian ethics a number of thoughtful essays dealing with methodological problems presented by the use of biblical materials in ethical thought. (Most of these are noted in part 6 of the bibliography.) These studies reflect full awareness of the complexity of interpretation. Specialists in the field are harboring no illusions about the difficulties of appropriating biblical understandings in constructive Christian ethics.

This study itself begins with methodology. Yet one more discussion of method is not likely to be of use to anyone, except perhaps its author. Methodology is fundamental. We must pay careful attention to its problems. However, the field of Christian ethics can now contribute to the interaction between ethical studies and biblical scholarship only by offering something more than reflection on method. We need a sustained examination of the results of biblical scholarship by means of the analytical tools developed within Christian ethics. The questions are essentially two. What can students of Christian ethics make of the results of biblical scholarship? How might those results figure in constructive efforts to interpret the Christian tradition in its bearing on contemporary realities? These questions do not yet take us to a systematic statement of a biblically informed ethic. Their intent is to advance a conversation. They are preparatory to a more comprehensive treatment of Christian ethics. The results to which they lead are poised between biblical scholarship and Christian ethics. Yet by developing linkages between these two sorts of inquiry, they enrich and deepen both.

Work on this project was initiated almost a decade ago when I was on academic leave from Vanderbilt University, studying European phenomenology. My aim was to clarify the interrelations between normative ethics and the social sciences in treatments of human action. Phenomenology can shed much light on this relation; it can also uncover the prereflective bases in the structures of awareness of understandings which figure in our various accounts of the moral life. In both respects phenomenology has much to offer contemporary ethical theory. I suggest some of its possible contributions in the second chapter of this book. Phenomenology, however, is no less pertinent in helping us grasp what is involved in the activity of interpreting, particularly when interpreting is associated with the mediation and appropriation of normative traditions. Phenomenology was not initially a hermeneutical discipline; but it soon opened up hermeneutical questions in a new manner. It made us aware of the fact that interpretation is a constituent in our most elemental way of being in the world, and not simply in our self-conscious attempts to make sense of texts. In this respect as well, phenomenology serves attempts to develop the connections between biblical studies and Christian ethics. The work as a whole is guided by a hermeneutic based on phenomenological investigations.

Not all readers will have an interest in the relatively technical scholarship which appears in chapter 2. Such readers may wish to turn directly to the discussion of biblical materials in chapters 3, 4, and 5. These chapters are, I believe, intelligible on their own terms. Yet the discussion in chapters 1 and 2 does make explicit the assumptions and critical principles which inform the reading of the biblical texts which follows. In this respect it is an essential part of the presentation as a whole.

The actual engagement with mid-twentieth-century biblical scholarship was facilitated by a faculty inquiry group at Vanderbilt University which devoted itself to the interrelationships of religious ethics and biblical studies. The group met regularly over a three-year period, sharing research in progress and reflecting on problems of substance and method that bear upon historical and contemporary conceptions of the moral life. I have a deep indebtedness to that group. It enabled me to make some appropriate selections in materials to be examined, and it also provided me with an opportunity to test some of my initial readings of those materials. Biblical scholars in the group included Walter Harrelson, James Crenshaw, Douglas Knight, and Daniel Patte, with occasional participation by Lou Silberman, John Donahue, and Gerd Lüdemann. Peter Paris, Howard Harrod, and I were the so-called specialists in religious ethics. I must offer particular thanks to Walter Harrelson, Peter Paris, and Howard Harrod, all of whom read earlier drafts of portions of the manuscript, offering encouragement and helpful suggestions.

Since moving to the Theological School of Drew University, I have found stimulating new colleagues who share my interest in the interface between ethics and biblical scholarship, especially Tom Oden, Ed Long, and Neill Hamilton, all of whom examined completed portions of the manuscript as it was moving toward its final form. Darrell Doughty was a helpful conversation partner as I sought to organize my discussion of Paul.

One can never adequately acknowledge all one's debts to the community of scholars. The numbers involved are too large and the occasions too numerous. Yet I must take note of the stimulus I have received from Stanley Hauerwas. He emphasized the importance of pushing beyond methodology and venturing particular interpretations of biblical materials, placing such an effort ahead of further work on technical problems in the field.

The preparation of a finished manuscript is itself a laborious task. How difficult it is to achieve accuracy and a measure of uniformity in putting a book together! My work in this regard has been much less tedious because of the able assistance of Kathy Bueker. Her alertness, her conscientious care, her general knowledge of appropriate scholarly forms, and above all, her cheerfulness in incorporating revisions of revisions into the typed manuscript have helped immeasurably.

The academic leave to study phenomenology was funded by a

Cross-Disciplinary grant from the Society for Values in Higher Education. Subsequent summers of research and writing were subsidized by successive grants from the University Research Council of Vanderbilt University. I began actually writing in the summer of 1980, residing at Westminster College in Cambridge, England. I was granted the privilege of working in the faculty room of the College, enjoying the hospitality of the Principal and his wife, the Rev. Martin Cressey and Dr. Pamela Cressey.

The book is dedicated to my wife, Mary-Lynn Ogletree. She is herself a student of the Scripture in her capacities as preacher, liturgist, and teacher. The former Associate Chaplain at Vanderbilt University, she is now claiming a sabbatical from professional activities to enter fully into the joys and challenges of motherhood. Our son, Tommy, is not the only beneficiary of her leave, however. In the process she has given me a level of backup support that active professionals are normally unable to provide their spouses. That support accounts for the fact that the book is coming out now rather than one or two years later.

Thomas W. Ogletree
Madison, New Jersey

THE USE
OF THE BIBLE
IN CHRISTIAN ETHICS

1

THE INTERPRETIVE TASK

The aim of ethical inquiry is to understand moral experience, not simply as a given, but with reference to human potentialities. Human potentialities are essential features of moral experience. They show themselves in the choices we make, in the priorities we set, and in the commitments which govern the investment of our resources and energies. Since potentiality belongs to moral experience, ethics can never be purely descriptive of patterns of life already in place. It must finally undertake normative proposals of human ways of being and acting in the world.

IN QUEST OF MORAL UNDERSTANDING

If we turn to the Bible in our ethical inquiries, it is because we believe that it can disclose something important about moral experience. The interest in the Bible is not simply historical, the attempt to re-present moral notions which are characteristic of an ancient cultural totality, for the sake, let us say, of an enlarged consciousness of the origins of our own culture. It is existential, the concern to make sense of the moral life in relation to possibilities opening up in our own setting. It is for the sake of truth and goodness that we turn to the Bible.

In directing our attention to the Bible in this fashion, we presume that it has something to say to us that we do not already know. On this presumption we dare to place our own convictions at risk in our reading of the biblical texts. Such receptivity to the world of the Bible does not in itself imply any dogma of biblical authority. It requires no more than the recognition of a phenomenon: that the biblical texts have in the course of our history been able to prove themselves over and over as saying something true. They represent that Hans-Georg Gadamer identifies as the classical, that is, "that which speaks in such a way that it is not a statement about what is past, a mere testimony to something that still needs to be interpreted, but says something to the present as if it were said specifically to it."[1] The classical fuses past and present. In so doing it discloses our historicity. It shows us that to understand is to situate oneself in a movement of tradition within which past and present constantly flow into each other.

If the Bible is to serve understanding, we cannot view it solely as a document from the past, still less as one whose meaning can be exhausted by strictly historical reconstructions. Such reconstructions are relevant for understanding. The Bible is, after all, made up of human documents written in the past against a background of quite different social and cultural milieus. To deal with it properly, we must keep its historical situatedness clearly in view. Even so, its meaning is not reducible to the conscious intentions of its authors in the original situations of production, nor to the senses it had for its initial readers. In becoming texts the biblical materials (as any texts) take on a life of their own which escapes the subjectivity of their authors and their first readers.[2] There is a surplus of meaning in texts beyond what is explicitly uttered. This surplus stems from that about which the texts speak. It is this subject matter which offers the possibility of a common ground for understanding between authors and interpreters.

Interpretation, therefore, does not consist simply in the exposition of original meanings. It finally involves an enlargement of the understanding of the interpreter concerning that about which the texts speak as a result of an encounter with the texts. In fact, if we do not reach this level of understanding, we cannot have much confidence that we have grasped what the texts are saying even in their original settings.

Gadamer proposes that we think of interpreting as a discourse with texts, analogous to the questioning and answering of a conversation.[3] Following R. G. Collingwood, he contends that we cannot comprehend what texts are saying until we discover the questions to which they offer themselves as answers. If the uncovering of these questions is to involve us, however, the questions cannot be treated as matters of significance only for other persons in some past time. They must express our own questions as well. Interpretation requires us to formulate the questions lying behind the texts in ways that are also real for us. A real question is one capable of shaking the hold of our taken-for-granted opinions. It is a question which places our own opinions in question. It opens up a region of ignorance, of not knowing, without which genuine inquiry would not be possible.

We begin our discourse with texts from within our own life situations. These situations involve meaning horizons which differ from those of the texts, even when the texts have already had considerable impact on our perceptions and our thoughts. The aim of the discourse is to realize a "fusion" of the two meaning horizons (Gadamer), our own and that of the texts. It is to reach a shared understanding of the subject matter which provides the common ground between the texts and our own inquiries.[4]

Such a shared understanding will be a new creation, a work of the productive imagination of the interpreter. It will raise what the texts are saying to a higher level of generality, one capable of expressing the interpreter's own sense of the truth. To capture what the texts are saying, we cannot simply repeat or paraphrase their explicit utterances. The language used in those utterances is no longer sustained by a concrete, human world. We must rather generate new utterances, new accounts of the subject matter of the texts, which also make sense to us. Here we come up against a basic paradox: to say the same thing as the texts, we must say something different, for that "same" thing can live again only if it is expressed in a way that is suited to the different reality within which we live. Insofar as we are able to accomplish this suitability, we will have realized the interpretive fusion of horizons.

We move toward this fusion of horizons by making explicit our own preunderstandings of the subject matter of the texts. By means of these preunderstandings, we venture reconstructions of the questions to which the texts under study can be read as answers. The

3

preunderstandings cannot remain unchallenged in the encounter with the texts, at least not if new understandings are to be gained. Their function is to establish a basis for taking up a conversation with the texts. We must, in turn, subject the preunderstandings themselves to questioning in terms of what the texts say. We must be prepared to modify them in light of this questioning, until we are able to give them a form which links us to the meanings uttered in the texts. In the process we grant to the texts the power to open up and transform our understanding of the matter under inquiry.

The task of this study is to venture formulations of the moral life which are congruent with central features of biblical faith. The formulations are offered as possible ways of gaining provisional closure on a substantive discourse between what the biblical texts are saying about the moral life and the presumptions and questions of contemporary ethical reflection. They will emerge as the outcome of three distinct yet interrelated stages of interpretation: an explicit account of salient preunderstandings of the moral life; a reconstruction of pivotal themes of biblical faith, ordered with reference to those preunderstandings; and constructive suggestions toward a "fusion" in contemporary life and thought of these two worlds of meaning.

Initially, I will sketch certain preunderstandings of the moral life which might help us discern the questions to which biblical texts can be read as answers. This sketch reflects a constructive ethical theory which is still in the process of development. The theory is based upon materials generated by phenomenological studies of the life world. The moral import of these studies will be made explicit under the guidance of three dominant conceptualizations of the moral life in Western thought. Various names are used to characterize these conceptions and they are formulated in variant ways, some more cogent and persuasive than others. I shall refer to them as consequentialist, deontological, and perfectionist perspectives.

These three perspectives have all found strong philosophical statement and defense in modern thought. Yet their significance is not simply philosophical. They have persisting importance in treatments of ethics because of their relative success in articulating elemental

4

facets of concrete moral experience. No less important, they have been institutionalized in particular arenas of modern social life, and they tend to function as the implicit ethic of human sciences which attend respectively to those arenas. I shall suggest in passing some of these latter connections in the course of my exposition. My primary interest, however, is to display in the structures that make up the life world the experiential bases of these three ethical perspectives. The accomplishments of the phenomenological movement fund that undertaking.

As will become apparent, I do not identify my own view with any of the perspectives already cited. I seek a theory which encompasses them all, locating them in a framework of thought which grants preeminence to human historicity. Following Gibson Winter, I shall label this view "historical contextualism."[5] Highlighting the historicity of existence not only permits us to see the essential interconnections among the facets of experience singled out in consequentialist, deontological, and perfectionist perspectives; it also enables us to discern the fundamental import of the interpretive task which makes up the central subject matter of this essay. In this respect it is a promising resource for preunderstandings which can equip us to engage the biblical texts in a discourse about the moral life.

The preunderstandings I shall delineate are by no means everyday prereflective understandings. They represent fairly advanced stages of thinking about the moral life. Nor has my treatment of them been worked out in isolation from biblical faith itself. In unfolding their meaning and significance I already have in view the distinctiveness of the world of the Bible. Given the role of the Bible in Western civilization, almost any of our moral notions will reflect its impact in some fashion. To its direct influence must be added the interpretive accomplishments of many predecessors, especially the great teachers of the church, and those who have contributed to the mediation of biblical faith in the practical ordering of human life. Nonetheless, the sketch I will offer still belongs under the rubric of preunderstandings. It attempts to make explicit some of our implicit understandings of moral experience; and its purpose is to orient us to the retrieval of biblical convictions about the moral life. In addition to evaluating its relative adequacy as a work of description, therefore, it is appropriate to assess its fruitfulness in giving us access to what the biblical texts are saying in the contexts of their original production. The final aim is to open up fresh understandings of human possibilities for being and acting in the world. In particular it is to uncover and set forth what biblical faith has to teach us about those possibilities.

BIBLICAL SCHOLARSHIP AND
CHRISTIAN ETHICS

The second stage of interpretation will consist in a re-presentation of classic biblical themes as they relate to moral understanding. In developing these themes, I will draw upon recent biblical scholarship, especially scholarship embodying or depending upon form and tradition criticism. In regard to Old Testament texts, the accomplishments of Martin Noth and Gerhard von Rad will be the central resource. For the New Testament, the studies that presuppose and build upon the work of Rudolf Bultmann, moving to and including the more recent redaction criticism, will occupy an analogous position.[6]

Traditio-historical studies are especially pertinent for Christian ethics. To begin with, their methods of interpretation keep in the forefront of attention the "life situations" which shaped the production, development, and transformation of materials found in the biblical texts. Consideration of the life situations of texts leads naturally to systematic treatments of the social worlds of ancient Israel and early Christianity and the role these worlds played in the formation of biblical understandings.[7] Insofar as these understandings express possibilities which hover before all determinant historical realities, they must be examined with their underlying social settings and institutional arrangements in view. It is as ingredients in the specific historical struggles of particular groups of human beings that they are of interest to the student of ethics, and it is in connection with similar struggles within contemporary life and society that we seek to apprehend their ongoing import.

This point of view does not imply a reduction of religious and moral notions to social processes. Such notions are not mere func-

6

tions of economic, social, and political forces. They have a shaping power of their own in the concrete life worlds of human beings. They impede and block certain kinds of developments which might otherwise be ready-to-hand as possibilities; they facilitate and reinforce others, virtually assuring their success. Even so, they do not operate in sovereign independence of the social forces at work in human affairs. In fact, their import is all the greater when they embody critical insight into the power of those forces to mold our perceptions and understandings. Apart from such insight, they are always in danger of serving as ideological cover for destructive and oppressive social patterns, or as utopian fantasies which provide little more than illusory compensation for a virtually intolerable existence.[8]

My own appropriation of biblical understandings will not be worked out fully in social and political terms, though I consider such a task to be a necessary undertaking. As has already been indicated, I am here seeking to display our essential connection with what the biblical texts are saying by means of the constitutive structures of the life world. These structures are more elemental than social, economic, and political arrangements as such. In fact, they order such arrangements as possible ways of forming a human world. Because they are more elemental, they can enable a discourse with texts initially produced in institutional settings quite different from our own. That discourse, provided it is productive, can in turn stimulate the kind of imaginative reconstruction of thought and practice that is needed if we are to deal critically with our own social existence. The key point here is that tradition criticism, by attending to the life situations underlying the transmission of traditions, provides data of particular interest to a hermeneutic governed by a life-world perspective.

The traditio-historical school is also of special importance to Christian ethics because it has been informed by significant theological interests. It is self-conscious about the hermeneutic problem. As I hope to make clear, an account of life-world structures furthers this theological interest. It enables us to thematize the religious dimensions of moral awareness in a fashion that puts us in critical contact with concerns addressed by the biblical texts. In this respect also it is in continuity with form and tradition criticism.

Many of the bolder generalizations of the traditio-historical school have in recent years been subjected to considerable criticism.[9] Scholars are calling attention to the ambiguity of the historical and textual data upon which those generalizations are based; and they are examining more closely features of the texts which were obscured or passed over by these seminal thinkers. I cannot see, however, that their accomplishments have yet been displaced by fundamentally different paradigms of interpretation, at least not any which bear comparable promise for the ethical appropriation of biblical understandings. What is called for is greater caution in making use of these generalizations, and fuller awareness of alternative ways of reconstructing the relevant history.

The accent on tradition history does not rule out attempts to grasp the meaning and import of the Bible as a completed work, for example, as the sacred Scriptures of Jewish and Christian communities. In this connection particular note might be taken of Brevard Childs's *Introduction to the Old Testament as Scripture.* Childs dramatizes the limitations of current modes of Old Testament study, including the Noth–von Rad consensus. He calls for a paradigm shift which centers in the recognition that the Hebrew Bible is of interest chiefly because it has functioned as sacred Scripture for Jewish and Christian communities. Rather than stressing the formation and mediation of Israel's historical traditions, he emphasizes the "canonical shaping" of the biblical texts. In keeping with this emphasis he grants preeminence to the final redactions of the biblical texts in a fashion that is not characteristic of earlier critical scholarship. The question is: how did the canonical status of biblical documents contribute to their composition? and what implications does that status have for the way we interpret them? Childs is not suggesting that we set aside attempts to reconstruct the history behind the present form of the biblical texts. His main interest is to subordinate historical reconstructions to the canonical orientation he commends.[10]

Childs's undertaking is legitimate insofar as we keep in view that the canonical shaping of the biblical texts is only one moment in the formation and transmission of the living traditions of a con-

8

crete human community. It is by no means the final moment, as Childs himself reminds us, for a history of exegesis follows which has its own extraordinary complexity; nor is it necessarily the most important moment. Indeed, once the Bible takes on the status of Scripture, the history it recalls ceases to be a living, open history. That history is idealized, and the texts which attest it are cut loose from its concreteness and specificity. "It is constitutive of the canon," Childs notes, "to seek to transmit the tradition in such a way as to prevent its being moored in the past."[11]

The problem is that tradition so understood tends to become a timeless deposit which floats above the ambiguous, historical struggles of human beings. As should be clear, my own approach to the Bible is governed by the conviction that the significance of the biblical texts cannot be confined to the past, to the original intentions of their authors, or to the intial contexts of their production. Yet it is precisely as moored in a particular history that they provide resources to help us deal with the quite particular history in which we presently find ourselves situated. In this respect reconstructions of the pilgrimages of the ancient Israelites and the early Christians contribute substantively to our interpretation and appropriation of what the texts of the Bible are saying.

How we assess Childs's proposal probably depends in the final analysis upon our view of the status of Scripture in contemporary communities of faith. Persons who see the Scripture principle as constitutive of such communities are apt to find in Childs's approach the most appropriate key to the meaning of the biblical texts. In general, his work accords with postcritical attempts to restore classic Jewish and Christian understandings of biblical authority. ("Israel defined itself in terms of a book," Childs contends.)[12] For those who have ceased to think in canonical terms of the traditioning processes which sustain communal life, however, Childs's work may bring to the fore the least interesting phase in the formation and transmission of the biblical texts. (This point would not hold as strongly for New Testament books since the history which underlies them is not nearly so extensive.) It is chiefly by restoring the lively connection of the texts with realities in the life worlds of concrete human communities that their import for contemporary moral

9

understanding is most clearly manifest. This latter position involves, of course, a critical reformulation of Christian attitudes toward the Bible on the basis of modern historical thinking.

Analogous comments might be made about the use of literary criticism in studies of biblical texts. Such criticism directs us to the texts as completed works having an integrity of their own. It helps us appreciate the unity of form and content in the constitution and mediation of meaning. It disciplines us to read carefully what appears as it appears. In particular it challenges the tendency of earlier scholarship to see texts principally as evidence for possible reconstructions of an underlying social and literary history.[13]

The semiotic accent on the deep structure of the text serves a similar end. It shows us how to complement our surface readings of texts with attention to their preconscious impact on understanding, an impact which is a function of structural features in the text.[14] In both cases we are encouraged to work with the extant forms of the texts.

As an aspect of biblical interpretation, these emphases also are sound and important. The Bible is literature. As such it requires literary analysis and interpretation. In fact, literary studies may help us locate those problematic features of texts which call for historical explanations of various kinds. Even so, the meaning of the Bible is not in the final analysis strictly literary; it is historical and existential. It does not concern imaginatively constructed worlds of meaning, but actual social and historical existence in the full scope of its moral and religious significance. Insofar as literary criticism becomes a more or less self-sufficient approach to the texts, its effect too is to idealize them and to abstract them from their social and historical matrix. Such idealism obscures the deep involvement of our ideas with the social, economic, and political bases of our worldly existence. It is precisely the latter which form and tradition criticism permit us to thematize and bring explicitly into view. As a result, these methods hold special interest for an appropriation of biblical understandings into Christian ethics.

In a brief study one cannot, of course, do justice to the full range of biblical materials. They cover too much history, are too diverse in form and content, and in many cases reflect lengthy periods of development. In discussing the Old Testament I will concentrate on the Pentateuch, especially its legal traditions, and on the eighth-and seventh-century (B.C.E.) literary prophets. References to other texts will serve chiefly to highlight — perhaps by way of contrast — what is contained in these materials. In the New Testament, I will focus on the Synoptic Gospels and the Pauline corpus, with only occasional references to other texts.

This selection is not simply arbitrary. It represents a judgment concerning what is most distinctive and interesting about the Bible so far as contemporary Christian ethics is concerned. In these materials we find the most significant challenges to the conventional wisdom of contemporary society and culture. The judgment is in some respects personal, though it is capable, I believe, of a reasoned defense; and in some respects it accords with much actual usage in the long history of Jewish and Christian communities. Even so, the discussion which follows is in no way dependent on the judiciousness of this selection. The primary aim is to set forth an approach and a set of hermeneutical understandings for utilizing biblical materials in Christian ethics. It is, moreover, to test the fruitfulness of that approach in relation to a selected set of themes which are widely recognized to have importance in the Bible.

The Old Testament materials will be set forth under the heading, "Covenant and Commandment," and New Testament materials, in terms of "Eschatology and Community." In part I shall attend to the Old Testament on its own terms, as a complete way of understanding in itself. Yet I shall also highlight the emergence of motifs which subsequently enjoy central importance in the New Testament writings. In this respect I shall deal with the Old and New Testaments as discrete elements in one basic orientation to moral existence, in accord with classical Christian presuppositions. I shall presume a certain thematic unity to the biblical witness, though, I hope, not one which is reductive of its rich diversity. The intent is not to belittle the diversity which is found in the Bible; it is to show how that diversity is ordered around some shared understandings of a fundamental sort. The diversity, thus, is not sheer multiplicity, but a set of variations, counterpoints, even discordant oppositions, which are bound up with certain shared convictions. Indeed, the unity of the Bible finally resides more in the unfolding identity of a people, and of a church arising in relation

11

to that people, than in particular themes, beliefs, or ways of thinking as such. My interest is to articulate the complexity of biblical understandings in a fashion which, nonetheless, has determinate shape, and hence, critical power.

The final task is to suggest constructive appropriations in Christian ethics of the moral understandings uncovered in the biblical texts. Interpretations which are suitable cannot merely accommodate biblical modes of life and thought to modern ones. Indeed, they will reflect insight into the relativity, provisionality, ambiguity, even dubiousness of our own presumed truths and values. They will presuppose receptivity to instruction on these most basic matters. On the other hand, they cannot involve a suspension of belief in what we genuinely take to be true and good. They do not in any sense call for a sacrifice of either intellect or conscience. They rather consist in a set of formulations which display our essential unity with the biblical texts, which effect a fusion of horizons of the biblical world and our own life world. Such formulations require boldness and imagination in stating anew what is at stake in biblical understandings, surpassing biblical utterances as such and attaining a level of generality capable of addressing our own sense of reality.

This last portion of the study will be relatively brief. It will primarily make explicit notions emerging throughout the exposition. From the beginning the first two stages of interpretation will be oriented to the third. A fuller and more complete explication of the third phase of interpretation would involve nothing short of a systematic account of the constitutive themes of Christian ethics, an undertaking which must await a later day. I shall be content, however, if the study as a whole provides a stimulus to further reflection on the use of the Bible in Christian ethics.[15]

NOTES

1. Hans-Georg Gadamer, *Truth and Method* (New York: Seabury Press, 1975), 257.
2. On this point see particularly Paul Ricoeur's account of the semantic autonomy of texts in his *Interpretation Theory* (Fort Worth: Texas Christian University Press, 1976), 25–44.

3. Cf. Gadamer, *Truth and Method*, 333–41.

4. Ibid., 258.

5. Cf. Gibson Winter, *Elements for a Social Ethic: Scientific and Ethical Perspectives on Social Process* (New York: Macmillan Co., 1966), 244.

6. Of special importance are Martin Noth, *The Laws in the Pentateuch and Other Studies* (Philadelphia: Fortress Press, 1966); Gerhard von Rad, *The Problem of the Hexateuch and Other Essays* (New York: McGraw-Hill, 1966) and *Old Testament Theology*, 2 vols. (New York: Harper & Row, 1962, 1965). For work in redaction criticism, attention is called to James M. Robinson, *The Problem of History in Mark and Other Marcan Studies* (Philadelphia: Fortress Press, 1982); Norman Perrin, *What Is Redaction Criticism?* (Philadelphia: Fortress Press, 1969); Willi Marxsen, *Mark the Evangelist* (Nashville: Abingdon Press, 1969); Günther Bornkamm, Gerhard Barth, and H. J. Held, *Tradition and Interpretation in Matthew* (Philadelphia: Westminster Press, 1963); Hans Conzelmann, *The Theology of St. Luke* (Philadelphia: Fortress Press, 1982); Jacob Jervell, *Luke and the People of God, A New Look at Luke-Acts* (Minneapolis: Augsburg Pub. House, 1972); and Luke T. Johnson, *The Literary Function of Possessions in Luke-Acts* (Missoula, Mont.; Scholars Press, 1977). Special mention should be made of three studies by Victor Paul Furnish: *Theology and Ethics in Paul, The Love Command in the New Testament,* and *The Moral Teaching of Paul: Selected Issues* (Nashville: Abingdon Press, 1968, 1972, and 1979 respectively). Finally, J. Christiaan Beker, in *Paul the Apostle: The Triumph of God in Life and Thought* (Philadelphia: Fortress Press, 1980), has been most helpful in suggesting a way to order the discussion of Paul's moral understandings. For useful secondary literature, see Douglas A. Knight, *Rediscovering the Traditions of Israel: The Development of the Traditio-Historical Research of the Old Testament, with Special Consideration of Scandinavian Contributions,* Society of Biblical Literature Dissertation Series 9 (Missoula, Mont.: Scholars Press, 1976); Douglas A. Knight, ed., *Tradition and Theology in the Old Testament* (Philadelphia: Fortress Press, 1977); and James L. Crenshaw, *Gerhard von Rad* (Waco, Tex.: Word Books, 1978).

7. See in particular Norman K. Gottwald, *The Tribes of Yahweh* (Maryknoll, N.Y.: Orbis Books, 1979), and John G. Gager, *Kingdom and Community: The Social World of Early Christianity* (Englewood Cliffs, N.J.: Prentice-Hall, 1975). Gager, for the most part, maintains fairly strictly a stance of sociological explanation in discussing the emergence and eventual social and cultural success of Christianity. Gottwald's study is more clearly informed by a theological interest in the liberating promise of ancient Israelite faith. See esp. 700–706.

8. The view of the relation between moral and religious ideas and social forces which informs my work can be found in Ernst Troeltsch's introduction to his monumental *Social Teaching of the Christian Churches*, Eng.

13

trans. Olive Wyon, Harper Torchbooks (New York: Harper & Row, 1960), 1:27–34. Troeltsch's work draws upon the sociological theory of Max Weber, but unlike Weber, he gives central place to the task of mediating constructively our moral and religious traditions.

9. For a discussion of some of the relevant literature, see Brevard S. Childs, *Introduction to the Old Testament as Scripture* (Philadelphia: Fortress Press, 1979), 125–27.

10. Ibid., 72–79.

11. Ibid., 79.

12. Ibid., 78.

13. For a good example of literary criticism, see James L. Crenshaw, *Samson: A Secret Betrayed, A Vow Ignored* (Atlanta: John Knox Press, 1978). Crenshaw is sensitive to the limits of literary criticism, though he makes skillful use of it. See also Mary Ann Tolbert, *Perspectives on the Parables: An Approach to Multiple Interpretations* (Philadelphia: Fortress Press, 1979).

14. For a discussion of structuralism in biblical interpretation, see Daniel Patte, *What Is Structural Exegesis?* (Philadelphia: Fortress Press, 1976).

15. Special note should be taken of the helpful book by Bruce C. Birch and Larry L. Rasmussen, *Bible and Ethics in the Christian Life* (Minneapolis: Augsburg Pub. House, 1976). I see my own work as a continuation of their important contribution. Where my work differs, it is chiefly that I have undertaken a more comprehensive account of the moral life and have looked in greater detail at the major strands of biblical tradition.

2

PREUNDERSTANDINGS OF THE MORAL LIFE

As we undertake a critical engagement with the Bible on the nature of moral experience, our first task is to gain greater self-awareness about our own taken-for-granted beliefs and convictions. In questioning the Bible about its moral understandings, or in seeking to uncover the questions to which it presents itself as an answer, what do we conceive the subject matter of the inquiry to be? What preunderstandings guide it? What presuppositions govern our angle of vision on it? What are the bases for these preunderstandings? How sound are they? It may, of course, turn out that the Bible has little or no interest in what we take to be the crucial moral issues, that it is in fact preoccupied with matters of a quite different sort. If so, then a profound discourse with the Bible on the nature of the moral life will not materialize at all. Yet we proceed with the presumption that what we are asking and what the biblical texts are saying will intersect productively in some fashion, though perhaps not exactly as we initially suppose. We prepare ourselves for testing this presumption by reminding ourselves of some of our own ways of thinking about the subject matter which brings us to the biblical texts. In the course of the inquiry these ways of thinking will themselves be at risk in the encounter with those texts, all in the interest of arriving at understandings which appear more profound, more true, more suited to our human reality. Nonetheless, our preunderstandings initially orient and guide our investigation.

Even at this stage we confront profound difficulties. Amid the plurality of modern cultures, it is apparent that we do not hold in common many important preunderstandings about the moral life, and those which function significantly in our individual perspectives may not be particularly clear. Our preunderstandings lack precise, coherent, and public articulation. At first glance this circumstance may appear to be an advantage. If nothing is particularly certain about the moral life in contemporary experience, then we may be more open to whatever the biblical texts may have to say, at least as candidates for attention. Unfortunately, this happy plurality tends to conceal the debilitating presumption that whatever morality might be, it has little basis other than social convention, or perhaps the idiosyncratic preferences of this or that individual. To deal effectively with what the biblical texts have to say about the moral life, we must first address the plurality of views in our own intellectual context. We must place ourselves in relation to thoughtful discussions of the moral life at play in contemporary culture, assessing them critically and assimilating them to frames of reference which enjoy the accent of reality in our own experience.

For the purposes of the present study, I shall develop an account of the moral life which reflects a critical consideration of three dominant conceptions of the moral life in modern Western thought. I have in view consequentialist, deontological, and perfectionist perspectives. Consequentialist thought is represented by the utilitarian commitment to promote the "greatest happiness of the greatest number"; it embraces as well the meliorist emphasis in American pragmatism: the continual, incremental improvement of the overall conditions of human life. Deontological views are generally associated with Immanuel Kant and with the neo-Kantian insistence on the clarity, consistency, publicness, and universality of moral principles. I shall include among such views, however, any perspectives which seek to identify and formulate the duties, both negative and positive, which are requisite to human social existence. Perfectionism takes us back to Aristotle's interest in the cultivation of those excellencies (virtues) which actualize human potential. It also finds expression, albeit in a quite different form, in Friedrich Nietzsche's vision of *Übermensch*, an ecstatic celebration of human powers of

16

self-transcendence. In general its focus is on perfecting human powers and on creating social conditions which facilitate such perfection.

As I have indicated, I do not consider any of these conceptions to be adequate, taken separately. What we require is a synthesis of the three determined by the temporal horizon of experience. It is in terms of the structures and dynamics of human historicity that the dominant conceptions gain their significance. Thus, the pre-understandings of the moral life which govern this study take the form of historical contextualism. Ernst Troeltsch has given this point of view its most comprehensive and forceful treatment,[1] though it has roots as well in the philosophical accomplishment of G. F. W. Hegel. More recently it has found expression in H. Richard Niebuhr's account of an ethics of responsibility and in Gibson Winter's foundational work in social ethics. It underlies a good deal of recent liberation thought, including thought which occupies itself with the critical retrieval of the deeper and richer traditions which belong to the American civil religion. The importance for ethics of the phenomenological movement is that it offers resources for placing this general orientation on a sounder theoretical footing.

With the exception of Aristotelian perfectionism, the classic formulations of the three dominant conceptions of the moral life originated in the Enlightenment. In fact, Troeltsch's own form of historical consciousness itself reflects the impact of the Enlightenment on human thought. Insofar as abstract uses of reason determine the practical operation of these conceptions, whether the formal accent is on universalizability, or the rational calculation of the fit between means and ends, they probably cannot enter into a fruitful conversation with biblical texts. In their Enlightenment and post-Enlightenment forms, these views of morality set forth an autonomous reason sufficient unto itself as the basis of the moral life. Autonomous reason has no need of what ancient texts may have to say, especially those that do not equate moral understanding with rational choice or with practical reason. To be sure, even in highly rational models of moral understanding one can inquire into the religious grounding of moral sensitivities and concerns. Such grounding will doubtless have motivational significance for par-

17

ticular human actors. The Bible may have relevance for these facets of moral experience. But moral understanding in the strict sense remains beyond the need of biblical instruction, having achieved its full self-sufficiency.[2]

More is going on, however, in these three conceptualizations of the moral life than comes to light in their highly rational formulations. They have a persistence in human thought because they are rooted in fundamental structures which order our being in the world as human beings. In fact, they can properly be viewed as specific articulations of possibilities present in these fundamental structures. Rather than expounding critically their classical expressions and their more important contemporary modifications, therefore, I will direct attention to the underlying structures on which they are founded.

In this undertaking I will be guided by phenomenological descriptions of constitutive features of our worldly being, especially intentionality and intersubjectivity, and the implication of the self in these two basic structures. Reference will also be made to embodiment, especially in relation to the selfhood of the moral actor. Finally, an account of temporality will highlight the larger meaning horizon which gives unity and significance to these basic structures and the modes of understanding they bear.[3] It is chiefly the temporal structure of experience which leads us to seek a synthesis of the dominant models of moral understanding on the basis of historical contextualism.

The task is to display the ways in which the various accounts of morality reside in structures which provide the conditions for the kinds of experiences we in fact have. If this account succeeds in uncovering something which is fundamental in moral experience, it will provide a basis for approaching the biblical texts which can enable their understandings to inform and transform the horizons of meaning which encompass our own orientations to the world.

GOAL-ORIENTED ACTIONS

The Intentional Structure of Action

Consequentialist theories of the moral life presuppose and articulate the intentional structure of human action. In phenomenology *intentionality* does not refer in the first instance to conscious purposes, to what we have in mind to do. It refers to the prereflective orientation of consciousness to the diverse forms of sense which present the world and its realities to awareness. It indicates that consciousness is always "conscious of . . . something," and that the modalities of sense which appear are correlative to corresponding consciousness acts.[4]

Where action is the theme, the intended meanings of interest are organized as projects and as deeds which implement them. Action embraces the distinction and the relation of project and deed.[5] A project is an image or conception of an action which I am entertaining as a possibility for myself, one that is within my power to accomplish. It is correlative to deciding and to deliberation on the grounds of deciding. A deed involves bodily movement, an actual, material intervention in the ongoing course of worldly events. It has enduring consequences for subsequent developments.

A deed is made up of a complex array of meanings of various kinds: sense percepts which convey salient aspects of the world, bodily sensations announcing sensible contact with worldly realities, kinesthetic feelings associated with bodily movement.[6] The meanings of primary importance in the deed, however, are those indicating that the project to which I previously committed myself is on the way to realization. The deed refers itself, that is, to the project which initially set it in motion. Insofar as the meanings which make up the concrete reality of the deed fulfill the expectations belonging to the project, I know the deed as my own, as something brought into being by my own initiatives.[7] Of course, my expectations are not infrequently disappointed, especially when my projects depart significantly from familiar, highly routinized actions. These disappointments signal how little I am able to grasp the almost indefinite array of variables at play in worldly happenings. Even less am I able to predict and control what follows from my deeds, especially in the responses of others to them.

Actions involve values. We adopt projects because of the values we expect to promote or protect by means of them. Values supply the essential content of our reasons for committing ourselves to our chosen projects. They enable us to justify our actions to ourselves and others. To decide upon a course of action is, then, to decide upon the values to be honored and served in a particular situation.

19

The values in question may be only implicit, elements in realities concretely experienced as good. Here we must distinguish goods and values.[8] Goods are objects, processes, relations, and states of affairs which we find to be desirable on the basis of the positive affects which accompany our experience of them. Values have an ideal status vis-à-vis concrete goods. They articulate what is good about concrete realities. They permit us to interpret the significance of the positive affects which accompany our experience of those goods. Insofar as values become explicit, they figure prominently in our attempts to express the overall meaning of our worldly being. They specify what we have come to acknowledge as desirable, as worthy of the investment of our energies, indeed, in some cases, of our devotion.

In our ordinary activities we generally do not thematize the values which are involved in our projects. They remain implicit or perhaps taken for granted. Our actions themselves are for the most part routine and typical. As such we normally carry them out without deliberation or self-conscious processes of decision-making. Only a few matters can become themes for explicit deliberation: for weighing carefully the value issues at stake in the decisions we must make, for tracing the likely outcomes of various courses of action. And even this sort of deliberation is possible only because the greater part of our action options are, for all practical purposes, settled, at least for the time being. Yet innovative actions and actions in response to novel situations do manifest the whole range of aspects which figure in a fully developed account of the intentional structure of action.

Consequentialist Ethical Theory
Consequentialist theories derive their persuasiveness from the fact that they articulate what is morally at stake in the intentional structure of action. They call attention to the fact that our actions are in our power and that we are answerable for their consequences. Indeed, we are no less accountable for the consequences of *inaction*, for not to decide is in effect to decide, in this case, to do nothing. Consequentialist views challenge us, therefore, to calculate the likely results of our actions, and to assess their relative goodness

(or badness) for human well-being. They drive home the point that the quality of the overall outcome of action is what counts, however that outcome may be achieved. The central issue is to determine which course of action among the available options is in a given instance likely to enhance human life the most or at least to minimize to the highest degree possible the hurt and pain so common to life. Such views also accent the fact that value issues are inherent features in any decisions we make, indeed, in any projects which we entertain even as possibilities. They stimulate us to become more self-conscious about our value commitments, and more critical about the optimal means of promoting those values in human affairs.[9]

Consequentialist theories have their characteristic weaknesses. They tempt us to exaggerate our capacity to predict and control the results of our actions. They tend to obscure the difficulties involved in surfacing our operative values, taking insufficient account of how much escapes our notice and how often we deceive ourselves in the course of our worldly engagements. In some instances—for example, utilitarianism—they may play down unduly the diversity and heterogeneity of values and value types. This tendency stems from the desire to establish a common measure for weighing values against one another.

When the quest for a common calculus becomes pressing, we are apt to reduce the richness and complexity of the value realm to something quantifiable. Usually we have in mind economic values (jobs, income, consumer goods and services, aggregate wealth) and perhaps certain measurable indices of political preferences (the vote, or the results of public opinion polls). At least where public policy is concerned, one then assumes that the good consists in policies which maximize economic resources and implement to the greatest extent possible the expressed preferences of relevant constituencies. When we reflect concretely on the material content of the values we honor, however, we do not so easily find a common measure for assessing them, at least not without articulating with some fullness the meaning horizon which gives shape to our total understanding of existence.

In response to this last problem, some students of value theory

21

have sought to identify the diverse types of values which lay claim to our regard, and to set forth the patterns which display their proper interrelations, their rankings, their priority orderings.[10] However, the more the diversity of values is noted, and the more the resistance of values to a general hierarchical arrangement is taken into account, the more complex becomes the attempt to work out and implement consequentialist ethical perspectives. The latter are most helpful when only a limited number of values and action options are under active consideration. The all-encompassing interest in utility is then translated into the more manageable pragmatist interest in achieving incremental improvements with respect to particular types of problems which have come to our attention in particular situations.[11]

Consequentialist thinking is most clearly institutionalized in the economic and political sectors of modern society, especially in policy making, for example, business planning or legislative activity at the various levels of government. Here above all the calculation of consequences and their assessment in terms of shared values is germane to the moral life. Quite naturally, the sciences most directly engaged in the study of these facets of human life tend to have a consequentialist bias in their implicit or explicit ethic. I have in mind notions of welfare and efficiency in economics; and in political science, the weighing of competing interests and of public acceptability, tempered perhaps by a consideration of the public interest.[12]

Consequentialist ethical theories bring to the fore an important feature of the moral life: its concern with goal-oriented actions and with the relative merits of their probable results. Such theories are especially appealing when we believe the course of events is reasonably predictable and that we can significantly direct its movement toward desired ends. They would seem to be indispensable for high-technology civilizations, for these civilizations are founded on the human capacity to create and order complex mechanisms of control over natural and social processes. However, such theories cannot safely be generalized into total and all-encompassing accounts of the moral life. By themselves, they oversimplify moral experience. They require other perspectives to supplement what they are able to grasp with peculiar clarity.

22

HUMAN INTERACTIONS

Intersubjectivity

Deontological theories derive their force from the intersubjective structure of action. They focus on the constraints and imperatives of action which are generated by the presence of other persons in our field of action. They articulate the basic moral fact that we can never treat these others as mere means, but must always also regard them as ends in themselves, as distinctive centers of meaning and valuation toward the world in their own right.[13] Consequentialist theories direct attention to the values which provide the final justification for our action choices; deontological theories bring to light the regulative principles which establish the basic ground rules of action. These principles cut across goal-oriented activity and its value basis. They accent considerations which interrupt our preoccupation with our own goals and with strategies for achieving them. They force us to attend to human interactions as such.

Here too the intentional orientation of consciousness remains basic. But the meanings of interest are not those which make up our actions—our projects and the deeds which implement them. They are those which disclose to us the presence of others having a dignity like our own, a dignity requiring our respect and beneficence.[14] They are those which enter into play in communicative processes, in discourse between human beings.

Attention to human interactions and the grounds of their possibility surfaces certain obligations which we must honor whatever else we might also have in view. Fundamental justice and fairness toward persons here takes priority over more encompassing visions of human well-being.

The claim is not that consequentialist theories are unable to factor into the overall value calculus a concern for others. After all, according to the principle of utility, I count as only one person alongside the many others in the determination of the wider social good, though I do count as one. And if we indeed had the ability to discern the good of each—truly approximating the wisdom and knowledge of the "ideal observer" of utilitarian thought—and to predict and manage the results of action, then the interests and needs of others could perhaps receive sufficient and appropriate attention within consequentialist thought. But we lack such powers of discernment and foreknowledge and also such capacities to control the course of events. We may in considerable measure be able to control our own actions, but we are essentially unable to manage the responses of others to them. These limitations suggest the need for a shift in orientation: away from exclusive attention to goal-oriented action toward more careful consideration of human interaction as such. Strategic action must be qualified and limited by the requirements of communicative interactions.[15] The strength of deontological theories lies in their ability to articulate the ground rules which order these interactions.

Deontology in Ethical Theory

Immanuel Kant sought to base the sense of duty which regulates action on the principle of a rational being.[16] The understanding of practical reason which is suggested by the conception of such a being makes the notion of universalizability foundational to morality. It makes law (and its associated notions) the proper form for expressing the moral imperative. Regard for others, who are also rational beings, is then derivative from the principle of universalizability. Logic takes precedence over concrete human interactions in the determination of duty.

The difficulty with this way of determining our duty is as follows: what I universalize in working out the content of my moral obligations is precisely my own vantage point on the world. In effect I assimilate others to that vantage point, despite my formal recognition of their otherness. I presume that they are in all relevant respects like me. However, insofar as the dignity and originality of the other is the theme, then communicative processes must be prior to the rational articulation of my own vantage point. The others whom I initially perceive to be like me must be able to present themselves in their own fashion, to speak for themselves out of their own worldly involvements. Such openness to others involves a decentering of my perspective on the world, a shock of recognition that my sense of the good is finite and relative, and stands in need of correction and supplementation by what others have to offer.

24

Moral awareness is founded, then, not on the principle of a rational being as such—on logic—but on a primal encounter with others, on communicative interactions. Morality consists essentially in taking others into account in our deliberations, our decision-making, our action.

Logic is not displaced by the accent on human interactions. Logic is, after all, requisite to comprehensibility, without which intelligible discourse would not be possible. And when we work out through concrete discourse the ground rules for social cooperation, the form most suited, in a practical sense, for articulating the constraints and imperatives of action is the universalizable principle. Formulations of this sort do not have any intrinsic moral authority. Their significance is that they provide the continuity and order which ongoing human interactions require, especially since many different persons—perhaps millions—are near or remote parties to those interactions. We characteristically express our obligations, therefore, in terms of laws, codes, and regulations, in terms of general principles and rules.[17]

These formulations are, to be sure, relative and finite, not absolute and final. They remain subject to continual modification and reformulation, not only in response to changed circumstances, but also in recognition of new insights and learnings emerging in human discourse. In this respect, relations remain primary in moral understandings. Principles and rules are subordinate to relationships. They are justified by their service to relationships. Yet so long as a principle or rule is in effect, its form is that of the general regulator of action which admits of no unspecifiable exceptions. The problem is to state the rule or principle appropriately—at the relevant level of generality—and to apply it aptly in concrete life situations.

What is displaced by attention to interaction is a monologic conception of the moral life.[18] Instead of arriving at the content of the moral law by universalizing our own maxims of action, we gain it through discourse. It is through discourse itself that we arrive at the ground rules of social cooperation, though these ground rules necessarily encompass the imperatives which make discourse possible in the first place.[19] The discourse in question, moreover, must be actual, concrete, historical — not simply hypothetical. A purely hypothetical discourse remains essentially monological, sealed off from the interventions of those differently placed in the world. The aim of the discourse is a workable social consensus which both allows space for diverse human vantage points and also reflects a richness of life generated by their ongoing mutual engagement with one another. It establishes the bases for personal community.[20]

Deontological perspectives are strongest in calling attention to those obligations which are entailed by the basic requisites of human life. In regard to these requisites they are largely regulative in significance. They set inviolable limits to action. In this function they are predominately negative. Their theme is: "harm not." They also assert minimal duties, one's necessary share of responsibility in the human enterprise: in labor and work, in truthfulness and fidelity. In contrast, consequentialist theories more readily bring to consciousness the positive values which provide the justifying grounds of action, the "for-the-sake-of-which" that renders action humanly important. When linked to a general theory of values, they articulate the total good to which a human being aspires. They state not simply what we are obliged to do, but what it might be desirable or worthwhile to do. Both of these aspects of the moral life are, however, grounded in fundamental structures which are constitutive of human life and being: consequentialist theories, in the intentionality of acting; deontological theories, in intersubjectivity, or more concretely, in the sociality of human life and action.

Deontological theories have their characteristic weaknesses as well. The most obvious of these is related to the abstractness of the principles and rules we formulate to express the content of our moral obligation. The formal principle can in the nature of the case never embrace the concrete reality. It treats the concrete solely in terms of some of its aspects, presumably the most salient ones from a moral point of view. But the concrete as such ever surpasses its grasp. In the effort to overcome this distance from concrete experience, or at least to reduce it, one is tempted to introduce ever greater specificity into the principle itself: perhaps by identifying and stating typical exceptions to its binding force, or by providing rules for its

26

application, and additional rules for ranking and ordering those rules in anticipated situations of conflict. In the process, the rules become ever more numerous and complex without in fact overcoming the gap between reality and the legal form. The result is that one becomes preoccupied with the rules as such, the massive book of detailed regulations, and ceases to attend as carefully to what is actually going on. A major problem for moral understanding is to assess the extent to which principles and rules need to be spelled out in various situations. Yet in no case can the rules displace the need for prudent judgment by mature moral actors, a central theme of perfectionist theories of the moral life.

A second weakness common to deontological theories is more subtle. Since the principles which state the content of our moral obligations are universal in form, we are tempted to assume that our more concrete sense of their meaning is similarly universal. We conceal from ourselves the presuppositions and taken-for-granted assumptions that actually control our application of the principles. For example, we may attend inadequately to the presumption of individualism which guides our reading of the principle of equality of opportunity. Consequently, we have difficulty seeing how socially reinforced prejudices of a most pervasive sort might affect its application. We are inclined to bestow on our quite particularist readings of our principles the grandeur appropriate only to their universal form, or better, to those basic conditions for human relationships which underlie the principles themselves.[21]

When moral principles are refracted through unexamined and uncriticized assumptions, they can serve the violation of the moral good they are supposed to protect. Here too, it is only in a living, ongoing discourse that the sense of our moral principles can be unfolded, for it is from such discourse and the human relationships it articulates that these principles derive their authority.

In modern society, deontological perspectives on the moral life are most clearly institutionalized in courts of law, especially where constitutional issues are at stake. Yet administrative agencies of government which have a predominantly regulatory function — for example, the Food and Drug Administration or the Interstate Commerce Commission — similarly tend to be informed by deontological thinking. Where sociology occupies itself with the integrative mechanisms of society, with the patterned operation of its functional requisites, it is the human science most likely to reflect a deontological bias. As an example, we might call to mind studies dealing with the differentiation and integration of social roles, and of the behavior expectations linked to those roles. One could quite appropriately speak of these "expectations" as having an imperative force for human actors by virtue of their import for the stability and order of society.

The special significance of deontological perspectives on the moral life is their ability to articulate the basic requisites of human life and dignity. Attention to these requisites takes priority in moral understanding over the more encompassing visions of human good in consequentialist thought.

THE FORMATION OF THE SELF

The Implication of the Self in Action

Perfectionist theories of the moral life highlight the personhood of the moral actor.[22] They derive their significance from their attention to the self in its actions and interactions. In making the self as agent the theme of our inquiries, we underscore the fact that human actions are not discrete and isolated occurrences. They are linked to stabilities and continuities in the beings of concrete actors. They express the kinds of persons we have already become and are becoming. They enter into the ongoing formation and reformation of our beings as persons. What we do is formative of who we are.

The focus on the self permits us to unfold the fundamental moral intuition that concrete persons make up the paramount locus of value. It is finally for the sake of concrete persons, the maximal realization of their potential as centers of meaning and value, that obligations are to be assumed and values honored. Perfectionist theories direct us to what is involved in the development and formation of persons.

The notion of virtue expresses the ethical interest in the cultivation of those excellencies which are appropriate to our potentialities as human beings, both in our capacities for acting and in our ability to make discerning judgments in concrete life situations. The values which provide the justifying grounds for our actions, and the obligations which order and regulate our interactions with others also come into play in accounts of virtue, but now as constituents in the kinds of persons we are. They appear as the dispositions, attitudes, purposes, hopes, convictions, and commitments of individual human actors.[23]

The self as the agent of action cannot easily be made a theme of inquiry. Our elemental orientation is always in the first instance toward the world, which includes our projects and our deeds, and the others with whom we interact. There is, to be sure, a kind of awareness of self which accompanies this primary orientation, but it is an elusive, shadowy one, more latent than manifest. To bring the self to the center of our deliberations, a reflexive move is required in which consciousness turns back upon itself and becomes self-consciousness. Paradoxically, however, we cannot in this fashion bring ourselves into view as active subjectivities. We can only catch ourselves retrospectively, in terms of what has already occurred. We still miss the act of consciousness by which we are conscious of ourselves.[24] (Though we can, as it were, objectify ourselves in the imagination, making use of materials already disclosed to reflection.) On the basis of what is given to this retrospective glance, supplemented and in no small measure shaped by the perceptions of others which have been communicated to us, we build up a sense of self, a sense of those habitualities and continuities that form our identities. These identities make up the content of our consciousness of our powers of judgment and action.

Even this sense of self, despite its importance for moral understanding, does not embrace the totality of human being. In particular it is unable to encompass the unconscious and preconscious dimensions of selfhood, dimensions rooted in our needs and desires, in our social location and function, in socialization processes which have drawn us into a common culture. These dimensions of self are by no means insignificant as determinants of behavior. The more we can bring them to awareness and incorporate them positively into our self-understandings, the stronger we are and the greater our powers of acting. Yet consciousness can never begin to lay hold of all that is going on in the depths of the unconscious, nor can it make fully explicit what we already apprehend at a preconscious level. What is important about the self of which we are conscious, however, is that it defines those aspects of our being that we can most readily subject to explicit moral and ethical reflection. It delineates the self insofar as we can gain some possession of it, and hence, become accountable for it.

The being of the self as body is crucial to self-identity. My body bears a region of self-experience which is uniquely my own, even though the language I use in speaking of it enables me to associate it with a comparable region in the experiences of others.[25] My body locates me in the world, marking my orientation to it. With its sensibilities and needs, it is the bearer of some of my values, those which we might term "sensible" and "organic," and it is the ground of the affectivity which colors all valuing experience. With its diverse powers and capacities (both preformed and fully developed) it is a primordial condition of my possibility of acting at all.

All acting involves the body. My relative mastery of my body is a crucial feature in my ability to determine the content and direction of my own acts. I must be able to limit and direct its demands and also to render it available to my wishes if I am to promote the values I hold in esteem and fulfill my obligations to my fellow human beings. The classic virtues of temperance and courage thematize these necessities. An account of moral agency embraces, therefore, a consideration of embodiment, both with reference to the apprehension of value meanings and to the capacities for action. These themes are not in themselves distinctive of perfectionist theories, though they may receive more sustained and systematic attention in such theories.

Self-identity above all involves temporality, the cumulative experiences, habitualities, and memories built up over time which give the self settled form.[26] The settled form does not close out new possibilities for growth and development, perhaps quite drastic conversions in our fundamental perceptions, attitudes, and commitments. But it does determine our placement with respect to those possibilities, and it provides an underlying continuity to experience even in the face of substantial shifts in orientation. Apart from these continuities and habitualities, we would lack that self-possession which is requisite to action. We would be a mere function of the interplay of organic, psychic, and social forces upon us, rather than agents with a capacity to intervene in the course of the world's events in terms of our own purposes.

Even so, this self-possession, though requisite to action, remains fragile, ever subject to disruption by forces beyond our control. Our being as agents is always vulnerable, finite, subject to distortion and dissolution. For its persistence and stability it stands ever in need of substantial, ongoing supports of various kinds, especially the supports provided by human relationships, by human community. Perfectionist theories have a tendency to underestimate this vulnerability and to overplay our ability to shape our own being and becoming as selves.[27]

Deontological and consequentialist theories taken by themselves entail theories of character and virtue, but such theories, when worked out, tend to be assimilated to notions of obligation and of values. In consequentialist theories, the virtuous person is the one able to discern the appropriate value priorities in the selection of the ends of action, and to link those ends critically to appropriate means. In classic utilitarianism, moral maturity involves both a fully developed sense of fellow feeling and the ability to discriminate between various qualities and levels of good: short-term and long-term goods; relatively simple, immediate goods, and richer, more nuanced ones. In deontological theories the virtuous person is the one who is ready and able to do his or her duty. It is the person who subjects his or her inclinations to the requirements of the moral law. It is the person who in all contexts acts respectfully and beneficently toward others.

Perfectionist Ethical Theory

More strongly than consequentialist or deontological theories, perfectionist theories stress the remoteness of value concepts and moral principles from concrete experience. If we are to apprehend what is going on in concrete situations and respond appropriately to them, we need more than our abstract moral notions, no matter how clear and precise they may be. We need a developed capacity

31

for moral discernment; we need prudence, "practical wisdom" (Aristotle). Practical wisdom makes use of critically formulated moral notions, but not as definitive determinants of good and right action. It treats them rather as guides for action whose concrete significance for each situation can finally be assessed only by a mature moral actor. The concrete judgments of such an actor, moreover, are by no means simply functions of these moral notions, that is, astute practical applications of them. They bring into play the full richness of the actor's accumulated experience and insight, and the full resources of his or her powers of acting. They are a function of the totality of understanding and being which forms that actor's worldly existence.[28]

What may be most distinctive about perfectionist theories is the central place they give to the maximization of the powers of selected individual persons as ends in themselves. For perfectionism, the virtues of excellent persons, their doing well and their faring well, cannot properly be assimilated either to the performance of social duty or to the promotion of overall human well-being, for example, in the "greatest happiness of the greatest number." The primary interest is that some at least shall be able to realize in their own beings what it is possible for human beings to become. Social duties and social goods are relative to this central interest.[29]

Perfectionist theories, we could say, are aristocratic rather than democratic in their tendency. They may as a result have a certain tolerance for human misery, inequality, and servitude provided the possibility for the accomplishment of human excellence is present for the worthy. The worthy are the persons of talent, those who exercise discipline, who are enterprising, who are ready to chart their own paths, who risk scorn, ridicule, and suffering for the sake of their own visions of good, and so on. Such persons will in appropriate ways be socially responsible; they will also seek significant associations with other human beings who have attained comparable levels of excellence. Still, their excellence can never be contained within a social group. Their reach ever pushes them beyond the social good as it is conventionally understood.

For perfectionist theories, it is the fullest realization of virtue by concrete human persons which is the primary substance of the

32

ethical. Resolving the competing claims of a general social good and the self-actualization of concrete persons is, of course, a persistent problem of paramount importance for ethical theory. Ideally, we manage to hold the two together in the unity of experience.

Like consequentialist and deontological theories, perfectionist theories also have their characteristic weaknesses. I have mentioned their tendency to overstate our control over the direction of our own development as persons, particularly when the perfection of our powers is seen chiefly as the result of the habitual practice of virtue. Similarly, the attention to individual persons as privileged centers of meaning and value inclines such theories to take insufficient note of the role relationships play in human selfhood. The social good becomes secondary to individual attainment. This tendency would seem to be especially strong in cultures already marked by an individualistic bias. And from some standpoints, the aristocratic leanings of perfectionist thought may themselves be problematic, obscuring the degree to which our destinies as human beings are interlocked. When some fare well and attain much, it is almost always at the expense of others, indeed, not infrequently by virtue of the domination and exploitation of those others. Excellence achieved at such a price is morally dubious at best. It takes on a morally negative cast insofar as it is a function of structural forms of social injustice.[30]

In modern societies, perfectionist perspectives on the moral life are most clearly institutionalized in those social units directly engaged in the care and nurture of the young: families, schools, churches, and voluntary associations devoted to social and recreational activities for children and youth. The sciences most likely to reflect perfectionist interests are psychology and social psychology, especially developmental psychology.

The strength of perfectionist theories is their ability to develop the implications of agency for human actions and interactions, and to unfold the signficance in moral understanding of our elemental recognition that human persons are the paramount locus of value.

I have sketched three basic models for conceptualizing the moral life: consequentialist, deontological, and perfectionist. These three models, I have suggested, give prominence respectively to language about values, duties and obligations, and virtues. They are usually in a competitive relationship with one another, each seeking to do justice to all essential features of the moral life, but within a framework dominated by one of the three types of concern. In contrast, I have associated these theories with fundamental structures which are constitutive of human life and being. These structures, I am arguing, permit us to see the distinctive strengths and limits of the competing theories. They also help us to move toward a view of the moral life which unites their central elements into a single, complex theory.[31]

Thus, I associated consequentialist theories with the intentional structure of acting, deontological theories with intersubjectivity and human sociality, and perfectionist theories with continuities in the being of the agent of action. I also noted briefly the special connection notions of character and virtue have to embodiment and · temporality. The final task is to show how the temporal horizon of human being stretches out before each of these elements, and is the structural basis of their essential unity.

THE TEMPORAL HORIZON
OF EXPERIENCE

Temporality figures in each of the structures I have discussed. Indeed, were it not a feature of these structures, it could not provide the basis for their unity. It is present in the intentionality of acting as the futurity of the project to which I commit myself in deciding upon a course of action. It is present in sociality as established social institutions and as a common stock of knowledge already in operation prior to my formation as a concrete human actor. Barring some cataclysm, this same social world will endure beyond my life span, albeit in a modified way. It is present in my being as actor in habitualities built up over time which order my actions and my judgments, and in my future possibilities for altering and transforming those habitualities. Even so, new dimensions of moral understanding enter into view when temporality becomes the central theme of investigation. These dimensions direct us to historical contextualism as a fourth perspective on the moral life.

For historical contextualism, two matters take on special impor-

34

tance: the concrete historicity of our moral notions, and the question of the meaning of being. The latter question forms the decisive meaning context within which we interpret and assess distinctively moral notions.

The Historicity of Moral Understanding

Historical contextualism accents the fact that the possibilities of moral understanding given with the constitutive structures of human being always appear in historically determinate forms. They reflect a common culture shared by the members of a particular social group. This culture articulates in specific ways the value realm that is latent in the human way of being in the world. It sets in relief certain of the value possibilities belonging to that realm; it actively blocks some out of consideration, identifying them as demonic or dangerous or reprehensible; it largely passes over others, leaving them wholly undeveloped; it grants still others only marginal standing in the total economy of life.

Similarly, the common culture has distinctive ways of ordering human interactions. It specifies how human beings are to be regarded, and the proper manner of exercising respect toward others. It establishes and limits human discourse. In most cases it will, unfortunately, make distinctions between the fully human, the marginally human, and the subhuman; it will consign outsiders and enemies, and perhaps subordinates, to one of the latter groups. Finally, the common culture bears images and definitions of virtue, specifying the nature of true human excellence. It has its saints and heroes, celebrated persons who model its sense of a fully actualized human life. In short, the culture historializes the possibilities of moral understanding which belong to human being.

We never take up our ethical inquiries in a purely rational form, certainly not in abstraction from the temporal flow of consciousness. Our inquiries are always shaped and conditioned by a particular history. History gives concreteness to human understandings of the moral life. Therefore, moral understandings are always relative to a particular history, to the possibilities it has actualized, to the limits it sets to further developments, to the openings for movement and creative growth it has brought into being. It is always in the context of our concrete situatedness that we respond to the moral claims and opportunities of the present.

Normally we take for granted the culturally defined contours of our situatedness. These contours constitute reality for us, until a crisis places them in question. Even then we are equipped to deal with the challenges presented by crisis only by means of resources already at our disposal, those mediated to us by our past. Perhaps we can only respond defensively, coping with threat by clinging all the more tenaciously to received traditions, lest all that is good and right and proper be lost. Perhaps more productive possibilities present themselves to us, so that we draw upon our resources to create something new, something more suited to new realities. We then take crisis as an occasion for growth, for moving beyond past wrongs and injustices toward a more humane future. We project novel "hypotheses of fulfillment" (Winter) for dealing with current difficulties. These hypotheses both utilize and take us beyond what has already been accomplished. They manifest the workings of a productive imagination in transforming problematic situations into more promising patterns of social order. Yet even this creativity will not cease to reflect our historicity, our movement toward an open future on the basis of what has already been effected in the past.[32]

Thus, though there is a structure to moral understanding which is derived from constitutive features of the human way of being in the world, that structure always appears concretely in forms and modes which are relative to a given history with its unique experiences and its distinctive cultural legacy. It is only with reference to such a history and by means of its traditions and achievements that we are able to articulate and enact moral understandings suited to the peculiarities of emerging life settings. Attention to the temporal structure of experience alerts us to our historicity and its role in the constitution of meaning.

Historical perspectives on the moral life do not themselves escape the vulnerabilities which characterize all human thought. Pursued in a thoroughgoing way, they tend toward a morally debilitating relativism, the sense that our moral notions are radically contingent

36

and so without authority in our lives. And if we resist such skeptical conclusions by bringing into view the structures which order the flux of human life, we still do not easily isolate principles of criticism which can facilitate our constructive appropriation of our cultural legacy. As a result, historically oriented accounts of the moral life are subject to wide swings between a moral positivism and a moral utopianism. The former accents the historical givenness of moral norms at the expense of the moral imagination; the latter celebrates novelty and innovation at the expense of the continuity of experience. In neither case are tight, rigorous arguments readily available for the defense of our material judgments. In this respect, historical modes of moral reasoning depend heavily on intuitive judgments of appropriateness, however much they may be informed by critical thought and well-founded knowledge.

Historical contextualism is not readily subject to institutionalization within the basic arrangements of society. In the nature of the case it takes on marked significance only in times of social crisis, when established social arrangements are proving inadequate and are under stress. In some measure, modern societies do provide special spaces for selected persons and groups to question social conventions and to experiment with innovative visions and life patterns. These spaces include institutions and organizations devoted to "high culture": universities, the theater, study groups, foundations concerned with the arts. To these more established contexts must be added utopian communities, prophetic religious groups, and issue-oriented voluntary associations. To become operational within society, historical contextualism finally requires effective voluntary associations engaged in political education and action. These associations strive to alter standardized social perceptions and to bring into being conditions for social change. Almost invariably they find themselves immersed in social conflict—in extreme cases, in revolutionary struggle with human life at risk.

In the human sciences, historical contextualism is most apt to appear in critical theories of society. Such theories occupy themselves with the investigation of the contradictions of society. They seek to identify potential crisis situations which might provide openings for constructive social change. These theories receive considerable supporting materials from social and political histories, and from comparative and evolutionary studies of human society.

The strength of historical contextualism is that it directs us to concrete experience and to the meanings which form it. In so doing it serves a lively discourse about what is going on in our common world, and about the proper response to it.

The Question of the Meaning of Being

Historical contextualism not only alerts us to the concrete historializations of moral understanding. It also calls attention to the wider matrix of meaning within which the moral life itself is situated. In our worldly being we have to do not simply with our practical, everyday engagements: goal-oriented actions, communicative interactions, struggles for identity and self-possession, and the concrete social and cultural situatedness of these three. We have to do, implicitly at least, with the question of the meaning of being.[33] This question concerns the ultimate sense and significance of the human pilgrimage. Only if we can discover some final meaning to human life are we likely to gain clear confirmation for peculiarly moral meanings: the values we honor, the obligations we assume, the virtues we would inculcate. Indeed, our way of apprehending the meaning of being will materially inform the moral meanings themselves.

Some examples may clarify this last claim. If our sense of the meaning of being is articulated in a tragic vision, then the moral meanings which order our lives will, quite likely, have an ironic cast to them. At some point we will expect our most conscientious efforts at accomplishing the good to ensnare us in the evil we would avoid. If our sense of the meaning of being is characterized by grace, especially grace which provisionally permits, perennially struggles with, and finally overcomes evil, then we will receive the promises and claims of the moral life as gift, as opportunity. We will experience a certain enlargement of our obligations and perhaps a profound release from self-absorption. We will live in hope toward the goodness we esteem, accepting with sobriety and humility, even grief, our persistent resistance to the fullness of being it offers. And if we find a void at the center of being, an emptiness which mocks the seriousness of our concerns, then the values we hold and the obligations we accept are apt to be reduced in scope — to survival, to the protection and promotion of those matters which are most clearly in our personal interest, perhaps to a kind of suspicion of human claims to altruistic concern. All else is likely to appear as folly and deceit. The larger meaning horizon which provides the matrix for our moral understandings is in no case neutral in its import for the latter.

The question of the meaning of being does not first come into play against the backdrop of the temporal horizon of experience. It hovers before all of the structures of awareness, and before all of the dimensions and facets of the moral life which have previously been treated. Consideration of the value realm drives us sooner or later to inquire into the center of values, the ultimate basis of the unity of valuative experiences. It sets before us the supreme value of the Good (Plato) or the Holy (Max Scheler). It announces radical monotheism (H. R. Niebuhr). Similarly, sensitivity to the originality of the claims of the other activates, at least in personalist traditions, a sense of the radically Other in reference to whom alone we can find final justification for our being. The concrete thou mediates the Holy Thou (Martin Buber), the source and ground of the personal. Finally, the quest for self-identity and self-possession founders on human finitude, frailty, duplicity, and transience, until we find a way to be at peace with its elusiveness and ultimate futility. Paradoxically, the "desire and effort to exist" (Jean Nabert) finds its completion only when it is given up, surrendered to the confirmation which comes when we acknowledge that the power and meaning of being does not finally reside in ourselves, certainly not as our possession.[34] It is present to us as gift, as grace. It frees us to be at home in the world, to "dwell" in the earth, precisely as the finite, vulnerable, flawed creatures we are.

One can deal with the discrete meanings which make up specifically moral understandings without moving explicitly to this final horizon. In many contexts, the presence of that horizon can and doubtless will be left unnoticed and unnamed. Our everyday, practical engagements will on those occasions occupy us almost totally. Nonetheless, this meaning horizon hovers before these engagements, at least as a question, a possibility; it belongs inextricably to that totality of understanding which is the distinctive promise and threat of the human way of being in the world. Without some sense of this question and its import for our existence, we cannot satisfactorily articulate all that is at stake in the moral life.

The suggestion here is that temporality brings to the fore with special acuteness the question of the meaning of being.[35] It draws into the unity of present awareness a sense of the ultimate whence and whither of our being, which both precedes and surpasses all that we are able to weigh, to judge, to determine, to manage. It suggests that a comprehension of our totality requires and rests upon a horizon of meaning which ever reaches beyond us and finally dislodges us from our everyday preoccupations, only to establish them again in a new light, one that is not and cannot be at our disposal. It keeps us open to disclosures of this meaning horizon in our quest for moral understanding. When such disclosures take place in our midst, they occur in historical concreteness: in the word of the poet, in the vision of the seer, in the sagas and legends of the storyteller, in the riddles of the sage and the parables of the prophet, in the sermons of the preacher, in the myths ritually reenacted by the priest at the special times and places of our common life. The interpretation, appropriation, and mediation of such materials is an essential aspect of our attempts to apprehend and pass on to others the moral understandings which have been given to us.

Processes of this kind are most apt to be institutionalized in organizations which specifically concern themselves with religious matters: churches, synagogues, temples, religious societies. They appear as well, however, in ritualistic political events and in the activities of organizations occupied with the mediation of a cultural legacy.

To sum up, we have goal-oriented actions, communicative interactions, and processes of self-formation. To these three aspects of our practical worldly engagements correspond three modalities of meaning: values, obligations, and virtues. These types of meaning in their historialized forms make up the substantive content of the moral life. The moral life in turn is framed by the question of the meaning of being. It is the latter question which directs us to that totality of understanding within which we are able to establish and confirm the significance of the more discrete meanings which belong to moral awareness. In authorizing our specific moral notions, this ultimate meaning horizon also materially affects the manner of their appearance to us and the role they play in the total economy of our lives.

NOTES

1. In particular I would cite Ernst Troeltsch's posthumously published study, "Ethics and the Philosophy of History," in *Christian Thought: Its History and Application*, ed. with an introduction by Baron Friedrich von Hügel (New York: Meridian Books, 1957). This is an elegant essay which has not received the attention it deserves.

2. To take a classic example, Immanuel Kant, in his *Critique of Practical Reason* (New York: Bobbs-Merrill, 1956), 128–36, argues for the importance of belief in God and the immortality of the soul for sustaining and giving full intelligibility to the moral life. These beliefs, however, can in no way shape the moral law itself, which is determinative for moral judgment. The autonomy of the moral law is strictly maintained. Specifically religious motifs can be substantively significant only "within the limits of reason alone."

3. I have identified and briefly characterized these structures elsewhere. See T. W. Ogletree, "The Activity of Interpreting in Moral Judgment," *Journal of Religious Ethics* (Spring 1980): 1–26. Some of the more important literature has been cited in that study.

4. This point is fundamental to phenomenology. It is reiterated in each of Edmund Husserl's introductory presentations of phenomenology. Cf., e.g., *The Crisis of European Sciences and Transcendental Phenomenology* (Evanston, Ill.: Northwestern University Press, 1970), par. 48, 165–67.

5. For the material which follows I am especially indebted to Paul Ricoeur's *Freedom and Nature: The Voluntary and the Involuntary* (Evanston, Ill.: Northwestern University Press, 1966), esp. 41–55, 66–84, 88–134.

6. The aspects of embodiment which are listed here are taken from a succinct discussion in Edmund Husserl's *Cartesian Meditations* (The Hague: Martinus Nijhoff, 1960), 97.

7. The suggestion that the meaning of the deed can be seen as the fulfillment (or lack thereof) of expectations generated by the project is an adaptation of Husserl's discussion of the relation between "meaning-intentions"

and "meaning-fulfillment" in perception and knowledge. See the sixth of his *Logical Investigations*, Eng. trans. J. N. Findlay (New York: Humanities Press, 1970), 2: 675–706. The study is entitled "Elements of a Phenomenological Elucidation of Knowledge."

8. For this distinction I am indebted to Max Scheler, *Formalism in Ethics and Non-Formal Ethics of Value* (Evanston, Ill.: Northwestern University Press, 1973), 12–23.

9. I particularly have in mind John Stuart Mill's classic essay, "Utilitarianism." Cf. *The Philosophy of John Stuart Mill*, ed. Marshall Cohen (New York: Modern Library, 1961). My account of utilitarian thought has been aided by David Lyons, *The Forms and Limits of Utilitarianism* (New York and London: Oxford University Press, 1965). What I am calling consequentialist thought is often labeled *teleological*. I have avoided this term, however, because it is ambiguously used to refer to both consequentialist and perfectionist thought, obscuring the distinction between them.

10. In addition to Scheler, *Formalism in Ethics*, esp. 86–110, I would mention Nicolai Hartmann, *Ethics*, vol. 2, *Moral Values*, Eng. trans. Stanton Coit (New York: Macmillan Co., 1932), 44–53, and the whole of sec. 8, 385–472. Hartmann stresses the complexity and heterogeneity of the value realm. He notes a number of different ways of thinking about the relations among values, each resulting in a somewhat different picture. I might add that many of the notions he discusses as values I would call virtues, e.g., wisdom, courage, self-control, truthfulness, fidelity, modesty, etc.

11. This attitude is embodied, e.g., in Charles E. Lindblom's much-cited account of the policy-making process, "The Science of Muddling Through," *Public Administration Review* 19 (Spring 1959): 17–27.

12. On the latter point, see Duncan MacRae, Jr., *The Social Function of Social Science* (New Haven, Conn.: Yale University Press, 1976), 107–202.

13. For my line of thinking, see T. W. Ogletree, "Hospitality to the Stranger: Reflections on the Role of the 'Other' in Moral Experience," in *The American Society of Christian Ethics, Selected Papers*, ed. Max Stackhouse (Waterloo, Ontario: Council on the Study of Religion, 1977), 16–40.

14. The classic phenomenological account of intersubjectivity is Husserl's *Cartesian Meditations*, 89–151. Husserl's central interest in this study is the nature and basis of our knowledge of other selves. He does not draw out the ethical implications of such knowledge. For the latter, I find Immanuel Levinas more helpful. See his *Totality and Infinity: An Essay on Exteriority*, Eng. trans. Alphonso Lingis (Pittsburgh: Duquesne University Press, 1969). I have discussed Levinas's work in the essay "Hospitality to the Stranger."

15. For the distinction between goal-oriented activity and communicative interaction, I am indebted to Jürgen Habermas. The distinction appears in many of his writings, beginning with his early study of Hegel's "Jena lectures," entitled "Labor and Interaction: Remarks on Hegel's Jena *Philosophy of Mind,*" in his *Theory and Practice* (Boston: Beacon Press, 1973), 142–69. It is prominent in *Knowledge and Human Interests* (Boston: Beacon Press, 1971), 25–63, 308–17. In the latter study it is associated with the distinction between empirical-analytic sciences and historical-hermeneutical sciences. It continues to organize his retrospective study of his intellectual pilgrimage. Cf. "Introduction: Some Difficulties in the Attempt to Link Theory and Praxis," also in *Theory and Practice.* Cf. esp. 16–19.

16. Cf. Immanuel Kant, *Fundamental Principles of the Metaphysics of Morals* (New York: Bobbs-Merrill, 1949), 24–30.

17. This discussion owes much to Jürgen Habermas's essay, "What is Universal Pragmatics?" in his *Communication and the Evolution of Society* (Boston: Beacon Press, 1979), 1–68.

18. Habermas makes the same point in his critique of Kant. See his "Labor and Interaction," in *Theory and Practice*, 150–51. Here Hegel is a major resource for his critique.

19. The list of these notions is not small. It includes comprehensibility, truthfulness, fidelity in commitments, regard or respect for others and their meaning worlds, community, and perhaps others as well. Cf. Habermas, "What is Universal Pragmatics?" in *Communication and the Evolution of Society*, 62–68. See also Gibson Winter's account of the norms implied in human sociality, especially freedom, justice, and harmony, in *Elements for a Social Ethic* (New York: Macmillan Co., 1966), 234–35.

20. My point here has close affinities with the argument of John Rawls, especially regarding the place and function of a theory of justice in human society. Cf. *A Theory of Justice* (Cambridge, Mass.: Harvard University Press, 1971), 7–11. I am, of course, calling into question Rawls's reliance on a hypothetical discourse in the "original situation" to establish the theory. The notion of "personal community" is taken from Scheler, *Formalism in Ethics and Non-Formal Ethics in Value*, 526–61, esp. 533ff. Scheler contrasts personal community, on the one hand, with a social solidarity in which the individual person is not yet clearly differentiated from the group, and, on the other hand, with a social order which is simply an aggregate of individuals, perhaps contracting individuals who agree to cooperate out of mutual self-interest. Personal community implies deep bonds formed in a common history, but the bonds involve persons who also understand themselves as centered beings in distinction from their group. Scheler sees the church as the most promising form for such a community in the modern world.

THE USE OF THE BIBLE IN CHRISTIAN ETHICS

21. I have discussed this point somewhat more fully elsewhere. See T. W. Ogletree, introduction to the essay, "The Activity of Interpreting in Moral Judgment."

22. Aristotle's *Nichomachaean Ethics* provides the basic model for what follows. I have also been helped considerably in thinking about these materials by Stanley Hauerwas, especially his *Character and the Christian Life: A Study in Theological Ethics* (San Antonio, Tex.: Trinity University Press, 1975).

23. James Gustafson calls attention to this point. See, e.g., the closing essay in *Christ and the Moral Life* (New York: Harper & Row, 1968), 238–71, esp. 240.

24. This problem is prominent in much post-Cartesian continental philosophy. For a phenomenological discussion of it, see Alfred Schutz, *Collected Papers*, vol. 1, *The Problem of Social Reality*, ed. Maurice Natanson (The Hague: Martinus Nijhoff, 1967), 167–75. The inability of consciousness to grasp itself in its active subjectivity underlies Husserl's important distinction between the transcendental ego and the psychological ego. In dealing with the constitutive acts of consciousness by which we have a world, Husserl is *not* focusing on concrete egos and the manifest contents of their consciousness. Nor is he pursuing philosophical psychology. He is attending to those prereflective acts of consciousness which are presupposed in any experience whatever. Phenomenological psychology in contrast is an enormously complex undertaking which presupposes and builds upon the results of transcendental phenomenology. Cf., e.g., *Crisis of European Sciences and Transcendental Phenomenology*, 191–265. For an important study in phenomenological psychology, see Aaron Gurwitsch, *Studies in Phenomenology and Psychology* (Evanston, Ill.: Northwestern University Press, 1966).

25. For this notion, see Husserl's *Cartesian Meditations*, 97. For a phenomenological treatment of embodiment, see Richard M. Zaner, *The Problem of Embodiment* (The Hague: Martinus Nijhoff, 1971), esp. 250–61.

26. In this respect, I consider it quite appropriate to link character and virtue to narrative, especially autobiography. See Stanley Hauerwas, *Truthfulness and Tragedy: Further Investigations in Christian Ethics* (Notre Dame, Ind.: University of Notre Dame Press, 1966), 27–34.

27. Gene Outka dramatizes the self's vulnerability to harm. See his review of Stanley Hauerwas's work in "Character, Vision, and Narrative," *Religious Studies Review* 6 (April 1980): 110–18, esp. 111–12. See also his "On Harming Others," *Interpretation* 34 (October 1980): 381–93.

28. See especially James Gustafson's discussion of "discernment" in "Moral Discernment in the Christian Life," in his *Theology and Christian Ethics* (Philadelphia: Pilgrim Press, 1974), 99–119.

29. I read both Aristotle and Nietzsche in this fashion.

30. This characterization is more true of popular understandings of perfectionism than of its more careful philosophical articulations.

31. Edward L. Long, Jr., reaches a similar conclusion in his *Survey of Christian Ethics* (New York and London: Oxford University Press, 1967). Having analyzed various approaches in Christian ethics to the "formulation of the ethical norm" and the "implementation of ethical decisions," he criticizes the "polemical exclusion" of the insights of some approaches on the basis of commitments to others. Each approach tends to lift up some motifs in moral understanding and underplay others, when in fact the various motifs are complementary. He calls for "comprehensive complementarity" in ethical theory. What we need, he argues, is "a phenomenological understanding of moral decision-making as carried out in relation to Christian commitments. Such an understanding could contribute to our awareness of what Underwood calls the 'actual basis of the grounds' of moral actions" (312).

My own study is an attempt to provide such a phenomenology, not simply of decision-making, but of the moral life in all of its dimensions.

32. On this point, cf. H. Richard Niebuhr, *The Responsible Self* (New York: Harper & Row, 1963), 94–107, and Gibson Winter, *Elements for a Social Ethic*, 254–58.

33. In general I have in mind Martin Heidegger's discussion of this theme in *On Time and Being* (New York: Harper & Row, 1972), 2–24. Cf. also Heidegger's "Letter on Humanism," in William Barrett and Henry D. Aiken, ed., *Philosophy in the Twentieth Century: An Anthology* (New York: Random House, 1962), 3: 270–302, esp. 281–94.

34. The point is crucial to Paul Ricoeur's critical appropriation of the thought of Jean Nabert. See his *Freud and Philosophy: An Essay on Interpretation*, Eng. trans. Denis Savage (New Haven, Conn.: Yale University Press, 1970), 528–29. For a central statement of Nabert's views, see *Elements for an Ethic*, Eng. trans. Wm. J. Petrek (Evanston, Ill.: Northwestern University Press, 1969).

35. Heidegger gives temporality this favored position in *Being and Time* (London: SCM Press, 1962). See the whole of div. 2, 274–488. One might also note Paul Tillich's use of temporal categories (origin and expectation) in his *The Socialist Decision*, Eng. trans. Franklin Sherman (New York: Harper & Row, 1977), 1–9. Temporality is, of course, dominant in the extensive literature on eschatology and hope in continental theology, recent Marxist philosophy, and liberation theology.

3

COVENANT AND COMMANDMENT: OLD TESTAMENT UNDERSTANDINGS OF THE MORAL LIFE

I have been sketching certain preunderstandings of the moral life which might guide our investigation of biblical materials. This account is not an end in itself. It represents a provisional attempt to uncover a common ground for our dialogue with the biblical texts—not to control what they may be permitted to say to us, but to suggest a way of thinking about the subject matter of the texts which might permit the texts to address us in our present. The intent is not to bypass or leap over a historical treatment of the texts, but to move beyond a mere re-presentation of what the texts are saying to a "fusion of horizons" (biblical and contemporary) which can open up and transform our own understandings.

The task of this chapter is to characterize the basic patterns of moral understanding which appear in the Pentateuch and the writings of the eighth- and seventh-century prophets. I shall examine these patterns in the context of the social evolution of Israelite life. I shall formulate them at a fairly high level of generality, making contact, on the one hand, with preunderstandings already articulated, and anticipating, on the other hand, a constructive appropriation of the truth they disclose.

It is my thesis that these writings display a precritical version of the historical contextualism set forth in the previous chapter. The moral life of the ancient Israelites, that is to say, is bound up with a sense of their concrete history. Within this basic frame of reference, deontological motifs are dominant. What we principally find are specifications of those duties and obligations which are requisite to the ongoing life of the people Israel. Consequentialist thought in the modern sense does not appear at all, that is, the weighing of possible courses of action in terms of the impact of their probable consequences on critically assessed value priorities. One can presume that calculations of this sort may have gone on, especially in the context of the monarchy where diplomatic and military policies would have had to be worked out. If so, however, such thinking does not show itself explicitly within the biblical literature. Nor for that matter do we find self-reflective discussions of values and value relationships. The values recognized and honored by the people are for all practical purposes taken for granted, and they are submerged in the dominant deontological interest. Perfectionist thinking is present in this literature, but not as something significant in its own right. It deals with the training and equipment of persons for their social and religious obligations. In this respect, it too is subordinate to deontological considerations: the health and well-being of the community in its ordered life. On this last point, the picture does shift somewhat in the postexilic literature, where the realization of human excellence emerges as a relatively autonomous theme. I shall note some instances of this latter emphasis. For the preexilic literature, however, a historically oriented form of deontology is pervasive. It is in this mode of understanding that the creativity and originality of Israelite thought shows itself most forcefully.

The chapter falls into five parts: (1) an account of the covenantal context of Israel's moral obligations; (2) a characterization of the content of the legal traditions which express those obligations, accenting the requirement of exclusive allegiance to Yahweh; (3) a discussion of the moral and religious issues at stake in Israel's struggles to maintain its allegiance to Yahweh, especially in relation to social and cultural challenges presented by Baalism and the establishment of the monarchy; (4) an examination of prophetic treatments of these pentateuchal themes, highlighting their essential continuity, but also calling attention to the distinctive emphasis they place on divine judgment, eschatology, and the human heart, and their attempts to reinterpret in a world setting the moral ramifications of convenantal fidelity; and (5) a brief consideration, chiefly by way of contrast, of some postexilic adjustments of Israelite understandings to the new realities of the world empires, stressing in particular the emergence of perfectionist motifs as relatively independent modes of moral understanding.

THE COVENANTAL CONTEXT OF
MORAL OBLIGATION

In the Pentateuch, the obligations of the people are inseparably linked to the covenant with Yahweh on Mt. Sinai. The basic picture is as follows. The obligations regulating the lives of the people are set forth as divinely given commandments, laws, and ordinances. Moses is the agent through whom they are given. Their presentation is prefaced by a recital of Yahweh's saving acts, especially the deliverance of the Hebrew people from Egypt. They presuppose as well Yahweh's self-disclosure to Moses in a theophany on Mt. Sinai. Their immediate occasion is an act of covenant making to which Yahweh through Moses has summoned the people. They delineate the manner of life Yahweh expects of Israel in the covenant he graciously offers.[1] The people accept the covenant and bind themselves to its obligations in a solemn act of covenant making. This action sets the conditions for the future life of the people in the land of Canaan. Yahweh promises the people blessing if they are faithful to the covenant and fulfill its requirements; he assures them curses if they are not.[2]

This complex set of actions and themes establishes an essential link between the commandments which express the obligations of the people and the covenant at Sinai. These obligations, that is to say, are covenant obligations. The covenant is their basis and the narratives which tell of the covenant and its placement in Israel's total pilgrimage disclose their authority in the lives of the people.

The covenant is not simply a political compact, though it does have important political dimensions, and not simply in the story of the miraculous escape from Egypt. Noteworthy, for example, is the prominence of the elders of the people in the accounts of covenant making (e.g., Exodus 24). Despite the centrality of Moses' charisma, these traditional leaders of the Israelite clans clearly have a role to play where the ground rules of social cooperation are at stake. Their presence in the narratives signals the operation of political processes. Yet the covenant is broader and deeper than politics as such. It is certainly richer than the modern notion of a social contract among autonomous, self-interested, rational individuals! It embraces the whole complex fabric of the people's lives, their shared experiences and interactions over time. The substantive obligations of the people are not simply functions of a formal agreement; they are integral features of their concrete social and historical reality taken in its totality.

In this connection, the covenant at Sinai does not appear as an absolute beginning for Israel, though it does mark a new phase of existence. It presupposes a prior history of Yahweh's involvements with the ancestors of the people gathered in that place. To the Sinai narratives are prefixed legends of a patriarchal prehistory: the stories of Abraham, Isaac, and Jacob (Genesis 12—50). This prehistory is set in relation to ancient sagas of human origins which recount God's primal dealings with the whole of humanity, especially divine attempts to cope with the pervasiveness of human evil (Genesis 1—11). The covenant at Sinai has a great deal behind it. In a sense it simply confirms and makes explicit what was already implicit in the prior history. It brings into relief what is at stake in the pilgrimage of this people, those who are the offspring of Abraham, Isaac, and Jacob.

Even Yahweh is apprehended and interpreted in terms of the concrete reality of the people: Yahweh is the one who accompanies the people, and has done so from the beginning (e.g., Exodus 3). Just as an awareness of the divine presence furnishes the larger meaning horizon for Israel's self-understandings, so the peculiar history of this people gives material content to their sense of the nature and character of that presence. Their moral notions are of a piece with their total history. The dramatic portrayal of the historical connection between covenant and commandment articulates the placement of Israel's moral understandings in the concrete reality of a people.

The emphasis on the historical reality of a people presents a striking contrast to philosophical attempts to derive moral understandings from human rationality as such, or to ground them in an anthropology. Reasoning patterns of this sort are not necessarily ruled out by the peculiar logic of the Sinai narratives. They may even be invited and encouraged by the sagas of human origins, which suggest that something akin to covenant relationships is latent in the structure of human creatureliness as such. Yet this reasoning is remote and abstract in comparison with interpretations of the actual social reality of an existing people. It becomes important chiefly when the moral substance of a people has itself become problematic in some fashion, so that one requires a more fundamental reference point as a way of regaining one's bearings. Nonetheless, it is in terms of living human communities and societies that moral notions have vividness and power, and can effectively shape and guide human action. This insight is implicit in the Israelite presumption that their obligations stem from the events at Sinai.

The materials in the Hexateuch display Israel's concrete reality as a manifestation of divine grace. The Hebrew term is *tsedakah*, usually translated "righteousness." It refers to Yahweh's activity on behalf of a people. Yahweh delivers the people from bondage and preserves them from peril. He binds himself to them in the covenant, which is the culmination of his saving activity. Indeed, the commandments, laws, and ordinances are in themselves grace. They do not simply specify obligations which the people must take upon themselves *because* Yahweh has been gracious to them. After all, grace as such implies no obligations whatever. It refers to what is freely offered, a gift without strings. If anything, the obligations become effective through nothing more than a sheer acknowledgment of the sovereign majesty of the one whose will they express. Thus, the solemn declaration of the Holiness Code, "I am the Lord," suffices to establish the authority of the commandments (cf., e.g., Leviticus 19). What comes to the fore in the texts, however, is that Yahweh gives commandments, laws, and ordinances for the sake of the people. They are a sign of divine care; they set forth that pattern of human existence which leads to blessedness.

According to this understanding, there is nothing about the moral life which is fundamentally alien to human powers and possibilities. It does not violate basic human needs, desires, and aspirations. Still less is it an arbitrary imposition on the human spirit by an all-

51

powerful deity. It can become burdensome and demanding; it often involves suffering and anguish, sometimes even death; it frequently blocks and frustrates immediate wants; it continually puts people to the test, and it certainly stretches them. In its deepest meanings, however, it is wholly congruent with human reality and its potentialities. Moreover, its requirements are in principle within the reach of human powers and capacities. The possibility of infidelity is ever present, and temptations will surely come, but where the people are diligent, they can keep the covenant and its obligations, to their ultimate benefit.

The narratives which recount the happenings upon which these formative understandings are based cannot be taken as accurate records of the actual course of events, certainly not as a critical historian might reconstruct them. In their present form they are a composite of traditional materials which initially existed quite independently of one another. Gerhard von Rad identifies three distinct bodies of tradition within the larger narrative framework, one dealing with the exodus from Egypt, a second with the theophany and covenant at Sinai, and a third with the conquest and occupation of the land of Canaan. Apart from the possibility that some version of the Decalogue might have figured in the Sinai traditions, the laws and regulations now found in the Pentateuch seem not to have belonged to any of these units in their earliest forms.[3] These three bodies of tradition, according to von Rad, took shape initially as cult legends associated with particular local shrines, that is, Shechem or Gilgal. In time they were brought together in-to a single story. That story presents a highly condensed, selective, and idealized version of Israelite history. It is laden with insertions, novel associations, and interpretations stemming from later periods in its transmission. Its composition is not the accomplishment of a single author. In fact, it does not involve an author at all in the modern sense. It is rather the work of collectors, redactors, and editors of traditional material, the most noteworthy of whom we know only as the "Yahwist" and "Elohist" of pentateuchal source criticism.[4] We have before us then not the thoughts and insights of gifted individuals but the collective memories of a people regarding their own past, to be sure, gathered and set forth by creative individuals. These memories were passed from generation to generation and were periodically rehearsed in the context of cultic activity. They articulate the larger meaning horizon which establishes the authority of the moral notions the people shared in common.

The discrete laws and ordinances which eventually made up the content of Israel's covenant obligations are organized in a number of identifiable collections: the Decalogue (Exodus 24 and Deuteronomy 5; cf. Lev. 19:1-4, 11-18), the Book of the Covenant (Exod. 20:23 – 23:19), the Holiness Code (Leviticus 17 – 26), the Deuteronomic Code (Deuteronomy 12 – 16), various units of cultic regulations, later part of the Priestly Code (e.g., Exod. 12:1-20, 43-49; Exodus 34; Leviticus 1 – 7, 11 – 15, 16; Numbers 28 – 29, passim). These collections themselves existed as independent units with their own purposes and spheres of validity before being brought together and placed in their present narrative setting. Their development involved lengthy, complex, and diverse histories. The striking point, however, is that all of these materials now appear as elements in the events at Sinai. For the ancient Israelites, Moses is the prototypical lawgiver, and the covenant defines the framework within which the commandments, laws, and ordinances are to be understood.[5] The prophet Jeremiah states succinctly the inner meaning of this essential link between covenant and commandment:

> Thus says the Lord of hosts, the God of Israel: . . . "Obey my voice, and I will be your God, and you shall be my people; and walk in all the ways that I command you, that it may be well with you" (Jer. 7:21, 23).

THE CONTENT OF ISRAEL'S
LEGAL TRADITIONS
Apodictic Commands and Casuistic Regulations
A detailed exposition of Old Testament legal materials is not possible in this context. However, several generalizations are in order. First, we find that Israel's obligations are sometimes formulated as broad prohibitions and commands, without specific stipulations

about the consequences of disobedience. The outstanding instance is the Decalogue. It sets forth the unequivocal constraints and demands of covenant fidelity. Its language is "Thou shalt . . ." and "Thou shalt not . . . ," chiefly the latter. Apodictic utterances of this sort are primarily suited for liturgical or instructional purposes, for example, in the training of the young. Other materials appear as fully developed legal statutes, as "case law." Representative is the Covenant Code of Exod. 20:23 – 23:19. This code identifies certain typical life situations, specifies how one is to deal with them, and indicates penalties for noncompliance. Casuistic utterances of this sort have practical usefulness for concrete judicial processes, the meting out of justice "in the gate."[6]

According to Martin Noth, the casuistic laws of the Old Testament reflect materials which were common to the ancient Near East, perhaps as mediated through Canaanite culture. The prohibitions and commands display the apodictic form which was normal for the earliest traditions of the Israelite tribes.[7] Despite their diverse origins, both of these modes of expression played a role in specifying the content of Israel's covenantal responsibilities. In Noth's language, we find in the Old Testament "general prohibitions of transgressions against the foundations of human community life," and also the casuistic "regulation of important regions of life in the daily round."[8] The former set forth the basic moral substance of the people; the latter gives that substance practical reality in everyday human interactions. While the specific form and content of both are historically relative, the former, because they are more fundamental, express understandings of more enduring importance.

The Intermixture of Cultic and Social Regulations

Second, we discover that cultic and social regulations are intermixed. There is no sharp separation of religious and moral obligations. I will later call attention to prophetic criticism of the people's tendency to reduce covenant fidelity to correct cultic performance to the neglect of its vital social aspects. Here the primary point is to underscore the essential unity of these two interests.

Two considerations are important in assessing the significance of this unity. On the one hand, Israel's religious convictions themselves concern a moral relationship: a covenantal commitment between two parties. What we might call moral sensibilities penetrate the religious relation, just as the religious relation provides the determinative basis for moral relationships among human beings. One is thus *morally* obliged to incorporate the reality of the religious relation into the normal processes of life in some suitable fashion, that is, in cultic activity. Laws dealing with the cult express this obligation. On the other hand, since the authority of the social laws presupposes not only the covenant, but also narrative accounts of the saving actions of God which first made the covenant possible, the rehearsal of these accounts in the context of the cult is itself integral to covenant fidelity. To speak in general terms: insofar as we appreciate the material connection between our moral notions and that wider horizon of meaning which displays their authority, then some sort of recognition and articulation of that meaning horizon in ritual activity is a feature in the moral life itself. A religious ethic which is wholly abstracted from the cult is a religious ethic without historical and social substance.

It would be misleading to suggest that Israel's cult centered exclusively in the ritual narration of decisive occurrences in its history. It reflected in considerable measure human attempts to cope with basic life rhythms, especially those linked to the production and reproduction of the conditions of existence. It involved animal and cereal offerings oriented to fertility and material abundance as well as actions concerned with the reiteration and restoration of the covenantal basis of life. These two concerns existed together as elements in a larger fabric of meaning. Even so, there are some indications that Israel tended to assimilate the natural elements in its religion to the historical, as in its adaptation of the great agricultural festivals to occasions for the recitation of its sacral traditions in rituals of covenant renewal.[9]

The Special Status of the Vulnerable
Most of the social regulations found in the Old Testament are not in themselves remarkable. They protect human life and property, they call for fairness in commercial transactions and in the adjudication of disputes, and they provide for the stability of the family and

its primary relationships.[10] Matters of this sort are quite basic. They concern the fundamental conditions of an ordered human world. It is doubtful that any society could long exist which did not have equivalent regulations of human interactions. Much of what we find in these materials can be found in other cultures of the ancient Near East.

What is of interest is the degree to which particularly vulnerable members of the society are singled out for special protection: widows, fatherless children, the poor, strangers in the land. The Israelites are obliged to maintain conditions which assure their subsistence. The great eighth-century prophets denounce Israel for faithlessness at this point. What is more striking is that Israel's sacral traditions are manifest in the substantive content of these special obligations. Care for the vulnerable members of society is the human counterpart to Yahweh's compassion for the vulnerable elect in Egypt:

> You shall not wrong a stranger or oppress him, for you were strangers in the land of Egypt. You shall not afflict any widow or orphan. If you do afflict them, and they cry out to me, I will surely hear their cry . . . (Exod. 22:21-23; cf. also Lev. 19:33-34).

Similarly, though ancient Israelite law allowed for a status of human servitude, it was for a limited time only. In the Holiness Code, this limitation is grounded in Yahweh's earlier regard for Hebrew slaves in Egypt: "They are my servants, whom I brought forth out of the land of Egypt; they shall not be sold as slaves" (Lev. 25:42). Unfortunately, the "nations round about" did not at that time enjoy a similar protection (cf. Lev. 25:44-46).

We must not romanticize these materials. Compassion for the vulnerable may presuppose structures of domination and subordination within society which permit and reinforce their vulnerability in the first place. It was the patriarchal structure of society, for example, that placed widows in an exposed position. Preferable from a moral point of view is a society which does not foster such vulnerability, but provides persons with resources to protect their own vital interests. Even so, human beings can never devise a society without some vulnerable members, for example, the aged, the seriously handicapped, the sick, infants, and children. Social arrangements suitable for their protection are essential ingredients in the moral health of a society, at least from the standpoint of these ancient traditions.

The important point here is that Israel's sacral traditions do not simply provide a warrant for its moral understandings. They also inform those understandings in a material way. Examples such as I have cited later take on special importance as resources for the prophetic criticism of society.

Exclusiveness

The most important characteristic of Israel's legal traditions is their insistence upon the exclusiveness of Israelite allegiance to Yahweh. To paraphrase Martin Noth: to the extent that the Old Testament laws are not simply "examples in individual dress" of basic regulations of the social and religious life of the ancient Near East, or of humanity generally, they consistently have as their aim the protection of the basic identity of the twelve-tribe confederation and prevention of its breakup.[11] What is finally at stake in the commandments, laws, and ordinances is Israel's loyalty to the foundational principles of its own existence.

For many students of religion, the emphasis on exclusive attachment to Yahweh is highly problematic. It suggests the cutting off of possibilities, intolerance of what is different, a refusal of communication and fellowship with others. It connotes a certain rigidity, inflexibility, and resistance to change. It may entail dichotomies and sharp oppositions where polar tensions are more appropriate: history versus nature, revelation versus reason, unity versus multiplicity (or plurality), masculinity versus femininity. It does not help much to note that the one who is alleged to demand such exclusiveness is believed to be the creator and preserver of the universe, the font of all wisdom and truth, for even such a divine being is apprehended only in terms of the transient, historical perspectives of one people. The modern interpreter is strongly tempted, therefore, to underplay this feature of Israelite understanding, concentrating instead on motifs which stand up more readily under contemporary tests of universalizability.

57

Exclusive fidelity to Yahweh is, however, quite essential to Israelite views of the moral life. Such fidelity is congruent with the historically oriented mode of thought which is characteristic of a good deal of the Old Testament. In general, historically oriented understandings grant centrality to social and cultural particularity in a fashion not found in perspectives which base themselves upon an anthropology, or a cosmology, or a conception of language or practical reason. For such understandings the moral life is integrally linked to the concrete reality of a people in their historical existence. When exclusiveness is viewed with reference to the concreteness of a people, some of its negative connotations begin to fall away. It then concerns the distinctive identity of a people, their self-definition and self-preservation in the face of pressures and attractions which might result in self-betrayal or self-dissolution. Even this sense of exclusiveness is not without ambiguities. It translates all too easily into dubious presumptions of moral and spiritual superiority; and when sufficient political and military power is present, it can function to legitimate imperialist domination over the lives of others. Nonetheless, no human community or society is able to accomplish anything special or make any distinctive contribution to the human stock of knowledge apart from exclusive attachment to its foundational understandings. The task before us is to grasp more fully what is at stake in Israel's zealous protection of its own particularity; it is to explore resources in that particularity for movement toward the building of a common world with others differently situated.

THE STRUGGLE FOR
COVENANT FIDELITY:
BAALISM AND THE MONARCHY

The exclusiveness of the covenant concerns Israel's development and preservation of its unique legacy, its peculiar truth. In the earlier centuries, what was at stake was a struggle for identity as a people. Israel had to find its way among the nations, resisting social and cultural assimilation into the common patterns of the ancient Near East. This way was not simply pregiven with Israel's origins. It took shape only through an extended development. It was a function of Israel's total pilgrimage. It also incorporated much from a wider environment, by no means foreclosing all positive contact with neighboring peoples. Nonetheless, it expressed a distinct tendency, a fundamental direction, which gained clearer definition in the social and cultural changes through which Israel passed. Once the basic contours of covenant fidelity gained clarity, the problem shifted somewhat. In recognition of Yahweh's lordship over all peoples, the leading questions began to deal with Israel's special status among the nations, and perhaps its mission to them. At this point Israel is portrayed as the bearer and protector of understandings which provide the basis for peace and justice among all peoples. A particular people comes to embody a proposal for the gathering together of all peoples in one human family.

To grasp the significance of covenantal exclusiveness, we need to examine Israel's struggles for identity in response to "crises" generated by major economic and political transitions: initially, the shift from pastoral to agricultural existence, and later, from a tribal confederation to monarchy.[12] Both of these transitions posed critical problems for Israel's self-understanding; in regard to both, the people were in danger of surrendering their peculiar heritage, becoming fully assimilated to the ways of the nations.

The Challenge of Canaanite Culture

It is not essential that we resolve the important historical disputes about Israelite beginnings. Can we trace the roots of the Israelite clans to slaves who escaped from Egypt, first becoming constituted as a people at Sinai (Bright)? Were they originally seminomadic peoples — perhaps from the region of Kadesh — who subsequently moved into Canaan, there developing a settled agricultural existence among the Canaanites (Noth)? Did Israelite tribalism rather emerge as a reaction to Egyptian and Canaanite civilizations, perhaps using their technical advances to form independent settlements in the hill country of Palestine (Gottwald)?[13]

The essential historical point is that at a formative period we come across a profound conflict between Israelite and Canaanite ways of life. This conflict had a number of dimensions. It concerned modes of economic activity: pastoral versus agricultural. It concerned forms of social and political organization: the Israelite tribal confederation, where power and authority were dispersed among the clans, over against the more centralized and hierarchically ordered arrangements of the Canaanite city-states. It concerned primal religious orientations: the Israelite celebration of constitutive happenings in a history with Yahweh in contrast to the cyclic rhythms of Canaanite fertility religion. In the former, social, political, and legal symbolizations of the divine life are prominent; in the latter, organic and sexual ones. This sociocultural conflict was crucial for Israel's self-definition because the Israelite tribes, with their distinctive way of life, were seeking to establish themselves among the Canaanites. In the process they were appropriating features of Canaanite civilization. The problem was to determine which features could become compatible with Yahwism, and which had to be renounced, out of loyalty to the covenant with Yahweh.

The Israelites did borrow much from Canaanite culture, and not just economically and socially. Even their cult reflected Canaanite influence. In the final analysis, however, they sustained their commitment to Yahwism, and they rejected the Baalism of the Canaanites (and of other neighboring peoples as well), at times, violently so. (Consider Elijah's "war" with the prophets of Baal, 1 Kings 18:40, and Jehu's bloody coup against the house of Ahab, 2 Kings 9.) In this connection, Noth suggests that some of the Old Testament laws which now appear to be idiosyncratic (or repressive?), for example, regulations regarding clean and unclean foods, or the "chastity laws" of Leviticus 18, proscribe practices which were closely associated with the Canaanite cult. The function of such laws may have been to separate the people of Israel from aspects of an alien culture which appeared to pose a threat to covenant faithfulness.[14]

For social ethics, the most interesting feature of Yahwism was its link with the emergence of a twelve-tribe confederation. According to Noth, the constitutive traditions of Israelite life took shape in the social milieu of a tribal confederation. This confederation had roots in Israel's seminomadic prehistory. It gained settled form during the period of struggle with the Canaanite city-states. It was the social basis for the old covenant theology. That theology in turn gave significance to the confederation, displaying its grounding in the gracious activity of Yahweh.[15]

It may be too much to claim, as Gottwald does, that Israel was "an egalitarian society in the midst of stratified societies."[16] The Israelite tribes were, after all, patriarchal in structure, itself a form of hierarchy, and the elders of the tribes enjoyed considerable authority. Even so, the tribal confederation did disperse authority and power; individual tribes enjoyed considerable autonomy; extended family units were honored and protected within the clans and tribes; and the elders were responsible for the well-being of all members of their clans, including those who no longer had a secure place within a stable family setting. Responsibility in this context involved important moral constraints on what the elders could and could not do. These patterns were considerably more egalitarian than those of the Canaanite city-states, where the authority of the rulers was more apt to be absolute.[17]

Not less important, Israel's religious understandings reinforced its principles of social order. These understandings centered in solemn covenants involving reciprocal commitments and obligations. They provided resources for resisting any religious sanctification of what might otherwise appear to be "natural" hierarchies among human beings. The emphasis on exclusive attachment to Yahweh concerned nothing less than the maintenance of these understandings and the social conditions they sanctioned.[18]

The victory of Yahwism over Baalism was not without cost. It may have resulted in overly repressive attitudes toward quite natural human processes, especially sexuality and diet. It seems to have entailed something like the suppression of "female power" in human religious consciousness.[19] Its patriarchal themes are an impediment to the egalitarian spirit of contemporary feminism. Allowing for the ambiguities, Israel's triumph over Baalism was still a major determinant of its religious and moral understandings. Israel's legacy to the nations is inconceivable apart from this triumph.

The Rise of the Monarchy
The establishment of the monarchy under Saul and David raised issues equally fundamental to Israel's faith. It brought into being a host of new political institutions: a state bureaucracy, taxes, the conscription of men and women for service to the state, a rationalized military force, political alliances with foreign nations and em-

pires. The alliances implied royal marriages to foreigners and the provision of space within state sanctuaries for their native religious observances. Even the Jerusalem Temple later housed foreign cults in this fashion, becoming a channel for alien religious influences in Israel (cf., e.g., 2 Kings 16:10–18, 21:4–9, and 23:4–7). These developments amounted to a fundamental change in the organizing principle of Israelite society. They were associated with other important changes as well: a demographic shift from rural to town and urban life, an economic shift from agriculture to increased commercial activity, and finally, the rise of a new upper-class elite.

The creation of the monarchy may have been necessary for the preservation of Israel's political independence, not only in response to the immediate Philistine challenge, but also that of powerful new empires to the north and east. For the tribal confederation, however, the monarchy was problematic at best. It endangered the autonomy and equality of the tribes, and it compromised Yahweh's sovereignty over the people. Not surprisingly, an important stratum of Israelite tradition is decidedly antimonarchical.[20] This opposition, I would suggest, was altogether appropriate. It is far from clear that the traditional covenantal understandings could have concrete social substance apart from a structure somewhat like the tribal confederation. When that structure began to lose ground to fundamentally different social arrangements, the older notions were in danger of degenerating into an ideology, that is, a body of ideas cut loose from any basis in actual human interactions, and functioning chiefly to conceal the dynamics of a quite different state of affairs. Noth contends that the old tribal confederation continued to be a viable institution into the period of the monarchy, finally coming to an end only with the Babylonian exile.[21] If so, it could have provided the people with social resources to maintain the older traditions, and where necessary, to constrain the activities of the king.

Over against the resistance to monarchy, there arose traditions which sanctioned the new developments. Gerhard von Rad labels them the David-Zion traditions.[22] They incorporated the monarchy into Israel's ancestral faith, adapting that faith to contemporary social and political realities. Von Rad stresses their importance alongside the exodus-Sinai-occupation traditions. He suggests that they developed in a time when the older traditions were already in decline. Though less miraculous in form and content, these traditions also tell of saving actions of God on behalf of the people.

The David-Zion traditions are themselves a composite of previously independent materials. One strand tells of how Yahweh established the house of David as the chosen instrument for his governance of Israel. The other identifies Jerusalem as Yahweh's appointed dwelling place, making it the central shrine in Israelite worship. These traditions play a prominent role in the deuteronomic histories of the kings of Israel (1 and 2 Kings). They also make up the theological substance of the prophetic message of Isaiah of Jerusalem, indeed, of what we might call the Isaiah "school" of prophecy.[23] They apparently had importance chiefly among the Judahites, perhaps primarily within Jerusalem itself, the "City of David." They never gained a firm hold in the northern kingdom, where older traditions of local shrines and charismatic leadership remained dominant until the fall of Samaria in 722 B.C.E.

The David-Zion traditions bestow sacral authority on the house of David. Still, they do not grant absolute sovereignty to the king. The king remains subject to the word of the prophet, even on matters which elsewhere could have been his clear prerogative, for example, military strategy, diplomacy, claims upon the resources of the land and the services of the people. And though the king took on some cultic functions, these never gained paramount importance in Israel's religious life. Most striking of all, even the house of David was totally unable to penetrate Moses' domain as the prototypical lawgiver in Israel. Moses, and Moses alone, remained the one who delivers the divine law to the people.

Thus, while Israel adopted the monarchy, in this respect becoming "like the nations," it did so only in a limited, sometimes even equivocal, fashion. Israel's identity as a people was never bound up with the existence of the state. It always remained broader and deeper than political institutions, though the latter were explicitly included. In this respect, the celebration of Zion and the Davidic dynasty as "works" of Yahweh is more or less in continuity with the ancient traditions. Since Israel's being had a basis other than the state, the people had resources to survive the loss of political independence at the time of the exile.

I have elaborated the substantive import of covenantal exclusiveness in terms of Israel's struggle with Baalism and the monarchy. The next task is to trace the development of these motifs in the writings of the eighth- and seventh-century literary prophets: Amos, Hosea, Micah, Isaiah, Jeremiah, and Ezekiel.

PROPHETIC JUDGMENT ON COVENANTAL INFIDELITY

The literary prophets stand in continuity with the ancient legal traditions of the Pentateuch. They interpret those materials in the context of changed social, economic, and cultural conditions. Israel's covenantal obligations to Yahweh remain central. In addressing the problems of the times, Amos and Hosea appeal to the exodus, Sinai, and occupation traditions (Amos 2:9-10; Hos. 11:1-4, 12:13, 13:4-5); Isaiah and Micah, to the David-Zion traditions (e.g., Isa. 29:1-8, 11:1-8; Mic. 5:1-2). Micah and Isaiah differ, however, in their treatment of Zion. Micah pronounces doom upon Zion itself (e.g., Mic. 3:9-12), while Isaiah treats it as a stronghold to which Yahweh is committed, at least amid the tumultous events in the final third of the eighth century B.C.E. In all cases, the crucial issue is Israel's exclusive attachment to Yahweh; and the principal challenges to the ancestral faith continue to come from Baalism and the monarchy.

The prophets do bring important new elements into view in articulating Israel's moral understandings, especially by the seventh century. A productive imagination is at work in their mediation of received traditions. Even so, the new elements belong to the logic of the older traditions, bringing them to bear upon changing circumstances in Israel's pilgrimage. I shall highlight three points: the prominence of a word of judgment on Israel's infidelity; an eschatological recasting of Israel's hopes for fulfillment; and a tendency to read Israel's failures less in terms of surface temptations awakened by contacts with neighboring societies and cultures, and more in terms of their anthropological roots in the waywardness of the human heart. These themes transform the old traditions while handing them on to subsequent generations.

Finally, I shall note some new ways of portraying the meaning of Israel's exclusive allegiance to Yahweh. Of special interest is the material in Second and Third Isaiah (Isaiah 40—55 and 56—66, respectively). In these texts exclusiveness no longer concerns Israel's struggle for identity among the nations; it is linked instead to principles entrusted to Israel for the peaceful gathering of the whole human family. Bases are being found in Israel's peculiar legacy for a new inclusiveness, but these bases also indirectly confirm the legitimacy of the earlier insistence on exclusiveness. The search for national identity has become the broader and deeper search for historical integrity.[24]

Israel's Covenant Failure

The prophets proclaim Yahweh's radical judgment upon Israel. Israel has broken the covenant, so the God who once acted to deliver this people is now coming to punish and destroy. The notion of God's "mighty acts" takes a somber turn; the day of the Lord becomes darkness, and not light (Amos 5:18).[25]

Amos goes so far as to announce that Yahweh is finished with Israel (e.g., Amos 7:7–9, 8:1–3). He qualifies this awful word with no more than a slender "perhaps": it *may* be that the Lord will be gracious to the remnant (!) of Joseph, provided the people learn to hate evil and love good, and establish justice in the gate (Amos 5:15). In a similar vein, Hosea, at Yahweh's command, names his third child, a son, *Lo Ammi*: "Not my People!" In a stunning reversal of Israel's covenant identity, the word of Yahweh is now, "You are not my people and I am not your God." The Mosaic covenant is at an end. The divine curses reserved for infidelity are about to come to pass.

How had Israel broken the covenant? Why was the situation so grave? Old themes reappear in these texts, reinterpreted in a new setting. Hosea, more than the other prophets of the period, condemns the people for their involvement with the cult of Baal. They mistakenly credit Baal for their fertility (cf. Hos. 9:10–11) and their abundant harvests (Hos. 2:8). They do not understand that Yahweh is also sovereign over these life processes. No less vigorously, Hosea assaults the people's reliance on the monarchy and its trappings for their physical security: kings and princes, palaces and fortified cities, chariots and a multitude of warriors (Hos. 8:4, 14; 10:13; 13:10). In delivering this word, Hosea apparently speaks out of the tradition of charismatic leaders and citizen armies which had informed the old tribal confederation. As Hosea sees it, the people (called Ephraim) had "mixed themselves" with the nations in their cultic and political life (Hos. 7:8).[26]

Isaiah of Jerusalem echoes this second set of themes, not, however, in terms of the exodus and occupation traditions, but on the basis of the David-Zion traditions. God's election of the house of David in no way implies the wholesale adoption of ancient Near Eastern political styles. It does not involve trust in chariots and foreign alliances. It rather consists in total reliance upon Yahweh and his righteous actions (cf. Isa. 7:4, 8:11-15, 10:20). If Jerusalem is in danger because of foreign military moves, that danger is in any case Yahweh's own doing, his visitation in judgment. The people have no need, therefore, to fear Damascus or Samaria, not even Assyria; it is Yahweh whom they need to fear.[27] (Small wonder that Isaiah is accused of being a conspirator, perhaps even against the king of Judah! Cf. Isa. 8:12.) When these foreign powers, acting as instruments of Yahweh's wrath, overstep their bounds—as they will inevitably do—they too will be doomed before Yahweh's wrath (e.g., Isa. 10:12-19).

For Isaiah, it is Yahweh, not the kings and princes of the nations, who is the chief actor in history. The task of the anointed one of the house of David is not that of securing Judah's political independence, nor even Jerusalem's survival; it is to establish justice in the land (cf. 1:26, 11:1-9). Likewise, the business of the people is to trust in Yahweh, and to maintain covenant faithfulness. The true security of the people lies in their steadfast adherence to the foundational principles of their own existence. Where such steadfastness is missing, military expedients will be of no avail.

This point brings us to the most memorable feature of the prophetic message: above all Yahweh requires justice of the people in their dealings with one another. The prophets carry forward in their own setting the moral understandings of the Decalogue and the Book of the Covenant. Hosea's list of Israel's transgressions echoes the "second table" of the Decalogue: "there is swearing, lying, killing, stealing, and committing adultery; they break all bounds and murder follows murder" (Hos. 4:2; cf. Jer. 7:9–10). Amos, Micah, and Isaiah address evils which call to mind the laws and ordinances of the Book of the Covenant. They single out deceitful commercial transactions (Hos. 12:7; Mic. 6:11–12), and bias and corruption in judicial processes (Amos 5:10–12; Isa. 5:23, 10:1–2). They underscore God's special regard for vulnerable members of society. For Isaiah the defense of the fatherless and the widow is a paradigm of what it means to "seek justice" and "correct oppression" (cf. Isa. 1:17). The measure of the righteousness of a people is the degree to which they guarantee justice for those least able to secure it for themselves.

Structural Bases of Economic Injustice

These prophets assail in broad and vigorous strokes what appears to be a general pattern of economic oppression. They direct their indictment to the "heads" and "rulers" of the house of Israel, to the "princes" and "elders," to the prosperous landowners and merchants. Their images are jolting. Amos cites those who "trample the head of the poor into the dust" (Amos 2:7); Micah, those who "tear the skin from off my people, and their flesh from off their bones" (Mic. 3:2); Isaiah, those who "crush" the people and "grind the face of the poor" (Isa. 3:14–15).

What do we make of this indictment? We are not dealing simply with the attitudes and actions of a random collection of unusually selfish individuals. We are dealing with class oppression. Its basis is the social and economic arrangements of the monarchy.

The monarchy created structures in which it was possible to amass a good deal of wealth: through taxes and forced labor, through the spoils of successful political and military operations, perhaps also through the arrogant seizure of ancestral lands (cf. the story of Naboth's vineyard, 1 Kings 21). This wealth was concentrated in the hands of a small elite associated with court life. It was further increased by the intensified commercial activity it stimulated. By means of this wealth, members of the new elite bought up lands which once provided sustenance for the peasants, and they converted these lands to their own uses, to large estates

67

and luxuriant vineyards (cf. Mic. 2:2–9; Isa. 5:8–10). One can presume a substantial inflation in the market values of many everyday necessities as a result of altered patterns of consumption brought about by this concentration of wealth.

Under these circumstances many people would be effectively cut off from the means of subsistence. Even when their poverty stemmed from specific grievances against the powerful, they were apparently unable to gain a fair hearing for their complaint, for the new elite had considerable influence over the elders who conducted judicial hearings. Small wonder that the prophets considered the practice of bribing judges so heinous, so outrageously highhanded. The more fundamental problem, however, was that the tribal confederation, which had once protected peasant farmers from abuse and exploitation, was simply no longer effective as a social force. The people were at the mercy of new realities beyond their control.

The prophets seem not to have been able to identify the structural basis for the oppression they condemned — unless Hosea's attack on kings and princes amounts to that level of thinking. A critical perspective on institutional arrangements in human society probably requires the analytic tools of the social sciences. It cannot readily be achieved through prophetic discernment alone.

The prophet Isaiah even associates himself with the ruling elite he calls into question. He has no confidence in the capacities of the victims of oppression to order their own affairs. In fact, he projects social chaos should the present leaders in Jerusalem be taken away into exile (Isa. 3:1–8). His hope is for a new representative of the house of David who would occupy himself with peace, justice, and righteousness (Isaiah 11). In other words, the problem is seen not in structural or institutional terms, but in volitional terms. Its basis is not a particular arrangement of social roles, but the personal qualities, commitments, and convictions of those who occupy the roles. If justice is finally to be realized, it will be achieved in a paternal social order.

Nonetheless, these prophets did see that something was fundamentally wrong with the new opulence of the powerful, especially when placed alongside the destitution of the poor. They sensed an inner connection between this opulence and this destitution which they were not fully able to specify. By this insight they brought the moral legacy of their predecessors to bear upon the concrete realities they faced.

What especially incensed the prophets was the presumption of the powerful and well-to-do that they could fulfill their covenant obligations simply by enthusiastic cultic performance, quite without regard for the human suffering caused by the extreme economic inequities of the times. Almost as one voice, Amos, Micah, and Isaiah condemn as useless, even as odious to Yahweh, a cult which is not accompanied by social righteousness.[28] The prophets are not opposed in principle to the traditional cult. They do not set aside the cultic regulations now found in the Pentateuch (i.e., those operative in their times). Even so, they accent the decisive importance of justice in human interactions in Israel's identity as the people of God. It is in their failure to heed this fundamental matter that the people have broken the covenant which Yahweh gave them. God's righteous judgment is, therefore, about to descend upon a disobedient people.

Eschatological Hopes

With the possible exception of Amos, the eighth-century prophets did not believe that God's coming judgment was to be his final action toward Israel. They envisaged a new action of God to redeem and restore Israel. The restoration, however, presupposed Israel's prior endurance of great national calamity. The first word is not deliverance, but ruin. Salvation is possible only on the other side of judgment (cf., e.g., Hos. 2:16–23).

According to von Rad, the orientation of these prophets to future saving actions of Yahweh introduced for the first time a genuinely eschatological motif into Israel's faith.[29] No longer shaped simply by the collective memories of past happenings, Israel began to direct itself to coming possibilities as the basis for worldly existence. This hope was itself informed by the ancient traditions. In fact, both of the major strands in Israel's classic heritage reappear. For Hosea,

Israel had to experience once more the deprivations of the wilderness as preparation for a new occupation of the land of promise. For Isaiah, Israel had to await a new David who would guarantee righteousness and peace. The prophets interpret their own difficult times as repetitions of what it must have been like before the original promises of God were set forth.

Over a century later, standing on the other side of the destruction of Jerusalem and in the presence of the strange new wilderness of Babylonian exile, Ezekiel and Jeremiah take up and expand these eschatological themes. More unequivocally than their predecessors, they underscore the qualitative newness of the saving actions Yahweh is to accomplish. Israel's hope of restoration requires that Yahweh create a new heart and a new spirit within the people (Ezek. 11:14–21), or that he make a totally new covenant, one engraved not on tablets of stone, but cut into human hearts (Jer. 31:31–34).

These new themes have enormous ramifications for moral understanding. The eschatological orientation introduces a remarkable tension, perhaps even a duality, into the moral life. One places one's hope in an order of life which in the nature of the case cannot be realized under existing worldly conditions. That order is not a mere dream, an empty wish, an idle fantasy; its basis is the power of the divine life, and its accomplishment is vital for human well-being. It alone assures peace, righteousness, and fullness of life for the creatures of the earth. Insofar as possible we are summoned to live by its promises and imperatives. However, since we cannot now inhabit a world governed by the hoped-for order, there is no way for us to escape deep suffering and tribulation in our present existence. To survive and to maintain our integrity in the present, we require a set of arrangements suited to existing conditions, no matter how difficult those conditions may be. We require moral and religious understandings adapted for survival in the interim, better still, designed for patient waiting and faithful enduring as we make the best of a bad situation. These two orders are not viewed as simply side by side, as belonging to two wholly separate spheres. They interpenetrate each other and pull at each other, setting up a complex field of forces in tension as the concrete matrix of moral and religious existence. A dialectic of this sort does not easily translate into the categories of Enlightenment ethics. Yet some version of it is indispensable to a biblically informed ethic.

The tensions here introduced are later stretched to the breaking point in apocalyptic treatments of the prophetic tradition, of which the book of Daniel is the best canonical example in the Old Testament. More strongly than ever these interpreters of Israel's faith dramatize the range and depth of the evils of the present age, thus radicalizing the scope of the upheavals implied in the coming of God's righteousness. For apocalyptic thought, we must endure in the present evil age; but our hope is in the totally different age of God's triumphant glory. This duality provides the salient elements in that meaning horizon which eventually became decisive for Christian understandings.

The Anthropological Roots of Human Evil

The accent on the new heart and the new spirit in Jeremiah and Ezekiel also has high importance for moral understanding. These motifs suggest that the crux of the problem in Israel's persistent transgression of covenant responsibilities is a flaw in human being itself: a hard heart, a stubborn heart, a heart slow to learn. The problem is not simply Baalism and its associations with agricultural life (or with fertility generally); nor is it the monarchy with its contradictions of clan autonomy and divine sovereignty. It is a weakness in humanity as such. Anthropology rather than social structures and institutions moves to the center of attention, a movement later intensified in the New Testament writings.

This move was not unprecedented. It was already prepared for by the ancient sagas of Genesis 1—11 which the Yahwist first put together and used as a preface to the legends of Israel's patriarchal prehistory. These sagas provided an anthropological frame of reference for the narration of Yahweh's dealings with Israel. They dramatized the pervasiveness of human wickedness among all peoples of the earth. They suggested that Yahweh had already made a fresh start with disobedient humanity in calling Abram and his family to leave Ur of the Chaldeans and go to Canaan (Gen. 11:31). For Jeremiah and Ezekiel, this deeper problem of the human inclination to evil becomes the focal issue in the definition of Israel's hope.

The Universal Lordship of Yahweh

One final matter in the prophetic message merits comment. For the prophets, Yahweh is not simply the God of Israel alongside of whom there are other gods for other peoples. He is the Lord of all peoples. Consequently, the prophets have to take up in a new and deeper fashion the meaning of Israel's exclusive ties to Yahweh. It is at least paradoxical to claim that the sovereign Lord over all should have a special relation with one particular group of people!

This problem did not surface as long as Israel's self-definition over against the nations was in the forefront of concern. As Israel's self-understanding matured, however, it required attention. The prophets have a good deal to say about the matter. Initially they stress Israel's unique responsibility among the nations. Because of their distinctive knowledge of Yahweh, the people are especially accountable for their manner of life (e.g., Amos 3:2). Later, suggestions of Israel's mission to the nations come to the fore: Zion shall be the place from which the teachings of Yahweh will go forth into the earth; and the nations shall gather to Zion to learn of the law of Yahweh (e.g., Isa. 2:1-4, which may be a postexilic oracle).

The message of the anonymous postexilic prophet, known to biblical critics only as Second Isaiah, is climactic. For this prophet, Israel has been called of Yahweh to be a "light to the nations": to open eyes that are blind, to bring prisoners out of the dungeon, to bring forth justice to the nations (Isa. 42:5-9). Israel's world mission provides a context for a fresh interpretation of its sufferings. This suffering is not preeminently a mark of divine wrath against a disobedient people. It is righteous suffering, the price of the special mission of the people. It is akin to labor pains, the prelude to a new birth of righteousness among all peoples (Isaiah 53, esp. vv. 10-11).

The urgency of Israel's exclusive attachment to Yahweh is then for the sake of establishing a basis for genuine human inclusiveness. This basis is not conquest or imperialism in any of its forms; it is righteousness and justice, that is, relations of mutual respect and caring among peoples.[30] It lets the oppressed go free, it breaks every yoke, it liberates the captives, it binds up the brokenhearted, it comforts those who mourn, it brings good news to the afflicted (Isa. 58:6-14; cf. Isa. 61:1-4).[31] It is for the sake of this hope that Israel has been called and appointed, and has lived out its peculiar history; it is in the fulfillment of this mission that Israel will find its distinctive joy.

The prophets carry forward the central thrust of Israel's traditions. They hold in view the covenantal context of Israel's obligations, both to Yahweh and to one another as the people of God. They understand these obligations as features in the exclusive loyalty which Yahweh requires of the people. Though this loyalty has crucial cultic components, it chiefly concerns elemental social, economic, and political matters: protection of the life and property of the people, fairness and justice in commercial transactions and in the adjudication of disputes, and special regard for the survival and well-being of the most vulnerable members of the society. It was failure on this last point which provoked the most severe of the prophetic indictments. As long as the people maintained covenant fidelity, so the prophets believed, they could trust in Yahweh to protect and deliver them from their enemies; where this fidelity was lacking, foreign alliances, chariots, and standing armies would be of no avail. It is Yahweh, not the nations, whom they finally have to fear.

The prophets participated in Israel's struggles to deal with covenantal obligations amid the tumultous political and economic developments of the times. They believed that Israel had violated the covenant, and hence, was doomed to suffer the judgment of God. They projected Israel's hopes for fulfillment into the future, portraying them increasingly in eschatological terms. They pressed the basis of Israel's failure to the inner life—beyond the social and cultural attractiveness of the nations to a flaw in the human heart. Even so, social structures and cultural patterns continued to figure prominently in their treatments of Israel's covenant identity. Finally, the growing world awareness of the prophets deepened and transformed their sense of the meaning of Israel's ties to Yahweh. Yahweh's special claims were no longer preeminently linked to

Israel's concrete particularity as such; they concerned as well a manner of being in the world, entrusted to Israel by Yahweh, which bore the potential of freeing and gathering in peace all peoples of the earth. The prophets dared to portray Israel as a light to the nations.

One final movement deserves mention prior to a summation of distinctive Old Testament contributions to moral understanding. We need to note briefly, at least by way of contrast, some of Israel's postexilic adaptations of the ancestral faith to the loss of political independence in the period of the great world empires.

POSTEXILIC ADAPTATIONS TO
THE WORLD EMPIRES

Beginning with the exile, the Jewish people had to find a way of surviving in an alien environment. Zion had been destroyed, and the house of David crushed; both Temple and political independence were at an end; and the tribal confederation was no more than a memory. The covenant people in the old sense had ceased to exist. Here we are in the presence of the deepest crisis in Israel's long and difficult pilgrimage.

For many, those belonging to the Diaspora, existence as God's people would from that time forth be accomplished without king or temple or tribal confederation; these persons would have at their disposal only a reduced body of commandments, laws, and ordinances: God's Torah as adapted for the family life of a minority community within a larger society. For others, there would for a time be a restored community in Jerusalem with a new temple and a renewed cult, but always under the auspices of the great world empires—Persian, Greek, Roman. There was a brief flicker of political independence under the Maccabees, and in modern times, we have witnessed the establishment of the Israeli state, in part as a Western response to the horrors of the Holocaust inflicted by the Nazis on the European Diaspora. But for the world disclosed in the biblical texts, political sovereignty was no longer to be. For the most part, what we find in this new situation is a theology and an ethics of patient waiting and faithful enduring.

A *People of the Book*

Martin Noth highlights the contrast between the ancient traditions and the understandings of the postexilic restoration community. For the former, the starting point was the concrete reality of a people, interpreted in sacral narratives of their origin and their pilgrimage over time. The commandments, laws, and ordinances which ordered the lives of the people had validity primarily with reference to this concrete existence. The narratives, in recounting the experiences of the people, displayed the authority of the commandments and laws in their lives. The twelve-tribe confederation, with its common cult and shared traditions, gave institutional form, and hence, social reality, to the understandings which informed their existence.

For the restoration community, the commandments, laws, and ordinances were in the forefront of attention. By virtue of their divine origin they were understood to be a body of authoritative and binding requirements in human life. Their authority was taken to be everlasting, even when their precise significance was unclear and required interpretation. Those who acknowledged the authority of these laws and diligently observed them made up the community of God's people. One belonged to the community by living in accordance with God's law. A shared history and the narration of collective memories were not irrelevant, but they were secondary to diligent observance of the statutes and ordinances given through Moses. The existence of a community of people committed to the observance of the law was a sign that the covenant continued in effect. This community gained its institutional reality in the temple cult, in family rituals, and in a cadre of teachers and interpreters of the law (i.e., the Levites).[32]

The laws and commandments in no way lacked religious and moral power in the new frame of reference, but that power was differently placed. What is most striking is that the formative traditions of the people seem to have lost their lively historical connection, both with the past and with the unfolding future. The point can be overstated. Haggai and Zechariah, for example, speak directly to the events of their times. Zechariah in particular echoes the great prophets in his sense of Israel's historical destiny. Also, apocalyptic literature later brings into view an eschatological future. In a formal sense, however, the laws and commandments which set forth the obligations of the people now present themselves as fixed once and for all. They take on independent reality over against the community. Henceforth, the community is to maintain its integrity chiefly by acknowledging and interpreting in changing situations what has already been given in an unchanging form. In this transition the Jewish people became, indeed, a people of the book.

It is not surprising to discover in this new frame of reference the emergence of what some have called a "torah mysticism," a celebration of law and commandment as a gracious gift which bears to the believer the glorious presence of the creator-God. Continual meditation on the law, diligent regard for its admonitions and warnings, and zealous attempts to embody its precepts in one's daily life amount in themselves to a participation in the majesty and goodness of God (e.g., Psalms 19, 119). In an equivalent fashion, religious thinkers, especially the sages, began to associate the commandments not so much with Moses as with creation, blending into one coherent picture of reality experientially based wisdom teachings, celebrations of the creative power of God, and the authority of law and commandment in human life. (See especially Proverbs 8, or the whole of chapters 1—9, and Sirach 1, 24.) Notions such as these maintain the religious power and depth of teachings which order the lives of the people. But they alter significantly the basic orientation of the older traditions.[33]

The Emergence of Perfectionist Themes

The postexilic literature not only reflects a somewhat different placement of the law within the total self-understanding of the people. It also discloses a certain redirection in the focal interest of the moral life itself. Instead of almost exclusive attention to the deontological concern with the requisites of social existence, we now find a perfectionist interest in the accomplishment of individual human excellence as something significant in its own right.

A perfectionist interest was by no means lacking in the preexilic literature. The book of Deuteronomy, for example, attends explicitly to the formation of persons. It admonishes the people to have the law constantly before their minds, and to teach it diligently to oncoming generations (cf. Deut. 6:4–9). The intent, however, was not to produce virtuous individuals as such; it was to create a people who had internalized their covenant obligations and so honored them as a kind of second nature. Thus, while a perfectionist emphasis was certainly present, it was wholly subordinated to the needs of the covenant community.

In a number of the postexilic Psalms we detect a slight change of focus. For the most part, the content of the moral life continues to be expressed in a legal form, in terms of statutes, laws, and ordinances. However, devoted attention to the law and diligent observance of its precepts are no longer directly linked to the integrity of the covenant community. Its point is to enable one to become a righteous human being; it is to help one find in such righteousness the joy and strength of one's life (cf., e.g., Pss. 1, 19:7–14, 119).[34] In these texts the laws and ordinances have been recast as personal virtues, as the habitual ways of acting of morally excellent individuals. No less important, such righteousness is apparently considered to be something which any genuinely committed person might achieve, regardless of the moral health of the community as a whole. It thus makes sense to distinguish righteous and wicked individuals within the community, to praise the former and condemn the latter.

Perfectionist motifs enjoy a similar independence in the book of Job. In the thirty-first chapter, Job describes in some detail his normal ways of acting in response to some typical life situations. What emerges is a portrait of a morally excellent human being, one who has internalized in his own life Israel's paramount moral teachings. Laws and ordinances are not explicitly mentioned in this text, but the moral content of Israel's legal traditions is manifest in what does appear. The purpose of Job's recitation, however, is to underscore his own virtue as an individual. It is not, let us say, to work out and establish basic principles of social cooperation. (Though one can certainly presume that persons having Job's virtues would contribute to the health and well-being of any human community!)

77

The presence of perfectionist themes in the postexilic texts indicates an increased sense of personal identity and destiny in the self-understandings of the people. This sensibility contrasts with the strong presumption of social solidarity in the earlier traditions. It attests a more complex and highly differentiated society. Even so, the conception of personal formation which is implicit in these texts continues to be one that is largely governed by socially mediated traditions. Human excellence is by no means presented as the creativity and self-transcendence of fully individuated selves, as in post-Enlightenment thought. It is set forth as strict conformity to a divinely revealed pattern of life.

In the Book of Proverbs perfectionist thinking comes more clearly into its own. In these texts it finds a form which is suited for its distinctive subject matter. Even in Proverbs we discover what may be echoes of the commandments and regulations of the ancient legal codes. These echoes are especially apparent in the "instruction" materials, the admonitions of the father to his son (e.g., Prov. 22:20–24). Erhard Gerstenberger has cited materials of this sort to reinforce his suggestion that the Decalogue originated in the context of the clan, as the instructions of the elders, the "fathers," to the young.[35]

More common in Proverbs, however, are not the "instructions," but the pithy sayings expressing a kind of practical wisdom about the good life. These sayings do not take the form of authoritative utterances, not even from the fathers, still less as God's direct revelation. With their interesting analogies, comparisons and contrasts, and their pointed observations, they invite readers (or hearers) to consult their own experiences, to become themselves astute observers of life. The aim is to develop in the novice a capacity for discerning judgments. The result is not a set of laws and ordinances, or even of principles and rules, which are to be applied to various life situations. We get instead a kind of gestalt, a portrait, of a person who has learned to live judiciously and well. This person knows the trials and temptations of life and can manage them; this person is attuned to the surface attractions of life, but can see through them to its more abiding values; this person is one who has a properly ordered set of priorities.[36]

This style of thinking is in touch with the distinctive strength of a perfectionist perspective on the moral life. The pity is that it was not articulated in a fashion more fully integrated with Israel's classic traditions. Points of contact are suggested in the wisdom literature, but for the most part these materials stand alongside the distinctive thrust of the Pentateuch and of the great literary prophets. It appears almost as an alternative viewpoint, a minority report, within the biblical literature. It offers a touch of down-to-earth human concerns amid the epochal visions of a people of destiny.

In general, perfectionism is not a dominant mode of moral understanding in the Old Testament literature. Dominant rather is the deontological interest in the constitutive obligations of a covenant people. And the form of deontological interest which presents the most striking challenge to contemporary religious thought is that embodied in the historical thrust of the ancient pentateuchal traditions and the message of the great eighth- and seventh-century B.C.E. prophets.

THE CHALLENGE
TO MORAL UNDERSTANDING
IN ISRAEL'S LEGACY

Where moral understanding is at stake, Israel's distinctive legacy can be seen in terms of two major categories: historicity and sociality. In the first, the key point is that Israel's moral obligations are linked to its concrete particularity as the covenant people of Yahweh. The major issues confronting Israel concern its struggle to work out the meaning of that particularity and to maintain it with fidelity in the face of alternative possibilities which threatened to compromise or undermine it.

Two aspects of Israel's historical particularity are of special interest. First, as the prophets came to appreciate the flawed nature of Israelite life, they projected the fulfillment of Israel's destiny into an eschatological future. The eschatological orientation called forth a dual perspective on the moral life: one perspective directed to a vision of future fulfillment which bestowed meaning on an ambiguous, even tragic, history; the other, to an ethics of survival — of patient waiting and faithful enduring — within an alien world order. A dual perspective of this kind is an essential feature of an ethic governed by a sense of human historicity. Second, the more deeply the prophets reflected upon the import of Israel's particularity, the more that particularity came to be seen not as a denial of universality or even of social and cultural otherness, but as a concretely historical way into universality. The universal takes on concrete reality, that is to say, not by abstracting from history, but by following the promise which is latent in its open horizon. When we attempt to take shortcuts to universality by logical refinements of our basic moral notions, we will invariably conceal in the result unacknowledged prejudices of one sort or another. The movement to universality is, to be sure, neither automatic nor inevitable; even so, it belongs to historical existence as one of its pregiven possibilities. Thus, by fidelity to its founding principles, Israel was contributing to the broader human quest for the bases of a humane world order under the divine sovereignty. For the prophets, the crucial requisite for such an order is justice; yet in their view the struggle for justice becomes concrete only when it is pursued from the vantage point of the vulnerable and the oppressed. The hope for the world resides in that order of life which provides hope for the hungry, the thirsty, the afflicted, the enslaved, the downtrodden.

Regarding sociality, a number of considerations are at stake. Morally speaking, the key point is social solidarity. According to Israelite understandings, it is not as isolated individuals, but as members of a community that we realize our being. Even our individuality is through and through social. Consequently, our wholeness as moral beings cannot be abstracted from the moral soundness of the community to which we belong. The moral soundness of the community, moreover, is most clearly manifest in its treatment of its most vulnerable members. As individuals, we share in the accomplishments of the community; but we are no less implicated in its failures. Individual responsibility is not ruled out by this sense of sociality; yet it gains an essentially social meaning. I act not simply for myself, but for the well-being of the whole people. I am answerable not simply to myself and my own principles, but to the whole people and its foundational principles. I am finally answerable for the people as well, for I am called to measure the corporate life of the people to whom I belong in terms of its founding principles, and in terms of the resources they offer for dealing with ever-changing social circumstances.

Sociality involves more than a moral vision, however. It involves as well the struggle for social arrangements congruent with that vision. The vision cannot itself take effective form apart from practical experience in working out its requisite social arrangements. In the biblical tradition, insight into this fundamental connection is most clearly manifest in the early resistance to monarchy, and in the prophetic critique of the economic, social, and political patterns subsequently generated by the monarchy. It is perhaps also manifest in Israelite attempts to devise a form of monarchy compatible with the social and religious institutions of premonarchical existence. What emerges in these materials is a strong awareness that Israel's reality, though profoundly political, is yet deeper than its political forms. It is certainly deeper than the specific instrumentalities which order the operations of the state. Crucial to this deeper reality are the institutions which took their form under the tribal confederation: cultic, social, judicial, and military. Because these institutions persisted into the period of the monarchy, they undergirded prophetic criticism of those distortions in Israelite life which were brought about by the monarchy. The same institutions later provided Israel with resources to survive the loss of political independence.

Despite the grandeur of Isaiah's messianic visions, it is doubtful that Israel could have sustained its ancient traditions without distortion under the conditions of the monarchy. Monarchy inevitably implied a hierarchical social and political order which ran counter to the ancient concern for the solidarity and well-being of all members of the community. At the time of its founding, it may likewise have appeared doubtful that Israel could survive without the monarchy. Military pressures from neighboring peoples very likely made the newer institutions seem necessary to Israel's ongoing life. In order to solidify and sustain its ancient traditions, Israel may have required political forms which contradicted those same traditions. Under circumstances of this kind the temptation is great to minimize the moral significance of institutional considerations. One then accounts for social failure not in institutional terms, but in terms of a flawed heart. And one hopes for a renewal of life not in the reconstruction of basic institutions but in the emergence of a new generation of leaders. The anthropological dimensions of

Israelite failure and the messianic bases of Israelite hopes are by no means uninteresting or unimportant for contemporary appropriations of the Old Testament legacy. Yet these dimensions appear in their proper light only when they deepen institutional issues, not when they displace them or render them irrelevant to moral concern. In any case, Israel's moral vision seems to have surpassed what it was able to build into its basic institutions during the periods in which it flourished economically and politically. In this respect, it presents a continuing challenge to human imagination and creativity.

NOTES

1. In recounting the faith of ancient Israel, it is difficult to avoid the masculine pronoun in references to deity, even though I consider it essential in contemporary reconstruction to move beyond the patriarchal bias of our Jewish and Christian roots. I applaud the efforts of biblical scholars to highlight the presence of feminine images and metaphors in biblical portrayals of the activity and character of God. See especially Phyllis Trible, *God and the Rhetoric of Sexuality*, Overtures to Biblical Theology 2 (Philadelphia: Fortress Press, 1978).

2. For a discussion of this basic pattern, see Gerhard von Rad, *The Problem of the Hexateuch and Other Essays* (New York: McGraw-Hill, 1966), 27ff. Von Rad presents the structure I have set forth as the organizing principle of the book of Deuteronomy. A variant form is found in Exodus 19 – 24.

3. Von Rad, *Problem of the Hexateuch*, 13–26. On the separateness of covenant making and prohibitions and commandments, see Erhard Gerstenberger, *Wesen und Herkunft des 'Apodiktischen Rechts'* (Neukirchen: Neukirchener Verlag, 1966), 89ff.

4. Von Rad accents the decisive role of the Yahwist in establishing the model for the narration of Israel's sacral traditions. See his *Old Testament Theology* (New York: Harper & Row, 1962), 1:49–53. The Yahwist document provides the organizing framework for von Rad's exposition of "the theology of Israel's historical traditions."

5. See Martin Noth, *The Laws in the Pentateuch and Other Studies* (Philadelphia: Fortress Press, 1966), 6–7, 37–40. For a helpful survey of recent scholarly studies of Israel's legal traditions, see Walter Harrelson, *The Ten Commandments and Human Rights*, Overtures to Biblical Theology 8 (Philadelphia: Fortress Press, 1980), 19–48. I might note that the hermeneutic which informs Harrelson's study is not unlike the one ad-

vocated in this work, though Harrelson does not attempt to make fully explicit the preunderstandings which inform his interpretations of the texts.

6. The "gate" is the place where the elders and judges heard the complaints of the people and adjudicated disputes among them. For a discussion of the distinction between apodictic and casuistic formulations, see Gerstenberger, *Apodiktischen Rechts*, 23ff.

7. Noth, *Laws in the Pentateuch*, 7-8. Gerstenberger, *Apodiktischen Rechts*, argues that the Decalogue had its origin in the clan, and hence predated Moses, despite its subsequent importance in the cult. Cf. 89ff. See also 61ff.

8. Noth, *Laws in the Pentateuch*, 8.

9. On this point see von Rad, *Problem of the Hexateuch*, 43.

10. The family structure was, of course, patriarchal. The ramifications of this fact are extensive, reaching into primary symbolic representations of the being and activity of God. Mediating these traditions in a form which does not simply reinforce the subordination of women is a major challenge to Christian ethics.

11. Noth, *Laws in the Pentateuch*, 59.

12. Von Rad speaks of these transitions as "crises" in Israel's development. See his *Old Testament Theology*, 1:15-68.

13. See John Bright, *A History of Israel*, 3d ed. (Philadelphia: Westminster Press, 1981); Martin Noth, *The History of Israel*, 2d ed. (London: A & C Black, 1958); and Norman K. Gottwald, *The Tribes of Yahweh* (Maryknoll, N.Y.: Orbis Books, 1979).

14. Noth, *Laws in the Pentateuch*, 54-58. He cites in particular the role of the wild pig in Canaanite religion. Cf. Deut. 14:8 and Lev. 11:7.

15. Noth, *Laws in the Pentateuch*, 28-30.

16. Gottwald, *Tribes of Yahweh*, 693.

17. The story of Naboth's vineyard, though later in time and involving the Tyrian Baal of Jezebel, is instructive in this connection. Jezebel could not comprehend Ahab's inability to override Naboth's refusal to sell him an ancestral vineyard. For her, Ahab's inability to act was an indication of weakness, not moral restraint. "Do you not govern Israel?" she asked her husband. Without apparent scruples, she arranged Naboth's death and seized his vineyard for Ahab's use. Since Ahab was nurtured in the traditions of Yahwism, he was constrained from such action. Not even kings could set aside a familial legacy. Cf. 1 Kings 21.

18. On the underlying cultic issues, see Walter Harrelson, *From Fertility Cult to Worship* (Garden City, N.Y.: Doubleday & Co., 1969).

19. Carol Christ, "Heretics and Outsiders: The Struggle Over Female Power in Western Religion," *Soundings* 51 (1978): 263-66.

20. Cf. especially 1 Sam. 8:11-17 and the remarkable fable of Jotham, Judg. 9:8-21. Cf. also Hos. 8:4, 13:11. When David became king, he sought to build ties with the confederation, chiefly by bringing the ark of the cove-

nant from Shiloh to Jerusalem (2 Sam. 6:1–19). By this act he established Jerusalem as the cultic center of Israelite life. The beginning of his reign was further marked by direct dealings with the elders of the various Israelite clans. Cf. 2 Sam. 2:4, 5:3; cf. also 1 Kings 12:3–19. For a discussion of opposition to the monarchy, see von Rad, *Old Testament Theology*, 1:57–68.

21. Noth, *Laws in the Pentateuch*, 32–33.

22. Von Rad, *Old Testament Theology*, 1:39–49. Cf. 2 Samuel 7 for Nathan's prophetic endorsement of David's kingship. Von Rad appeals to preexilic material in the Psalms as supporting evidence for these traditions, especially Psalms 110 and 132.

23. Cf. von Rad, *Old Testament Theology*, 2:147. Von Rad organizes his discussion of Isaiah's prophetic message around the motifs of Zion and Yahweh's anointed one, 155–75. He accents Isaiah's theological scope and power.

24. The distinction between identity and integrity is taken from Erik Erikson's account of the psychosocial development of the healthy self. Identity is an adolescent issue. It confronts the threat of identity diffusion. Integrity is an issue of mature adulthood. It suggests one sufficiently sure. of his or her center to be able to respect and enter into fellowship with those who are different. It too is not beyond threat, but the threat is more profound: ultimate despair over the meaning and significance of existence. The issue is no longer "who am I?" but "does it matter at all?" In Israel's maturation as a people, the skepticism and resignation of Ecclesiastes properly belong with the grand vision of the Isaiah school. See Erik Erikson, "Growth and Crises of the Healthy Personality," in *Identity and the Life Cycle, Psychological Issues* I (1959): 50–100.

25. Cf. von Rad, *Old Testament Theology*, 2:178 ff. Von Rad says that the message of radical judgment has no basis in the old traditions. I am uncertain of his meaning since such judgment would seem to be continuous with the announcement of curses for disobedience to the covenant—or does this tradition itself reflect the influence of the eighth-century prophets?

26. Von Rad notes that Hosea is the only prophet from the northern kingdom whose writings have survived. His thought roots in the exodus-Sinai-occupation traditions. Hosea's thought provides supporting evidence for von Rad's claim that the exodus-Sinai-occupation traditions were initially preserved primarily in the northern kingdom. Cf. ibid., 2:139–40.

27. Von Rad develops the relation of Isaiah's attitudes toward military activity to ancient traditions of holy war. Cf. ibid., 2:153.

28. The passages I have in mind are such classics they scarcely need to be cited again here: Amos 5:21–24; Mic. 6:6–8; and Isa. 1:10–20.

29. Von Rad, *Old Testament Theology*, 2:185.

30. Note in this connection von Rad's discussion of the Hebrew term usually translated "righteousness," *Old Testament Theology*, 1:377–83. In

reference to God, the term designates divine activity in establishing and delivering a people. In reference to human activity, it designates covenant fidelity, honoring in appropriate ways the relationships brought into being by the covenant. It embraces obedience to the laws and commandments. In no way does it suggest setting aside the law; it rather expresses the spirit of the law. This point is clear in the close association between righteousness and justice (*mishpat*), where the latter concerns judicial processes among the people, especially "in the gate." At a concrete level, where there are complaints and disputes, righteousness consists in justice. In both cases what are at stake are right relationships among the people.

31. Critics credit these passages to yet a "third" Isaiah. In content they are fully congruent, however, with the message of Second Isaiah.

32. Noth, *Laws in the Pentateuch*, 80; cf. also 86–87. Materials in Ezra epitomize the latter mode of understanding.

33. Gerhard von Rad, *Wisdom in Israel* (Nashville: Abingdon Press, 1972), argues that there is a close link between Israel's wisdom and Yahwism, accenting in particular the central theme of Proverbs 1 – 9: "the fear of the Lord is the beginning of wisdom." James Crenshaw concedes that this claim may be a legitimate corrective to the overstatement in prior scholarship of the secularity of wisdom literature. Even so, he insists upon the distinctiveness of wisdom thinking within Israelite life: "Sages lived within the covenant community, to be sure, but they chose to ignore virtually every tradition known to prophets and priests. That silence speaks more eloquently than von Rad's immersion of sages into the Yahwistic font suggests." See J. L. Crenshaw's review of von Rad's study in *Religious Studies Review* 2 (April 1976): 8–9. For Crenshaw's own work, see his *Studies in Ancient Israelite Wisdom* (New York: KTAV, 1975).

34. Noth, *Laws in the Pentateuch*, 95–101.

35. Gerstenberger, *Apodiktischen Rechts*, 117ff.

36. In this discussion I have been guided by von Rad, *Old Testament Theology*, 1:418–41. See also his *Wisdom in Israel*, esp. 113–37.

4

SYNOPTIC PORTRAYALS OF ESCHATOLOGICAL EXISTENCE

The discussion of the New Testament will focus on the Synoptic Gospels and the letters of Paul, with brief consideration of contrasting orientations in other literature. Since the book of Acts is integral to Luke's narration of Jesus' ministry, its themes will be treated in the discussion of Luke's Gospel. In general, the materials selected for closer study enjoy a status in the New Testament comparable to "law" and "prophets" in the Old Testament.[1] I will turn first to the Synoptic Gospels and Acts even though their appearance is later in time than Paul's writings. This starting point enables us to bring the public ministry of Jesus into view at the outset. Paul himself presupposes Jesus' ministry, though he makes almost no explicit mention of it. Also, the Synoptics contain traditions which predate Paul's missionary activity. In this respect, they put us in touch with a primitive phase in the emergence of the Christian movement. The present chapter will be devoted to the Synoptics, drawing upon the accomplishments of redaction critics and literary critics. These approaches focus our attention on the distinctive points of view conveyed by the Gospels as completed documents. The following chapter will deal with the thought of Paul.

The New Testament writings continue a version of the historical contextualism found in the pentateuchal traditions and the prophetic literature. However, the sense of history present in these writings is profoundly marked by a distinctive eschatology: a conviction that the new age has already dawned. For Paul the arrival of the new age is linked to the death and resurrection of Jesus Christ.

It is manifest as the "fruits" of the Spirit in the lives of persons belonging to the new Christian communities. Its final consummation is at hand. It consists in the ultimate realization of God's dominion over all things (cf. 1 Cor. 15:24-28). It will bring a cataclysmic end to the present form of the world. For Mark the new age dawns in the public ministry of Jesus. It is the work of the Spirit. By the power of the Spirit Jesus challenges the destructive control Satan exercises over human affairs. Mark structures his account of Jesus in terms of the eschatological conflict between the Spirit and Satan.[2] Like Paul he believes that the coming of the Son of Man in power and glory is imminent (cf. Mark 13:28, 30-31), though he displays sensitivity to a certain apprehensiveness in his anticipated readers over the unexpected delay of that occurrence (Mark 13:32-37).

Matthew and Luke moderate the intensity of the eschatological expectations found in Paul and Mark. More strongly than Mark, Matthew reckons with the possibility that considerable time may pass before the kingdom of heaven is fully established. He maintains an orientation toward that hoped-for event, but he weighs more heavily daily concerns for the ordered life of developing communities of faith. In general, he gives greater prominence than Mark to the moral and religious substance of eschatological existence.

In Luke-Acts, eschatology is taken up into a broad scheme of salvation-history.[3] The scheme has three sharply delineated periods: the period of the law and the prophets, the period of Jesus (prefaced by the birth narratives and concluded with an account of Jesus' ascension into heaven), and the period of the missionary expansion of the church. Luke deals with the first period retrospectively; he narrates the second and the third. The latter periods have strong geographical associations as well: Jesus' ministry, with Galilee and Jerusalem; the church's expansion, with Jerusalem, Judea, and Samaria, then with the cities of Asia Minor, Macedonia, and Greece, eventually with Rome, and symbolically, with "the ends of the earth" (cf. Acts 1:8). In one sense eschatology has for Luke been dissolved into the church's missionary expansion. Thus, the book of Acts concludes not with a community awaiting Jesus' coming in power and glory, but with Paul preaching the kingdom of

God in Rome, "openly and unhindered" (Acts 28:31). The focal interest is in the spread of the message about Jesus to the ends of the earth, not in the consummation of God's sovereign reign. In another sense, the epoch of the church is itself eschatological. It is the age of the Spirit, which Luke, quoting the prophet Joel, portrays as having eschatological significance. Eschatology so understood deals with the inauguration of a new and decisive stage in historical development. This new stage has deep roots in the stabilities and continuities of preceding stages. Luke's feeling for historical continuities has important implications for his moral understandings. Even so, his conviction that something genuinely new has come into being with Jesus and the Spirit-filled apostolate places him on common ground with Paul and the other Gospel authors.

I noted that eschatology emerged as an important theme in the thought of Jeremiah, Ezekiel, and Second Isaiah, qualifying their understandings of Israel's destiny as the covenant people of Yahweh. In that context, I suggested, eschatology had the effect of generating a dual perspective in ethics: a vision of fulfillment in a coming new age, and an orientation to survival in the alien circumstances of the present age. In the New Testament, this duality becomes a dialectic. The coming new age takes on substantive though incomplete reality in the present. One is already summoned to live on its terms even while one must continue to endure the afflictions of the age which is passing away. A new community, oriented to and based upon the new age, takes form in the midst of institutions which remain under the sway of the old. Consequently, those who dare to live for the new inevitably find themselves in conflict with those who cling to the old. The latter use the resources of established institutions to harass, persecute, and subdue the former. Christian existence unfolds in the midst of historical expressions of eschatological conflict. If eschatology is an important qualifying theme in some Old Testament literature, it is the decisive feature of much New Testament thought. The paramount task facing those who would appropriate New Testament notions into constructive ethical thought is to clarify and comprehend the bearing of eschatology on ethics.[4]

Within the eschatological horizon of New Testament ethics,

perfectionist motifs enjoy noteworthy prominence. The central interest is not so much in doing the good or upholding the right as in becoming and being good. The moral life is not associated in the first instance with the conscientious observance of those duties which are requisite to social existence. It centers rather in personal transformations brought about by loyalty to Jesus and by the power at work in him. It consists in discipleship, dying and rising with Christ, being in and with Christ, having the mind of Christ, walking in the Spirit. In keeping with this emphasis, deontological language in the New Testament is sometimes assimilated to the perfectionist interest. Thus, laws and commandments function not simply as statements about what we are to do, but predominantly as specifications of who we are to become.

Eschatology is the basis for the prominence of perfectionist themes in the New Testament. Insofar as the new age is present in the midst of the old, those who respond to its imperatives are wrenched loose from the normal stabilities of institutional life. They are summoned to a new way of being in the world which does not yet have settled corporate form. That way has such urgency and overweening importance that those who take it up inevitably find themselves at odds with established patterns of social life. Fidelity to its claims may as a result cost them a great deal: suffering, social ostracism, persecution, imprisonment, even death. In this context the foremost concerns of New Testament writers properly relate to the "perfection" of persons in the new life to which they have been summoned.

The new way does involve community. The life of faith is corporate, and essentially so. As such it entails obligations to mutual recognition, care, support, and service within the community. It is chiefly with reference to the ordered life of emerging communities of faith that deontological thinking appears in the New Testament documents. The more a given author is attentive to the formation and building-up of such communities, the more his moral reasoning has a deontological cast.

New Testament communities are gathered communities. They are made up of individuals from many nations who have responded to the promises and demands of the dawning new age, who are bound to one another by virtue of the fact that they are bound to

Jesus Christ and his kingdom. Community is formed by mission, the summons to all people to participate in the appearing within history of the time of ultimate fulfillment. Thus, the social settings which have paramount importance in New Testament moral thought are gathered communities of like-minded individuals, not basic institutions into which persons have been born or by which they have been formed through established socialization processes. Institutions of the latter sort are not ignored. Indeed, they cannot be, for they continue to impinge on the new communities. An important task for New Testament authors is to work out an appropriate accommodation to the demands of such institutions, especially established religions—Jewish and Hellenistic—but also the state and the household. Even so, these institutional arrangements do not provide the crucial frames of reference for the moral thinking which comes to expression. Crucial rather is the development and maintenance of modes of communal life which accord with the eschatological horizon of Christian understanding. These modes of communal life presuppose persons who have given themselves in faith and obedience to the new reality accomplished in Jesus. In this respect the deontological thinking which is present in the New Testament tends to be subordinate to and dependent upon perfectionist motifs. As in the case of the Old Testament, consequentialist thought in the modern sense scarcely appears at all.[5]

In my treatment of the Synoptic Gospels I will highlight the category of discipleship, displaying its "perfectionist" thrust and linking it to the eschatological horizon of Christian faith. Following a general account of discipleship, I will give more detailed attention to its implications for the relation of early Christian communities to Jewish religious life. It is with reference to the religious institutions of Judaism that the radicalism of New Testament eschatology shows itself most clearly. Crucial to this discussion will be a consideration of the role of law in the Christian life. While the organizing themes of Old Testament ethics can be seen in terms of "covenant and commandment," the Synoptic authors, governed by eschatological expectations, venture to rethink the meaning and function of law in human existence. New Testament literature achieves no simple unanimity on this important matter, which may partially explain why interpreters of Christian ethics have throughout history repeatedly come to serious disagreements on the place of law in the moral life. The disagreements, I will argue, are as important and illuminating as the agreements. Finally, I will examine two motifs of special importance for social thought which appear respectively in Matthew and Luke: forgiveness as a requisite for community order, and the religious and social meaning of property. These motifs are linked to distinctive features in the life of the emerging communities of faith. They do not in themselves amount to political and economic theories. However, they do reflect experiential matrices which can under different circumstances give rise to significant social thought. As such, they have important implications for contemporary religious social ethics.

DISCIPLESHIP AND THE
COMMUNITY OF DISCIPLES

In the Synoptic Gospels discipleship emerges as the central category for setting forth the moral life. Discipleship consists in following Jesus. It involves participation in his activity and adherence to his teaching. Above all it entails sharing in his suffering. Jesus' ministry is determined by the presence of the coming kingdom of God. Discipleship is, therefore, eschatological existence. It is existence governed by the realities of the coming new age, but lived out under the conditions of the old.

In Mark the term "disciple" (*mathētēs*) refers to the Twelve, or at least to an inner circle gathered closely about Jesus (cf. Mark 3:13–19, 4:10). Not all who respond to Jesus' activity are encouraged to remain in close company with him. (The notable instance is the "Geresene demoniac," Mark 5:18–19.) More strongly than Luke, and quite in contrast to Matthew, Mark accents the unstable, even equivocal, nature of the disciples' commitment to Jesus. On the one hand, they leave all to follow him. They become active bearers of his ministry. They proclaim the kingdom, exorcise demons, anoint and heal the sick. They confess him as the Christ, witness the divine disclosure of his identity, and pledge him their total allegiance. On the other hand, they continually misunderstand the import of his sayings. They confuse his priorities, and are unable to grasp the radical newness of the power at work in him. Above all they underestimate the mortal nature of the conflict in which he is engaged. When their time of testing comes, they betray him, or deny him and abandon him to his enemies. And if verse 16:8 is Mark's original ending, the Gospel concludes with a description of the fear-induced silence of the women who came to the tomb to anoint Jesus' body.[6]

Mark's realistic portrayal of the first followers of Jesus functions to dispel any naive illusions anyone might have that discipleship is a simple, straightforward matter. In effect, Mark's Gospel is an admonition to later followers not to be so equivocal, so vacillating, so uncomprehending, but to bear steadfastly the costs of loyalty to Jesus and the coming kingdom. This admonition is intensified by Jesus' vindication in the resurrection. By virtue of the resurrection Jesus' messiahship is fully manifest to persons who have the eyes to see, so there are no more excuses for failures like those of the initial twelve. Even so, the life which followers of Jesus are to live is essentially continuous with that to which Jesus called his inner circle. They must be governed in their activity and their thinking by the presence of the coming kingdom. In their loyalty to that kingdom they must, like Jesus, endure trials, sufferings, and persecutions.

Mark does not give us as much information as we might like on the substantive content of discipleship. For the most part he takes such content for granted, accenting instead the formal obligation to fidelity. Yet he makes dramatically clear what is at stake institutionally in such fidelity: one finds oneself in conflict with family members, with synagogues and religious councils, and one may anticipate difficulties with the state as well. The Markan apocalypse states the point succinctly:

> But take heed to yourselves; for they will deliver you up to councils; and you will be beaten in synagogues; and you will stand before governors and kings for my sake, to bear testimony before them. . . . And brother will deliver up brother to death, and the father his child, and children will rise against parents and have them put to death; and you will be hated by all for my name's sake. But he [or she] who endures to the end will be saved (Mark 13:9, 12).

The disruptive impact of discipleship on family ties is especially striking. In ancient Israel, we have seen, the family formed the underlying social basis for the covenant community. Loyalty to Yahweh solidified rather than weakened family bonds. In Mark's account, familial claims and obligations have been relativized. The associations of primary importance are now those brought into being by the shared vocation to discipleship. When Jesus' mother and brothers come for him, Jesus asks: "Who are my mother and my brothers?" Answering his own question, he asserts, "Whoever does the will of God is my brother, and sister, and mother" (Mark 3:31, 35; cf. Matt. 12:46–50; Luke 8:9–20). When in another context Peter reminds Jesus that he and the other disciples have "left everything" and followed him, Jesus responds: "Truly, I say to you, there is no one who has left house or brothers and sisters or mother or father or children or lands, for my sake and for the gospel, who will not receive a hundredfold now in this time, houses and brothers and sisters and mothers and children and lands, with persecutions, and in the age to come eternal life" (Mark 10:29–30; cf. Matt. 19:27–30; Luke 18:28–30).

The present reality of the coming kingdom by no means nullifies all family obligations. Jesus chides the scribes and Pharisees for sanctioning the setting aside of duties of parental support on the grounds that the resources for such support have already been committed to God (Mark 7:9–13). The saying about the essential indissolubility of marriage, at least from the vantage point of God's creative purpose, moves in the same direction (Mark 10:2–9). Even so, the family along with other traditional institutions has been shaken by the impact of the kingdom. Taken-for-granted social arrangements have been placed in question, and new possibilities for communal existence have been set in motion. These new possibilities are eschatological.[7] Discipleship for Mark is existence in the cross fire of the ages.

Matthew uses the term disciple as a designation for all believers, not just the Twelve, though the Twelve are singled out for special instruction in preparation for apostolic leadership. Thus, as he narrates the "great commission" of Jesus, the charge to the "eleven" is to "make disciples of all nations" (Matt. 28:19). Matthew consistently removes any suggestion of a difference in the nature of discipleship prior to and following the resurrection. The time of

Jesus and the time of the church are identical in meaning.[8] In keeping with this perception Matthew omits the Markan stress on the misunderstandings of the disciples. Understanding is given with the call to become a follower of Jesus. "To you it has been given to know the secrets of the kingdom of heaven," Jesus says to his disciples. "But to them [the crowds] it has not been given" (Matt. 13:11). And he later adds, "Blessed are your eyes, for they see, and your ears, for they hear. Truly, I say to you, many prophets and righteous ones longed to see what you see, and did not see it, and to hear what you hear, and did not hear it" (Matt. 13:16–17, au. trans.).[9] Matthew does not unduly idealize the twelve, nor does he obscure the proneness to failure of any who would be disciples. The problem, however, is not lack of understanding but weakness of faith. Thus, Matthew's Jesus must deal with the "little faith" of his followers (cf. Matt. 6:30, 8:26, 14:31, 16:8, 17:20).[10] The challenge is to deeper trust, and hence, more unqualified obedience.

Matthew gives much greater attention than Mark to the substantive content of discipleship. This content is spelled out in terms of radical obedience to the law, interpreted from the vantage point of the love command. I will return to a fuller discussion of Matthew's view of the law. Otherwise, Matthew largely incorporates the major Markan themes about discipleship: its cost, its unsettling impact on the family, the primacy it implies for the community of disciples over all other associations.

Luke-Acts also uses the term disciple in an encompassing sense, though perhaps less characteristically than Matthew. He has special interest in the twelve, whom he calls apostles. His concern is to identify the leadership of the true Israel and the emerging gentile Christian community which is based upon it. His problem is to make sense of the almost total rejection of Jesus by the established leadership of the first-century Jewish community. The twelve are called and prepared to assume the responsibilities which were renounced by these leaders. Already in Jesus' lifetime they begin to share in his authority and power. Following the outpouring of the Spirit at Pentecost, they pick up and carry foward the work he was about, though in a later stage of its development. By virtue of their authority, the apostles are distinguished from the people. They are the bearers of the prophetic power which calls the church into being and sustains it in its ongoing life. At the same time, they model the manner of life to which all the people have been summoned.[11]

What is most distinctive about discipleship in Luke's account is its strong association with the poor, the sick, the disabled, and the outcast. These are the persons to whom Jesus comes bearing the good news of the kingdom. Jesus' citation of Isaiah 61 at the beginning of his public ministry functions in Luke as a kind of platform for his subsequent activity:

> The Spirit of the Lord is upon me, because he has anointed me to preach good news to the poor. He has sent me to proclaim release to the captives and recovering of sight to the blind, to set at liberty those who are oppressed, to proclaim the acceptable year of the Lord (Luke 4:18–19).

The chapters immediately following cite incident after incident in which Jesus concretely accomplishes what has been publicly announced: demons are exorcised, the sick and the lame are visited and healed, the defiled are cleansed, tax collectors and sinners are embraced, and the poor are comforted and blessed. When John's disciples inquire of Jesus whether he is the one to come, Jesus simply cites the deeds of his ministry: "Go and tell John what you have seen and heard: the blind receive their sight, the lame walk, lepers are cleansed, and the deaf hear, the dead are raised up, the poor have good news preached to them" (Luke 7:22).

In contrast, the rich, the powerful, the privileged, and those who occupy places of honor within the Jewish community are offended at Jesus and so find themselves rejected by God. More explicitly than any New Testament author, with the possible exception of James, Luke calls attention to the role of social class and social status in the responses of the people to Jesus. By and large the followers of Jesus are from the lower classes and from marginal positions in the society. The enemies of Jesus are the wealthy, the mighty, the highly esteemed. Such persons are unable to receive Jesus' message as good news, for as Luke puts it, they already have their consolation (Luke 6:24).

Like Matthew, Luke also makes use of Markan materials concerning the conflicts and stresses of discipleship, and the urgency of unqualified fidelity to its claims. The principal differences in his handling of these traditions stem from his distinctive theology of history, and from his view of the special status of Israel in that history. It is to this latter question that we now turn.

GATHERED COMMUNITIES AND
THE LEGACY OF ISRAEL

Mark: The Primacy of the Moral Law

The Synoptic authors unfold the meaning of discipleship in terms of the relations of the emerging Christian communities to Judaism and the legacy of Israel. Mark's gospel is the farthest removed from Judaism, reflecting the situation of the gentile church. The author finds it necessary to explain Jewish customs to his readers, and he summarizes these customs in ways that convey little interest in their details (e.g., Mark 7:3-4). He treats the ceremonial elements of the law as no longer binding, and grants little or no weight to rabbinic traditions. In a fashion reminiscent of the great prophets, he elevates the moral law over cultic performance. For Mark, however, the traditional Jewish cult has largely been set aside. In its stead are the distinctive cultic practices of gentile Christian communities. These center in table fellowship, especially the Eucharist (Mark 14:22-25, but see also 6:34-44, 8:1-9, 14-21, and 10:35-45).[12]

Mark's point of view is summarized in his treatment of the question about the greatest of the commandments. Jesus responds to his questioner by identifying the first and second among the commandments as the love of God and neighbor. A scribe then adds that this double obligation is "much more than all whole burnt offerings and sacrifices." Jesus endorses the scribe's comment by saying: "You are not far from the kingdom of God" (Mark 12:33, 34).[13]

The accent on the primacy of the love command reiterates themes which Mark introduced earlier in the Gospel by means of conflict stories. Two incidents involve presumed infractions of Sabbath ordinances: the disciples pluck grain as they pass through the grainfields on the Sabbath; and on the Sabbath Jesus heals a man with a withered hand. When challenged by the Pharisees concerning these matters, Jesus suggests in regard to the first that Sabbath observance can be set aside in instances of human need. He cites as precedent the incident in which David and his companions ate the "bread of the Presence" in the Temple, an exigency, incidentally, which would appear to have been far greater than that reflected in the more or less casual act of plucking grain as one walks through the fields (Mark 2:23–28). "The Sabbath is made for human beings," Jesus asserts, "and not human beings for the Sabbath; so the Son of man is lord even of the Sabbath" (Mark 2:27–28, au. trans.). In regard to the second incident, Jesus intuits the disapproval of the Pharisees and initiates the exchange: "Is it lawful on the Sabbath to do good or to do harm, to save life or to kill?" His opponents make no response. The rhetorical question accents the point that ritual correctness must not stand in the way of human compassion. What is interesting about these instances is that neither has to do with genuine emergency situations. The impression conveyed in both is that strict Sabbath observance is no longer of great importance.

In a similar vein we have the dispute about eating with "defiled hands" (Mark 7:1–23). In contrast to traditional concerns for ritual cleanliness, Jesus insists that it is not what goes into a person that defiles, but what comes out. From within, he continues, arise "evil thoughts, fornication, theft, murder, adultery, coveting, wickedness, deceit, licentiousness, envy, slander, pride, foolishness" (Mark 7:21–22). At issue is not cultic failure, but moral failure. Here especially it is evident that Mark is referring to customs which have ceased to have relevance for the Christian community.[14]

To summarize, moral traditions not only take precedence over cultic matters; the cultic practices of importance are distinctively Christian, wholly displacing analogous Jewish observances. For the most part, moreover, even the moral traditions are presented only in the most general terms. A noteworthy exception is the saying about divorce (Mark 10:2–9). What is of interest about this saying, however, is that it locates the authority for the prohibition of divorce not in the Mosaic law, but in God's original purpose in creation. Mark understands the gospel of Jesus Christ as something which fulfills the promises of God to ancient Israel. Even so, the fulfillment is in important respects an annulment as well. Many customary features of Jewish life are negated for the sake of a more inclusive gentile church.

Mark's treatment of the parable of the "wicked tenants" (Mark 12:1–11) provides what Robinson calls a "unified presentation" of his conception of the relation of the gentile church to Judaism.[15] The Jewish people, or at least their leaders, have repeatedly rejected God's servants. By rejecting God's son they are now themselves rejected, and their inheritance has passed to others, presumably those who have become disciples as a result of the gentile mission. We have here a striking variant of the vision of Second Isaiah. Israel is indeed a light to the nations, but in a paradoxical way. Jewish rejection of God's promises in Jesus is the occasion for divine action to fulfill Israel's legacy through the faithfulness of the gentiles. Yet the legacy is fulfilled not by the confirmation and maintenance of Jewish traditions and institutions. It is brought to fruition by their displacement, or at least by the displacement of their salient ritual elements. The moral and prophetic traditions endure, but in a new context determined by the imminence of the coming kingdom of God.

For Mark, it must be added, the kingdom entails a similar challenge to characteristic gentile practices (e.g., Mark 10:42). What is at stake, therefore, is eschatological criticism, not simply the preferring of one set of customs or national groupings to another. The principal point is that the people of God are henceforth to be made up of those who are willing to be disciples, to participate in the continuation of the struggles which marked Jesus' ministry. These struggles are a function of the fact that something new is coming into being. There is in Mark no brooding anguish, such as we find in Paul's letter to the Romans, over the fate of the Jews in God's plan of salvation. Judaism is rather being left behind in the gathering momentum of gentile Christian communities. It has itself become part of the residue of the age which is passing away.

Luke: The Continuing Authority of the Mosaic Law

Luke provides the sharpest contrast to Mark, though Luke-Acts is often read as presenting, like Mark, a pattern of Jewish rejection and gentile inclusion. In fact, Luke sees the restoration of the true

Israel as the basis of the possibility of the gentile mission. Jacob Jervell summarizes the salient points: (1) Luke does not describe a Jewish people who as a whole reject the early Christian message. What we get is a picture of a divided Israel with repentant and unrepentant elements. (Note in particular Luke's recurrent references in Acts to mass conversions of Jews, Acts 2:41, 4:4, 5:14, 6:1, 7, 9:42, 12:24, 13:43, 14:1, 17:10–12, 21:20.) (2) In Acts the term "Israel" continues to refer to the Jewish people. It is not a general designation for the church. The portion of Jews who believe in the Messiah and repent of their sins is the purified, restored, and true Israel. The unrepentant portion has forfeited its membership in the people of God. (3) The gentile mission is fully in accord with Scripture (cf. Luke 24:41; Acts 3:25, 13:47, 15:13–21, 10:43). The gathering of gentiles has been part of God's plan from the beginning. It is by no means an ad hoc response to the Jewish rejection of Jesus. For the gentiles, sharing in salvation means sharing in the promises of Israel. The promises must first be fulfilled in Israel before gentiles can enter into God's saving activity. "The mission to Jews," Jervell concludes, "is a necessary stage through which the history of salvation must pass in order that salvation might proceed from a restored Israel to the gentiles."[16] The new thing is not that salvation now includes the gentiles. What is new is that gentiles are now saved *as* gentiles, that is, without circumcision, without first becoming proselytes. (4) The mission to the Jews is essentially complete. The repentant Israel has been gathered, leaving no further obligation to those who have refused the messianic message. The continuing task is the gentile mission, which is central to Luke's own time.[17]

The belief that a restored Israel is the basis of the church's gentile mission has important implications for the status of the Mosaic law within the Christian life. Jervell makes clear what is at stake. The issue for Luke is not the Pauline concern: whether justification comes by faith or by steadfast adherence to the dictates of the law. Luke apparently believes that the forgiveness of sins proclaimed through Jesus does free believers in some measure from the Mosaic law (cf. Acts 13:38–39). The issue is to specify correctly the role of the Mosaic law in determining the identity of the Christian community. As we have seen, law and commandment are integral to Israel's existence as the people of God. The question is whether the Mosaic law is now simply a matter of history, a feature of an earlier stage in the salvation-history of God's people, or whether it also has some abiding significance within the Christian church.

Jervell contends, in contrast to many recent interpreters,[18] that Luke's outlook on this matter is the most conservative of the New Testament. Luke treats the Mosaic law as Israel's law. He is especially concerned with the ritual and ceremonial aspects of the law. In this respect, law is not essentially moral law, but the sign of Jewish identity, the mark of distinction between Jews and gentiles. At the heart of the matter is circumcision, though food laws and Temple observances also play a part. Luke does not seek to Christianize the law or to interpret it with a view to the church. He does not say that Jews misunderstand the law, nor that they desire to be justified by their strict obedience to it, though he does charge Jews with not keeping crucial features of the law. His main interest is to establish the indissoluble connection between Israel and the law. He stresses the fact that Christians in the primitive church of Jerusalem adhered universally to the dictates of the law.[19] Even the "apostolic decrees," which authorize a gentile Christianity without circumcision, are determined by an appeal to the law and the prophets. Gentile Christians are to "abstain from the pollutions of idols and from unchastity and from what is strangled and from blood" (Acts 15:20).[20] These special obligations, Jervell points out, state what the Mosaic law itself requires of strangers who sojourn among the Israelites (cf. Leviticus 17 – 18). For a people loyal to the Mosaic law, one might argue, it would be unlawful to impose on gentiles more than Moses himself demanded.

One cannot take the apostolic decrees to mean that absolutely nothing else is required of gentile Christians than the observance of the four stated prohibitions. What is at issue is the relation of gentile Christians to features of the Mosaic law which normally function to set Jews apart from gentiles. Gentile Christians who would associate themselves with Jews of the true Israel, with repentant Jews who accept Jesus as the Messiah, must pay heed to these four prohibitions, and only these four, in relating themselves to the distinguishing obligations of the Jewish people. Otherwise, Luke appears to take it for granted that gentile Christians will also honor those aspects of Israelite legal traditions which have echoes in the moral understandings of other cultures. Thus, Jervell concludes, Luke succeeds in establishing the necessity of full compliance with the law while also affirming the salvation of gentiles as gentiles.[21]

A major concern of Luke's is to answer charges, primarily from non-Christian Jews, that Christian Jews do not keep the law, or that Stephen and Jesus alter the "customs from Moses" and amend the law, or that Paul invalidates the law, preaches apostasy from Moses, speaks against Israel. Luke cites such charges no less than eight times; in each case he reports corresponding declarations of innocence (Acts 6:11, 13, 14, 18:13, 21:21, 28, 25:8, 28:17). Even Paul is depicted by Luke as the great missionary among the Jews, gathering the penitent Israel in the synagogues of the Diaspora and teaching them to adhere to circumcision and the law. In the concluding chapters of Acts, Paul is still the pious Pharisee faithful to the law.[22]

Jervell's central thesis is that Luke's view of the law is bound up with his ecclesiology. The basis of the church is a restored Israel, an Israel faithful in its observance of the law. The church also includes gentiles, and precisely as gentiles. Gentile Christians are relieved of certain aspects of the law, those strictly reserved for Israel. Yet they are the church not apart from Israel, still less over against Israel, but precisely in association with Israel. Israel remains the light for the nations through whom salvation extends to the uttermost parts of the earth (cf. Acts 14:47). Consequently, gentiles too are subject to the law, not, to be sure, as a way of salvation, but as an integral feature of their being as the people of God.[23]

Luke's treatment of traditions recounting Jesus' attitudes toward the law reflects his point of view. In introducing his discussion of the commands to love God and neighbor, the issue for Luke is not the determination of the greatest of the commandments (cf. Mark 12:28; Matt. 22:36). It concerns what one must do to inherit eternal life (Luke 10:25–28). Moreover, a lawyer, not Jesus, provides the answer. In the narration, the love command does not emerge as the essence of the law or as the interpretive clue to its central meaning (cf. Matt 22:40, also 5:43–48, 7:12). Nor is it elevated above sacrifices (cf. Mark 12:33). It appears as one command alongside many other equally binding laws and commandments.

Luke's Jesus condemns the Pharisees for scrupulously tithing even herbs and spices while neglecting justice and the love of God. Yet he does not, like Matthew, refer to the latter as "weightier matters of the law" (cf. Matt. 23:23). The tithes ought to be paid, but without neglecting other obligations (Luke 11:42). (On the latter point, Matthew is in agreement with Luke.) Luke wholly omits the Markan pericope on ritual cleanliness (Mark 7:1–23), though Luke 11:37–41 may be a variant, presumably from the non-Markan source which Matthew and Luke share. He mentions no critique of the Pharisees for rejecting God's commandments in favor of human traditions (cf. Mark 7:8; Matt. 15:3–7). He rather speaks of the "customs of the fathers" as being in harmony with the law (Acts 6:14, 21:21, 28:17; cf. 10:14–16, 11:3, 8). In presenting Jesus' words about divorce, he does not, as Mark, refer beyond Moses to a more elemental divine purpose (cf. Mark 10:1–12). Nor is the Mosaic law portrayed as a concession to the hardness of human hearts. The prohibition of divorce is a straightforward and binding commandment of God (Luke 16:18).

Finally, in narrating disputes about the Sabbath—Luke reports four incidents: 6:1–5, 6–11, 13:10–17, 14:16—Jesus' position in each case accords with the law, such that the Jewish leaders are unable to sustain any objection to his words or deeds. The point is not that the "Sabbath is made for human beings" (Mark 2:27), nor that one may transgress Sabbath observances to save a life. The point is that it is altogether lawful to do good on the Sabbath. Having healed on the Sabbath a woman who had been "bent over" for eighteen years, Jesus defends himself against the indignation of the ruler of the synagogue by asserting that it is no more unlawful to free a "daughter of Abraham" from her infirmity than to untie an ox or an ass and lead it to water (Luke 10:16). Sabbath laws, in other words, do not justify the ruler's indignation. That indignation is rather sheer hypocrisy (Luke 13:15). It conceals disregard of the imperatives of the law to heed the cries of the needy.

At every point Luke presents Jesus as one who diligently observes the law and urges others to do so as well. Jesus' critique of the Pharisees, scribes, and Sadducees is not that they misunderstand the law or elevate their traditions above the divine commands. It is that they do not fully observe what the law requires of them, especially with respect to almsgiving or compassion for the poor, the blind and the lame, the tax collectors and sinners. This last observation brings us once again to a central theme of Luke's gospel: Jesus brings good news to the poor. The point to be noted here is that regard for the poor, indeed, for marginal and outcast persons of all sorts, is an integral feature of adherence to the Mosaic law. Luke is reiterating in a new context an insight forcefully put forward by the eighth-century prophets: that the measure of Israelite covenant fidelity, of their righteousness and justice as the people of God, is the degree to which they concern themselves with the well-being of their most vulnerable members.

To sum up the argument thus far, Mark assumes a gentile church which has already effectively displaced Israel as the people of God. In accord with an important strand of prophetic teaching, Mark emphasizes the primacy of the moral law over cultic performance. In fact, however, traditional Jewish rituals have been set aside altogether. In their stead emerges the distinctive cult of the gentile Christian communities, especially the common meal and the Lord's Supper. Luke in contrast insists upon the continuity of the Christian church with Israel and its legacy. He focuses attention on a repentant Israel whose responsiveness to Jesus' messiahship and to the workings of the Spirit is the basis for the gathering of a gentile community from all the world. It is precisely through Israel that God brings salvation to the nations. The true Israel, moreover, is faithful to the Mosaic law in all respects. Gentile Christians likewise observe those aspects of the law which are addressed to them in their associations with a repentant Israel. For Luke, law articulates the manner of life of those who are the people of God. In its identity-bearing function, its ceremonial aspects — especially circumcision and the food laws — are quite as important as its moral injunctions.

Matthew: Law as the Perfection of Love

Matthew's Gospel would appear to occupy a mediating position between Mark and Luke. Most contemporary scholars identify

Matthew's initial audience as a Jewish-Christian community.[24] In such a community it would be urgent to think through carefully the continuities and discontinuities between Judaism and Christianity. Central to this task is a clarification of the nature and status of law: its authority, its placement in the life of faith, its essential meaning, its substantive content. Apart from the Pauline epistles, no New Testament text deals so fully with these problems.

On the one hand, Matthew's Jesus, like Luke's, insists upon obedience to the total law: ". . . till heaven and earth pass away, not an iota, not a dot, will pass away from the law until all is accomplished. Whoever then relaxes one of the least of these commandments and teaches others so, shall be called least in the kingdom of heaven; but the person who does them and teaches them shall be called great in the kingdom of heaven" (Matt. 5:18–19, au. trans.).[25] Discipleship consists in unqualified obedience to God. "Not every one who says to me, 'Lord, Lord,' shall enter the kingdom of heaven, but the one who does the will of my Father who is in heaven" (Matt. 7:21). The will of God is articulated as law, as commandment. Indeed, Matthew also has regard for oral tradition. Whereas Mark rejects rabbinic traditions (e.g., Mark 7:1–13), Matthew on occasion adopts them or appeals to them (cf. 5:21, 43, 12:11, 23:23).[26] Included are ceremonial traditions, for example, private sacrifices (Matt. 5:23–24), the temple tax (Matt. 17:24–27),[27] the tithing of spices (Matt. 23:23), and Sabbath observances (Matt. 12:1–14; cf. also Matt. 24:20).[28]

Matthew's Jesus does in some instances set the commandments of God over against the traditions of the "elders," preferring the former to the latter (e.g., Matt. 15:3–9). In one case he cites Isa. 29:13, implying that the traditions are not divinely given teachings, but only the "precepts of human beings." Also, Matthew clearly ranks moral goodness above ritual cleanliness, as in the dispute with the Pharisees over eating with defiled hands (Matt. 15:1–2, 10–20). Matthew modifies Mark's version of this story in an interesting way. Whereas Mark lists a whole series of defiling vices (Mark 7:21–22), Matthew cites only those which correspond to the "second table" of the ten commandments: murder, adultery, fornication, theft, false witness, and slander (Matt. 15:19). Even so, since Matthew appeals to tradition in other contexts, including references to ceremonial matters, we cannot read this passage as expressing a general opposition between commandment and tradition, or of moral and ceremonial aspects of the law. What is at issue is the right interpretation of the law. The binding authority of the total law is in view throughout the Gospel.

On the other hand, Matthew, unlike Luke, portrays Jesus as offering a fresh interpretation of the law. The keys to the content of the law are the commands to love God and the neighbor (Matt. 23:36–40). In terms of these commands, Matthew makes distinctions among various laws and ranks them in relation to one another. The command to love God, Jesus says, is the "great" and "first" commandment; the command to love the neighbor is "like it." Not only do these two commandments stand out from all the rest. Upon them depend ("hang," *krematai*) all the law and the prophets. Law and prophets explicate what the two commandments require, and these commandments provide the key to their meaning and import.

Matthew does not treat the love commands as sufficient guides to the will of God, such that one might dispense with all other laws and traditions. He is as troubled by antinomianism as by rabbinic formalism.[29] His insistence upon regard for the whole law reflects his belief that the law is divine revelation and, as such, eternally binding. His procedure, therefore, is not to deal directly with situations in terms of the love commands alone, viewed in abstraction from the total legal tradition; it is to approach situations by way of the teaching of law and prophets, interpreting the import of these materials on the basis of the love commands. The full sweep of the law is operative, but it is read as commanding love. In this respect, Matthew maintains a strong sense of the continuity of tradition, but he has a means of reassessing and reinterpreting it in changing social and cultural situations.

Matthew's sense of the pivotal importance of the love commands guides his treatment of the various conflict stories contained in the Synoptic traditions. I have already called attention to some of the relevant passages, for example, Matthew's association of the attitudes and desires that defile a person with the "second table" of the commandments, and his contention that justice and mercy are weightier than the tithing of spices. In both instances we find echoes of his claim that love is the key to the meaning of the law. Matthew's handling of the story of Jesus healing on the Sabbath accords with this general direction of thought (Matt. 12:9–14). The accent (as in the case of Luke) falls on the positive obligation to do good (vv. 11–12), not on a justifiable contravention of Sabbath regulations. The essence of the law is to do good, and that essence qualifies and clarifies the way obligations to Sabbath observance are to be understood and applied.

The story of the disciples plucking grain on the Sabbath holds special interest. Two things occur. First, Matthew emphasizes the disciples' hunger (Matt. 12:1). Their action is not wanton, but motivated by need. Second, Matthew cites Hos. 6:6: "And if you had known what this means, 'I desire mercy, and not sacrifice,' you would not have condemned the guiltless. For the Son of man is lord of the sabbath" (Matt. 12:7–8). The reference is puzzling since it is not clearly applicable to the situation. Is Sabbath observance like "sacrifices"? And who is called to show mercy? It would appear that the Hosea citation is addressed to the Pharisees, who are being asked to show mercy toward the hungry disciples rather than insist on strict Sabbath observance. Yet Matthew's Jesus also implies that the disciples are "guiltless," and, hence, in no need of mercy. They are guiltless apparently because of their association with the Son of man, whose presence among them is analogous to, yet greater than, the presence of the temple for the temple priests. The argument seems to be: just as temple priests are authorized to do on the Sabbath what would for others amount to a profanation of the Sabbath (Matt. 12:5; cf. Num. 28:9–10), so the disciples, by virtue of the presence of the Son of man, have permission to do what would normally be a violation of Sabbath ordinances. The analogy turns on a messianic claim, yet its link with the Hosea citation remains obscure. Perhaps the suggestion is that the dawning of the new age in Jesus discloses mercy as the central meaning of the law, and thus alters its practical operation in human affairs. Hosea announced beforehand the primacy of mercy (the Hebrew word is *chesed*). Had the Pharisees been able to grasp Hosea's meaning, they would not have condemned the disciples. Alas, however, they could not understand, so they could not properly interpret and

107

apply the law. As a result, they condemned the innocent. This reading, though not without problems, at least accords with Matthew's general orientation to the law. It underscores his consciousness that Jesus' ministry and teaching issue in a new way of understanding and enacting what the law commands.

The love commands pervade the Sermon on the Mount. The two major sections of this body of teaching material (Matt. 5:17–48, and Matt. 6:1 – 7:12) conclude with explicit treatments of neighbor love. In the first, the command to love the neighbor functions to extend traditional claims of the law. A rigorously limited right to avenge a wrong—an eye for an eye—is transformed into a mandate to nonresistance (Matt. 5:38–42); and neighbor love is set forth as including love of enemies (Matt. 5:43–48). The second major section ends with a formulation of the "golden rule": whatever you wish that others would do to you, do so to them. This, Jesus asserts, "is the law and the prophets" (Matt. 7:12). Yet the whole sermon can be read as explicating the two great commandments. In the first part, Jesus discusses prohibitions against killing, adultery, and lying under oath, all of which bear upon neighbor love. In the second, he speaks of various spiritual disciplines, of unqualified allegiance to God, and of trust in God, all of which belong to an understanding of the command to love God.

Two features in Matthew's handling of these materials call for special comment. The first concerns his contention that disciples are to make themselves wholly vulnerable to the actions of others, even enemies. What is one to make of this claim? Eschatology unquestionably plays a decisive role. If one believes the final consummation of God's kingdom to be imminent, it is not implausible that one might willingly endure all sorts of suffering, even unjust suffering, for the sake of that kingdom. Indeed, one's very survival might well be a matter of relatively slight consequence. If the force of the sayings depends, however, upon the literal form of this expectation, then the more or less indefinite postponement of its fulfillment would have the effect of rendering them psychologically and morally unacceptable. For a world such as ours, it is necessary to delineate a legitimate self-defense and to set appropriate limits to the claims which others may be permitted to make.

When we stress the substantive meaning of eschatology for ethics, however, these materials enjoy continuing importance whatever the temporal limits of human historical experience. Eschatology directs attention to new possibilities for human existence taking form in the midst of the old age. In this context, Matthew's Jesus offers a realistic assessment of what is entailed if we are to break the structures of destruction which presently order human life. A community of love can emerge in this setting only if persons through faith find resources to do more than simply what can under ordinary circumstances be considered reasonable, even to absorb the violence of others without recompense. Such love is not just a work of supererogation which displays in a special way the excellence of the one who embodies it. It is requisite to communities which are able to nourish human beings to that fullness of life which the gospel promises.

We may find ourselves unable to endure with dignity the level of injury implied by these sayings, still less to sustain our dignity over time. We may find it wholly inconceivable to envision an ordered social life constituted and maintained on the basis of such love. Matthew himself, we might note, seems to have assumed that most of his readers, like the original followers of Jesus, would be persons of little faith, not those who had realized the perfection to which the kingdom of heaven summons them. Even so, implied in Matthew's account is the insight that to meet violence with violence and to repay injury with injury is to remain embroiled in the cycle of destruction characteristic of the old order which is passing away. Such responses offer no possibility of a breakthrough to the promises of the kingdom. Even if we were to accomplish a social revolution which overcame particular kinds of entrenched structural injustice, the resulting world would still not partake of the hoped-for kingdom insofar as violence remained its underlying premise. In the final analysis, violence cannot be overcome by violence, only by its renunciation in a love which bears all things. Matthew's eschatology enables him to name the conditions for human community in a world where conflict, violence, oppression, and exploitation are the order of the day.

The second matter calling for special comment concerns

Matthew's insistence that obedience to the law involves not simply correct behavior, but the full investment of the total self. It encompasses subjective intentions, attitudes and feelings, and the workings of the imagination. Matthew not only lifts up the love commands as interpretive clues to the meaning of the law; guided by those commands he also suggests a new way of conceiving what is involved in obeying the law in the first place! Thus, the prohibition of killing now has to do with anger and insult, even the belief of another that he or she has been wronged. If you are offering a gift at the altar, Jesus says, and recall that your brother has something against you, leave the gift before the altar, go and be reconciled to your brother, and then come and offer your gift (Matt. 5:23–24). The point is not that you have something against this brother, but that he has something against you. You must make right the wrong done. In the text it is not even clear that the brother's complaint is a legitimate one. The only consideration is that he has "something against you." Thus, you must be prepared to attend to his perception that something is wrong whatever may be your own assessment of the situation. The outcome to be sought is neither self-vindication nor simply recompense for the other, but reconciliation.

In a similar vein, the commandment against adultery now includes the lustful gaze directed toward the spouse of another;[30] and the obligation to speak truthfully under oath becomes a mandate to truthfulness in all discourse whatever, making oaths superfluous. Indeed, the resort to oaths is disclosed as an index of human evil. Obedience to the law is not limited, then, to those behavioral requisites for a well-ordered social existence. It articulates the totality of the divine claims upon the lives of the disciples; and that totality touches the deepest levels of self-experience, levels which profoundly affect the quality of human interactions. "You, therefore, must be perfect," Jesus concludes, "as your heavenly Father is perfect" (Matt. 5:48).[31]

Parallel to the insistence upon totality in obedience to the law is a caution against public displays in almsgiving, prayer, and fasting. Such displays tempt one to trivialize spiritual exercises. Jesus urges the disciples self-consciously to avoid them in order that they might maintain an unwavering focus on the essential thing, their relations with "the Father who is in heaven." Here too the totality of one's being is called fully into play. The relation with God is unfolded as strict fidelity—"no one can serve two masters"—and as unlimited trust—"do not be anxious about your life, . . . but seek first his kingdom and his righteousness, and these things will be yours as well" (Matt. 6:33). Fidelity and trust are but two sides of a fundamental way of orienting one's life to God. They set forth what it means to love God with "all your heart, and with all your soul, and with all your mind" (Matt. 22:37).

In these passages Matthew is expressing in the language of law and commandment what might more appropriately be stated in the language of virtues. Matthew's Jesus is concerned less with action-guiding principles as such than with the elemental attitudes and orientations of persons. His theme is the perfection of the disciples in faith and love. To be sure, the "perfection" Matthew has in mind is not an end in itself; it consists in a readiness and a capacity for relationships, both with fellow human beings and with God. In particular Matthew calls attention to what is involved in establishing harmonious relationships where alienation, enmity, duplicity, and anxious care are the order of the day. Yet his focus is on the formation of disciples: equipping them to bear the social, psychic, and physical costs of realizing a community of love based on faith in the mercy of God.

One can question the suitability of the category of law for articulating these perfectionist motifs. In a formal sense, the category of law implies notions of univocal clarity and specificity, of consistency and coherence, of generality of form and universality of application, of publicness.[32] With reference to agency, it presupposes a notion of volition founded on a sharp distinction between actions which are within our power and those which are not. It assumes a capacity to deliberate on the proper application of the law in given situations, and to act in accord with the results of that deliberation.[33] Matthew's focal interest obscures some of these assumptions. In fact, he so stretches the category of law that we are forced to rethink what it might mean to observe its stipulations, or more generally, what might be entailed in taking responsibility for our own actions. Matthew presses us to attend to the affective dimensions of human actions and interactions. These dimensions emerge as the wellsprings of action. They empower action and generate criteria to measure its worth. More is involved, therefore, in keeping the commandments of God than a simple act of will guided by thoughtful deliberation on the proper application of the law to particular situations. It is the total self in all its dimensions to which the commandments are addressed.

A failure to appreciate Matthew's remarkable way of using legal language leads, I think, to some serious misreadings of these texts. The problem is whether commands can properly be addressed to feelings, desires, and fears. Such commands would at best appear to be impotent. At worst they are capable of causing psychic harm, both exacerbating guilt and generating pretense and self-deception. Thus, if I take seriously the words of Jesus in these texts, I simply find that I feel guilty about my anger or about my sexual desires; perhaps I condemn myself for my anxiety about the morrow, my self-protectiveness, or my need for recognition and esteem by others. Alternatively, I strive to deny these forbidden feelings in myself. I banish them to unconscious regions of my psyche, much as Matthew admonished us to pluck out an offending eye or cut off an unruly hand. In so doing I release them to work havoc in my life in unacknowledged ways.

The force of Matthew's presentation, however, is to dramatize the insufficiency — at least where vital relationships are involved — of behavior which merely conforms to the letter of the law, even when it stems from actions carried out (as Immanuel Kant would have it) for the sake of the law. In human relationships, feelings, desires, needs, and fears matter profoundly. They are not morally irrelevant subjective accompaniments of basic duties and obligations. If we would be perfect, and not merely formally correct, we must in our actions learn how to get in touch with our feelings and desires, bringing them positively and constructively into play in all aspects of our lives.

How are we to incorporate our feelings and passions into our volitional activity? How do we take responsibility for them? Matthew does not provide many clues here, which may account for the fact that his thought often functions to promote guilt and self-deception rather than the perfection of which he writes. The most promising suggestions occur in his description of procedures for handling inter-personal conflict within the church (Matt. 18:15–20). There Jesus admonishes his followers to talk out their problems, first privately, then in the presence of two or three witnesses, and, as a last resort, before the whole church. If a resolution of the conflict is achieved at any of these points, a reconciliation may result which dissipates anger and resentment and releases positive feelings of mutual af-fection. At the same time, the procedures also hold realistically in view the possibility that efforts at reconciliation may fail. What is noteworthy is that the aggrieved party is not under those circum-stances exhorted to continue bearing with patience the injury in-flicted upon him. Instead the offending brother is expelled from the church: "let him be to you as a gentile and a tax collector" (v. 17, an ironic choice of images since Jesus came for tax collec-tors and sinners, and his message is finally for gentiles as well as Jews).

While these procedures suggest concrete ways of dealing with negative and destructive feelings, they too have troubling limita-tions. For one thing, they assume that one person is wholly in the right and the other wholly in the wrong, obscuring the more characteristic dynamics of collusion in mutual hurt by persons closely associated with each other. The talking must in most cases be reciprocal. Second, they bestow more authority on the church's final action than would appear justifiable given the ambiguity of collective as well as individual judgments. "Whatever you bind on earth," Jesus says, "shall be bound in heaven, and whatever you loose on earth shall be loosed in heaven" (v. 18). More sober and cautious is the image of the church provided by the parable of grain and weeds growing together until the time of harvest (Matt. 13:24–30). Communities must learn to live with unresolved con-flicts even when efforts at reconciliation are vigorous.

Finally, the subtlety and difficulty of getting in touch with feel-ings is not addressed by these procedures at all. In most instances we probably cannot gain control over our feelings with the direct-ness suggested by the Matthean texts. The paradox is that we

113

generally must suspend the moral imperatives and their binding claims if we are to attend to what is going on at a feeling level in our various worldly involvements. Insofar as we are able to gain insight into these deeper dimensions of experience, we have a stronger possibility of drawing upon them as a positive resource for accomplishing the quality of relationships to which the commandments direct us in the first place. On this point, Paul, in insisting upon the justification of sinners by grace quite apart from works of the law, may be a more profound interpreter of the promise of the Christian gospel than Matthew. Yet Matthew himself has no illusions about the difficulty of entering into the perfection to which we are summoned as disciples. As I have noted, he acknowledges that disciples are for the most part persons of little faith—unable to love, to forgive, to risk, to trust. It is finally only by God's power that we can mature in that faith by which we enter the kingdom of heaven. Matthew's principal accomplishment, however, is to dramatize the fact that feelings, desires, and deep-seated attitudes have an essential role to play in the fulfillment of the commandments of God, especially when the law is interpreted as essentially commanding love.

To summarize, Matthew deals in an original way with the significance of the Mosaic law in the Christian life. Like Luke he stresses the continuing authority of the law. In contrast to Luke he sees in Jesus' teaching a thoroughgoing reinterpretation of the law and its place in human life. Not only are the two great commandments put forward as the key to the concrete application of the law in various life situations; these commandments also both intensify and alter the basic force of the laws. They transform a restricted right to avenge a wrong to a mandate to nonresistance, and they extend neighbor love to enemies. They also enlarge the scope of obligation to embrace the total self, especially elemental feelings, attitudes, and desires. Finally, Matthew's treatment of the law has the effect of changing its characteristic deontological thrust—the explication of the moral requisites of human social order—into a perfectionist thrust—the delineation of the wholeness of life to which God calls faithful disciples. As a resource for moral understanding, Matthew rivals Paul in importance. He fully appreciates the church's continuity with Judaism and with Israelite legal traditions; yet he labors to bring into view the discontinuities with traditional understandings which are constitutive of Christian existence. These discontinuities have their basis in the inauguration of the new age which has already begun in the midst of the old order which is passing away.

Though Matthew and Luke stress the continuity of the gathered Christian communities with Jewish life and thought, we must not overlook the fact that, like Mark, they finally interpret the Christian gospel as resulting in the displacement of Judaism, at least in its traditional forms. For Luke, the repentant Israel has already been incorporated into the church's life, or better, is the basis for its missionary activity. The unrepentant Israel, the Israel which has rejected Jesus' messiahship, has forfeited any further claim to the promises of God. It is like the faithless Israel which Hosea exposed by naming his child "Not My People." This Israel has become an enemy to God, a troublemaker, a persecutor of the church. Luke makes no attempt to discern any legitimate grounds for the Jewish rejection of Jesus. Such Jews are simply unrepentant. Likewise, Matthew assumes a transformation of the Jewish legacy through Jesus' messiahship, so that those who persist in classic forms of Jewish fidelity are taken to be incapable of comprehending the promises of the coming kingdom of heaven. Essentially, they are the hypocrites, the blind guides who mislead and destroy, the foolish ones who build their houses on sand.

The Synoptic writers do grasp the impulse to universality in the heritage of Israel. On this point they are one with Second Isaiah. This universality is embodied concretely, however, in a gentile mission in which persons from all nations are summoned to acknowledge Jesus as the Jewish messiah. The mission builds upon traditional Judaism. Yet it adapts Jewish life and thought to the social and cultural realities of the Hellenistic world. On this basis it gathers from the peoples of the earth, one person at a time, an eschatological people. A new people takes form amidst the decaying structures of the old age. Consequently, traditional Judaism, though once a bearer of the promises of God, now belongs to the world which is passing away. Of the New Testament authors, only

Paul persists in honoring the Jews in their Jewishness as the elect people of God. In Paul's view God remains faithful to the Jews whatever their explicit stance toward Jesus and the messianic claims of the early church. I shall subsequently elaborate this last observation in my treatment of Paul's thought.

SOCIAL MOTIFS IN
SYNOPTIC THOUGHT

The Locus of Institutional Creativity

The ethical creativity of the Synoptic authors resides chiefly in their accounts of discipleship. Their critical impulses are directed against established religious and familial patterns in Jewish life. Their constructive impulses consist in elaborations of new forms of association in Christian existence. There is only slight interest in the import of the Christian message for the economic and political arrangements of the time.

Economic and political life are not altogether neglected. There is a fair amount of comment on the state and on the relationship of the new communities to state authority. In general, however, Synoptic treatments of Jesus do not suggest a direct concern with political and economic institutions. Their tendency is to portray such institutions as givens of the old order which no longer hold major interest for communities of disciples. Though that order continues to provide structures within which Christian existence can take form, it is, nonetheless, an order which is passing away.

The center of attention is on eschatological communities which are self-consciously oriented to the coming kingdom of God. Thus, while Roman authorities are accomplices in the execution of Jesus, they are so without conviction, largely as a concession to the sensibilities and passions of the Jewish elite in Jerusalem. It is primarily with the established Jewish leadership that Jesus and his followers are in conflict. Luke seeks to establish the point that the Christian movement has no basic quarrel with Rome. Its troubles are with unrepentant Israel. The chief instigators of these troubles are Jews who reject Jesus' messiahship. The state has no cause to view this movement as a threat to its authority or to social stability in general. In fact, when the state plays its proper role, it provides indirect aid to the Christian movement, allowing it to propagate its good news in peace. The Christian movement in turn supports public order. Otherwise, affairs of state lie outside of substantive Christian concern.

With the possible exception of the system of tax collection, economic institutions receive even less attention. Standard economic practices do provide a rich resource for parabolic instruction; and there is a good deal of pointed comment on what people do with their material resources and what such resources mean for their spiritual lives. Still, economic institutions as such, in particular the systems for producing and distributing the means of subsistence, do not come into view as objects for critical thought. They are taken-for-granted features in the world which is passing away.

The relative disregard of economic and political arrangements contrasts with pentateuchal traditions and prophetic literature. Such disregard doubtless reflects the social location of the overwhelming majority of the first Christians. For the most part they were the marginal people, the poor of the land, and in some cases, social outcasts. They had no access to the ruling classes, nor could they easily conceive of such access. For them, the basic institutions of society were essentially external realities, beyond their social reach. They occupied themselves with what they could do something about: the ordered life of communities of faith, kinship ties, and household relationships. Even if a member of the ruling class were to become a disciple, he or she could not easily remain in such a position. To be a disciple was to cast one's lot with the little people.

Whatever their contemporary appeal, we cannot sustain claims that the Synoptic Gospels provide a direct basis for a social ethic, that is, an ethic which embraces primary economic and political institutions. They do not, as John Howard Yoder argues, offer a specific sociopolitical option.[34] What they provide is an ecclesiology, or better, reflection on a number of models for ordering the life of gathered communities of disciples. They do specify the stance persons in Christian community ought to take toward economic and political institutions. This accomplishment is by no means of slight importance, but it does not amount to a sociopolitical option, nor to a comprehensive social ethic in the sense of twentieth-century Christian ethics.

These observations do not imply that the Synoptics have no

positive contributions to make to Christian social ethics. They rather indicate that we cannot discover such contributions by focusing on what the texts say about the state or about the economic organization of Palestine under imperial Roman rule. We have to direct our attention to the creative accomplishments of the early churches in working out patterns of common life as ordered communities of faith and love. The task is to think through the ramifications these accomplishments might have for economic and political institutions. The suggestion is that the early Christian communities provided matrices of experience capable of generating insights and ideas which under different sociopolitical circumstances could take form as a fully articulated sociopolitical vision. The claim is not that such a vision is already present, though perhaps undeveloped, in the New Testament itself. What we find is material capable of giving rise to such a vision. There is always implicit in fertile images and ideas more than can be fully explicated; but the explication itself is, as I have argued, a work of the productive imagination. The Synoptics provide food for thought, the stimulus to go further in working out the meaning of Christian existence in quite different economic, social, and political circumstances.

The eschatological communities portrayed in the Gospels are not in essence small, marginal communities, incapable in principle of embracing and transforming economic and political activities in human society. Initially they were small and marginal, but not necessarily so. Their horizon was the whole inhabited earth. Their élan was missionary expansion. The possibility was present from the beginning that these communities might at some point become sufficiently successful in their evangelistic efforts so as to be thrust into the task of taking some kind of responsibility, appropriate or otherwise, for ordering the economic and political affairs of human society.

The primary thesis is that a social ethic based on the Synoptic Gospels must embody their distinctive eschatology. It cannot take its central clues from the economic and political realities of the old age, for that age is passing away. It may recognize the provisional validity of the old order, and within limits abide by its constraints. That order is ultimately subject to divine power and authority; indirectly it too does the work of God. It at least sustains the minimal conditions for human existence in a broken, alien world. Yet the Synoptic message has little of substantive importance to say about the old order except to call attention to its transient and ambiguous character, and to shake its pretensions to ultimacy. The originality of Synoptic thought shows itself in social understandings which are eschatologically determined, oriented to the promise of the coming kingdom of God. These understandings are developed in terms of the internal arrangements of developing Christian communities. If we are to construct a social ethic on New Testament thought, we must build upon the redemptive promise of the gospel rather than upon a notion of creation (orders of creation), or an account of the providential activity of God in preserving a world which has subjected itself to the power of evil (orders of necessity). Notions of the latter sort are not wholly illegitimate since the old order continues to enjoy provisional standing even for Christians. Yet they can be properly assessed only in relation to eschatological possibilities. Orders of creation and preservation are related to orders of redemption as the old age is related to the new, that is, dialectically.

To develop this line of thought, I wish to look briefly at two motifs, one in Matthew and the other in Luke-Acts. The first concerns Matthew's emphasis on mercy and forgiveness as integral to communal life. This motif points toward a political order founded not on the means of violence, not even as a state monopoly, but on mutual recognition, commitment, and forbearance. The second concerns Luke's treatment of possessions, especially the practice of almsgiving and the experiment with communal property. This motif initially expresses freedom from worldly entanglements; yet it issues in the conviction that material wealth is essentially social. It points toward a form of economic organization which challenges the individualistic assumptions of advanced capitalist societies and leads to a quest for ways of developing social control of material resources, placing them at the disposal of the total community.

Matthew: Mercy and Forbearance as a Basis of Community
The relevant materials in Matthew have already been cited. The task here is to call attention to their sociopolitical signficance. Matthew interprets the law as love, and elaborates the meaning of love

119

as mercy. Mercy involves forgiving those who have wronged you, and receiving them again into fellowship. In reciting the Lord's Prayer, Matthew comments on only one phrase, that concerning the forgiveness of debts (which he takes as equivalent to trespasses, *paraptomata*). "If you forgive others their trespasses," Jesus says, "your heavenly Father will also forgive you; but if you do not forgive others their trespasses, neither will your Father forgive your trespasses" (Matt. 6:14–15, au. trans.). The commentary discloses the centrality of forgiveness in Matthew's presentation of Jesus' teaching.

The relation between receiving and bestowing forgiveness is elaborated in the parable of the unforgiving servant. Though this servant had been forgiven an extraordinarily large debt by his king, he had one of his own servants cast into debtor's prison for his inability to repay a small debt. The king confronted him indignantly: "You wicked servant! I forgave you all that debt because you besought me; and should not you have had mercy on your fellow servant, as I had mercy on you?" (Matt. 18:32–33). For his refusal to show mercy, the king ordered the unforgiving servant delivered to the jailers. "So also my heavenly Father will do to every one of you," Jesus concluded, "if you do not forgive your brother from your heart" (Matt. 18:35).

The parable comes as an answer to a question from Peter. "Lord, how often shall I forgive one who sins against me? As many as seven times?" "Not seven times," Jesus replies, "but seventy times seven" (Matt. 18:22, paraphrased). The parable immediately follows, celebrating God's boundless mercy and reminding us that a readiness to bestow mercy is of a piece with receptivity to it. Jesus' exchange with Peter follows the description of procedures to be followed within communities of faith in seeking reconciliation between persons where one has wronged another (Matt. 18:15–20). The sequence of these materials suggests that mercy — mutual forbearance and forgiveness — is constitutive of eschatological community, and that such mercy has its basis in the mercy of God. Whereas coercion and violence assure social order in the world which is passing away, the promise of community in the coming kingdom of heaven stems from mercy and forgiveness.

120

The importance of this motif is intensified by the fact that the early church was a community gathered from the nations. Many natural supports for human association — family, kinship ties, a common language and culture, ethnic and racial identity — could no longer contribute directly to stable social order. The diversity of the community with regard to these factors actually increased the likelihood of unintended misunderstandings and injuries among those who confessed a common allegiance to Jesus Christ. Communities transcending family, language, culture, and national identity could only sustain themselves through continual acts of forgiveness, and through a readiness to bear hurt without reprisal.

Can such notions inform the quest for more humane forms of political life? Can they contribute to models of public life in pluralistic settings? Pertinent here is Hannah Arendt's claim that human action (as opposed to labor and work) presupposes a public setting of mutual respect and recognition where diverse individuals can in freedom distinguish themselves through speech directed to the common good.[35] The bases for such a public setting, Arendt argues, are essentially twofold: the ability to make and keep promises (covenant making) and the ability to forgive one another.[36] Both of these conditions figure in Matthew's accounts of community, and the latter is especially prominent. Matthew's interest is in community maintenance, in no small measure through the mediation and transformation of living traditions. He does not entertain the idea of a public setting or of public discourse oriented to a common good. In this respect, his thought never becomes political in any proper sense. Even so, the conditions of communal life in Matthew's understanding correspond to those in Arendt's account of a republic. These conditions make possible a form of political life where open discourse replaces tradition, language, custom, race, the struggle for survival, and especially violence, as the founding principle of social order. Such a republic is essentially a moral order, Arendt notes. Indeed, it founds a "new order of the world" for human life.[37] The vision, that is to say, is eschatological. It has to do with the emergence of a qualitatively new mode of politics in the midst of structures and arrangements determined by quite different principles. The new order in Arendt's view is fragile and highly vulnerable, an accomplishment which can be maintained only by continual renewal. Yet it persists as a genuine human possibility when suitable social and economic conditions are present.

The point of citing Arendt is not, as it were, to provide biblical authorization for her political philosophy. Still less is it to imply that her vision of public life already resides in Matthew's treatments of communal order. It is not even to suggest that Matthew and Arendt are finally compatible. In fact, if our imaginative development of Matthew's understandings were to issue in a constructive sociopolitical vision, that vision would surely give more weight than does Arendt to the formative importance of living traditions in the constitution of social existence. The point is that Matthew's treatment of factors crucial to the maintenance of gathered communities of disciples contains materials which make contact with original political thought, especially when that thought is itself eschatological. Such materials can be a stimulus to a social ethic governed by the eschatological horizon of New Testament faith.

Luke: Communal Uses of Possessions

If Matthew's account of communities of mutual forgiveness offers resources for political ethics, Luke's treatment of possessions and their role in the Christian life has an analogous promise for an ethic addressed to economic life. Students of Luke-Acts have given a good deal of attention to Luke's special regard for the poor, the disabled, and the outcast. For the most part, however, this important theme has not been treated in relation to the overall point of view of Luke-Acts. Luke Johnson has recently moved to fill this gap with his illuminating study of the "literary function of possessions in Luke-Acts."[38]

For Luke, Johnson argues, how one relates to one's possessions is a decisive factor in whether one accepts or rejects the good news Jesus brings. The general pattern is that the poor accept Jesus while the rich reject him. Poverty and riches are not simply economic designations, though they are preeminently that. They encompass as well physical well-being, social power, and social status. Zacchaeus, for example, is a "lost" rich man, a social outcast by virtue of his occupation as a tax collector. He responds joyfully to Jesus, pledges half of his goods to the poor, and promises to restore fourfold any goods that he has wrongfully acquired. In giving to the poor, Zacchaeus identifies himself with the poor and so casts his lot with them (Luke 19:1–10). His response contrasts sharply with that of the rich ruler, who claims to have observed all of the commandments from his youth, but is unwilling to sell what he has, distribute to the poor, and follow Jesus (Luke 18:18–30). By turning away from Jesus' call, the ruler numbers himself with those Pharisees, "lovers of money," who scoff at Jesus and his words (Luke 16:14). Jesus charges them with hypocrisy. "You are those who justify yourselves before human beings, but God knows your hearts; for what is exalted among human beings is an abomination in the sight of God" (Luke 16:15 au. trans.). When one clings to possessions, one is cut off from the good news. When one is free of possessions, and so is able to give them up, one is ready to receive the Lord.

The parable of the good Samaritan carries a similar meaning (Luke 10:29–37). The parable elaborates the love command. The question at issue is the way to eternal life, not the determination of the greatest of the commandments. The point of the parable is to characterize the demeanor of a person destined for eternal life, not to show how one might define the nature and extent of one's duties to one's fellow human beings. In asking how to identify his neighbor, the lawyer seems to have lost sight of his own initial question. Luke suggests that his second question is a self-justifying one. As the parable unfolds, what is important about the Samaritan is his freedom with respect to possessions. He is able to respond to the man who was mugged on the Jericho road because he does not cling to what he has. He places what he has at the disposal of a stranger in need. In so doing he provides a model of one destined for eternal life.

Luke sets forth two principal ways of dealing with possessions: the giving of alms and the community of goods. The giving of alms may mean the total disposition of one's goods in order to become a follower of Jesus. This understanding has been noted in the instance of the rich ruler. In a similar vein Jesus admonishes his disciples, "Sell your possessions, and give alms; provide yourselves with purses that do not grow old . . ." (Luke 12:33). The giving of alms also refers to persons of means who do not clutch at what they have, but share it with others, while yet retaining some control over their resources. We read, for example, of women (Mary Magdalene and Joanna, the wife of one of Herod's stewards, and "many others") who provide support from their own means for Jesus and the twelve (Luke 8:2–3). The mission of the twelve and later of the seventy likewise presupposes hearers ready to give alms. In both cases the disciples are instructed to take nothing for their journey, but to receive food and drink from the households they visit (Luke 9:3, 10:4–8). This instruction is the exact opposite of that which Jesus gives to the twelve shortly before his arrest. In the latter instance, Jesus tells those who have a purse to take it with them, and the one who has no sword to sell his mantle and buy one (Luke 22:36). Apparently Jesus and his followers can at this point no longer count on receptivity to the gospel message, and hence, a readiness to support its messengers. The twelve must provide for themselves. Other treatments of almsgiving in Jesus' public ministry have already been cited.[39]

The Acts of the Apostles reports similar patterns. The offering taken in the church at Antioch for needy Christians in Jerusalem is an instance of almsgiving, though the accent is on sharing with those already in the church. The occasion is a predicted famine. Each gives according to his or her ability. Saul and Barnabas deliver the gift (Acts 11:27–30).[40]

If almsgiving presupposes freedom with respect to one's possessions, the community of goods is correlative to a life together. Luke shows us, Johnson notes, the practice of sharing goods in Jesus' inner circle.[41] The most interesting passages, however, are brief characterizations of the church in the period immediately following Pentecost. "All who believed were together and had all things in common," Luke tells us; "and they sold their possessions and goods and distributed them to all, as any had need" (Acts 2:44–45). This same picture is repeated a second time, highlighting the relation between community feeling and the sharing of goods: "Those who believed were of one heart and soul, and no one said that any of the things which he [or she] possessed was his [or her] own ..." (Acts 4:32).

The second passage adds a new note. It identifies the apostles as the ones who take responsibility for the distribution of the community goods (Acts 4:35). Johnson notes that Luke already associates apostolic authority with the oversight of property in his account of Jesus' ministry, for example, in the feeding of the five thousand (Luke 9:10–17), and perhaps in the parable of the faithful steward "whom the master will set over the household, to give them their portion of food at the proper time" (Luke 12:42).[42] Ironically, when the apostles later appoint seven persons to manage the daily distribution in order that they might devote themselves to the preaching of the Word (Acts 6:2–6), Stephen, one of those appointed, comes to prominence precisely as a man full of the Spirit who continues and extends the apostolic preaching.

The community of goods is not altogether idyllic, as is illustrated by the abortive attempt of Ananias and Sapphira to withhold deceitfully from the community a portion of their own property (Acts 5:1–11). Also, the occasion for the appointment of the seven was that "hellenists" were complaining that their widows were being neglected in the daily distribution (Acts 6:1). Luke does not lift up the pattern as a continuing standard for the church. He reports it simply as a short-lived practice of the earliest Jerusalem community. Paul, for example, is portrayed as one who provides for himself, apparently as a tentmaker, and who maintains a measure of personal control over his resources (Acts 18:1–4, 21–24; 28:30). Almsgiving, in a form which falls short of the total disposition of one's resources, is treated as the more enduring practice.

Though these materials disclose important features of early Christian communities, they cannot be taken as equivalents to a sociopolitical option for human economic activity. They do not in any way address questions related to the production of the means of subsistence, only questions of distribution at the level of consumption.[43] Luke takes for granted the continued participation of Christians in the established economic arrangements of the first-century Roman world. Doubtless some activities would have been excluded, for example, usury. Luke's primary aim, however, is to portray the Christian as one who makes use of holdings without grasping at them or clinging to them, placing them rather at the disposal of those in need, especially within the community of faith. What is altered is not the economic system as such, but one's relations to possessions within that system.

Even so, the practice of almsgiving and experiments with communal property grow out of and give rise to experiences which potentially have important implications for the economic organization of human society. The tendency of both patterns is to dissolve within the communities of faith the class and status distinctions of the larger society. All believers are now numbered among the poor, the hungry, the sorrowful, and the despised for whom the gospel comes as good news. Power and status relations are similarly altered within the community insofar as the apostles use their special gifts for the well-being of all, to serve rather than be served (Luke 22:24-27). Within the mode of service, authority for the maintenance of understandings central to the ordered life of the community resides with the apostles. Since these gathered communities functioned as decisive reference groups for their members, taking priority over all other institutional involvements, their impact on the basic life relations of the people could have been profound.

Can such notions inform the quest for more humane patterns of economic life? Can they contribute to models of economic organization suitable for high-technology civilizations? At the least they challenge the aggressive individualism of capitalist ideology, including the claim that individuals are free to use and dispose of their property as they see fit so long as they do not interfere with a similar right for others. Property and wealth are essentially social for these communities. They exist for the well-being of all. Similarly, Lukan understandings are incompatible with the vast disparities of income and wealth which characterize both feudal and capitalist societies. Their impulse is toward equality, the overcoming of class distinctions. Freedom from the compulsions of possessive individualism is the freedom to place what one has at the disposal of others who need it.

Notions such as these cannot translate directly into a modern social vision, let us say, democratic socialism or a Marxist commitment to proletarian revolution. Their precise import for social ethics depends upon the critical and constructive judgments of contemporary thinkers who would mediate their truth in a new setting. Nonetheless, Lukan themes disclose a basis in the gospel itself for the continuing lure of socialist thought in Christian social ethics.

The challenge to interpreters of Christian ethics is to articulate these themes in a fashion that addresses the social forces at work in the modern world.

To sum up, the Synoptic Gospels do not offer a specific socio-political option, certainly not one capable of coming to grips with the dominant social forces at work in the modern world. However, they do reflect matrices of experience which generated ideas and understandings capable of development into original social thought. Matthew offers a vision of a gathered community whose cohesion is founded on mutual forbearance and forgiveness rather than kinship or a common culture. Violence in particular is displaced as a principle of social order. Luke points to a community in which property rights are no longer the exclusive prerogative of individuals but exist for the well-being of all. The conception of possessions is primarily manifest in almsgiving, though it includes as well the possibility of a community of goods. Even almsgiving is not optional, for example, a work of supererogation. It is a fundamental obligation of persons who have been freed from attachments to property in order to serve their fellow human beings.

These understandings provide only fragments and suggestions for social thought. We do not find in the New Testament a conceptual framework for developing their implications, nor for thinking through their internal relationships within the early Christian communities. Yet it is to such understandings as these, not explicit references to the state or the Palestinian economy, that we must look when we consider the resources offered by the New Testament for a contemporary Christian social ethic. These resources reflect the originality of early Christian social thinking, based on experiences with communal life oriented to the coming kingdom of God.

THE CHALLENGE TO
MORAL UNDERSTANDING IN
THE SYNOPTIC GOSPELS

I have been examining Synoptic treatments of the moral life, highlighting their distinctive eschatology. Central is a recognition of the presence of the coming kingdom in the midst of the continuities of the old age. This eschatology led to conflict within and around emerging Christian communities over the nature and status of established Jewish institutions: in general, over the Mosaic law and its traditional interpretations; more particularly, over Sabbath observances, food laws, family ties, and temple rites and customs.

In line with the prophetic tradition, Mark lifts up the primacy of the moral law over cultic and ceremonial law. At the same time, he takes for granted the displacement of traditional Jewish practices by the development of a distinctively Christian cult. Luke stresses the continuing authority of the Mosaic law in both its moral and cultic aspects. He sees strict adherence to that law as an identifying characteristic of a faithful and repentant Israel. He accents the obligation to respond to the needs of the poor, the hungry, the disabled, the prisoner, the stranger, the outcast. This classic obligation now has renewed force, for the new age has begun in Jesus' ministry and is gaining momentum through the workings of the Holy Spirit. Luke celebrates the Christian mission to the gentiles. Under the guidance of the Spirit, gentiles are being welcomed into association with the true and obedient Israel, and on terms already provided for in the Mosaic law itself. These terms are explicitly stated in the "apostolic decrees" (Acts 15:19–21). They indicate that gentiles are no longer required to practice circumcision as a condition of their entry into the people of God.

For the student of ethics Matthew's Gospel holds special interest. Like Luke it insists upon the continuing authority of Jewish legal traditions. However, it goes beyond Luke in calling for a thoroughgoing reinterpretation of those traditions on the basis of a Christian eschatology. For Matthew the law essentially commands love. Its stipulations are to be appropriated with this understanding in mind. Law also gains a perfectionist thrust in Matthew. Rather than functioning chiefly to describe the moral requisites of social order, its primary impulse is to portray the wholeness of existence to which disciples are summoned.

The institutional creativity of the Synoptic writers is most prominent in their attempts to shed light on the ordering principles of the new communities of faith. Mark dramatizes the central formal characteristic of these communities. They are gathered communities, not "natural" communities. Their basis is a readiness to follow Christ rather than kinship ties or national loyalties. They grow not by the propagation of offspring, but by an evangelical mission. In essence they are open to peoples of all races and nations.

Building upon Mark's contributions, Matthew fills in some of the substantive content of Christian communal existence. Noteworthy is his emphasis on mercy and mutual forgiveness in the maintenance of communities of disciples. Luke accents the import of possessions for one's readiness to become a disciple and to enter into new social relationships with fellow disciples. Almsgiving discloses a person's freedom from attachments to property, and hence, his or her freedom to follow Christ; the community of property brings into view the social nature of property, its function in providing for communal well-being. I suggested that these motifs in Matthew and Luke offer to critical imagination materials for constructive political and economic thought. It is in continuity with their impulses that distinctively Christian social thinking must unfold.

In comparison with their paramount interest in the internal relations of Christian communities, the Synoptic authors give relatively scant attention to established economic and political structures. By and large, they perceive these institutions to be external to immediate Christian concern; they consider them effectively out of reach of initiatives by the first disciples. Basically, the state and the economic order belong to the age which is passing away. They continue to have provisional validity, but only insofar as they provide a certain order which for the present makes human life possible. Luke speaks most pointedly about the positive good of the state, and also of the supportive stance of Christians toward state authority. He recognizes that imperial Rome maintains social conditions which make possible the spread of the gospel to the ends of the earth. As such it contributes to the Christian mission. Even so, Luke's conception of the state and its relation to the coming kingdom is not substantially different from that of the other Synoptic authors. If a Christian ethic is to make an original contribution to political and economic thought, therefore, it will not be by way of explicit Synoptic commentary on the state and its place in human life. It will be by elaborating and developing the political and economic implications of insights present in Synoptic attention to the internal affairs of the eschatological communities.

The next task is to examine Paul's treatment of Christian moral understandings, completing the study of selected New Testament materials.

NOTES

1. The most problematic feature of this selection is the lack of attention I give to the Johannine literature. This literature is quite influential in the life of the Christian church, yet its interpretation presents special problems to which I cannot do justice in the present essay.

2. Cf. James M. Robinson, *The Problem of History in Mark and Other Marcan Studies* (Philadelphia: Fortress Press, 1982), esp. 76–80.

3. Hans Conzelmann, *The Theology of St. Luke* (Philadelphia: Fortress Press, 1982), convincingly establishes this point. See esp. 149–51. The original German title, *Die Mitte der Zeit*, is more appropriate than that of the English translation. Conzelmann's study is sharply focused on Luke's theology of history, and only indirectly on other themes. His thesis is that Luke portrays Jesus as the center, or "middle" (*die Mitte*), of the historical process.

4. Jack T. Sanders, *Ethics in the New Testament* (Philadelphia: Fortress Press, 1975), concurs that eschatology presents the central problem for the interpreter of New Testament ethics. His opening chapter (1–29) provides a helpful overview of recent attempts in New Testament scholarship to deal with this problem, especially in reference to the teachings of Jesus. Following Albert Schweitzer and Henry J. Cadbury, Sanders argues that the eschatology of the New Testament renders its ethic irrelevant for contemporary human beings. In fact, the outcome of his study is to "relieve" us of the need or the temptation to begin with Jesus, or the early church, or the New Testament in seeking to develop coherent ethical positions (cf. 130). In effect, what the New Testament teaches us is that it has nothing to teach us about ethics. The thesis being argued here is that the New Testament has eschatology to teach us. What is of central interest about New Testament ethics is its thoroughgoing determination by eschatology.

My disagreements with Sanders stem from differing accounts of the moral life, and from contrasting approaches to the hermeneutic problem. Sanders does not lay out his preunderstandings of ethics, though he seems to identify ethics with the guidance of action, both in personal choices and in corporate involvements (cf. 19). The ethical theory I am offering certainly embraces an interest in concrete moral guidance, but it places that interest in a larger framework of thought. The New Testament is not a rich resource for the concrete guidance of action in present-day life; but it does set forth a horizon of understanding which presents no small challenge to contemporary taken-for-granted assumptions about the world.

Similarly, Sanders appears to identify the imminent expectation of the end of the world as the central feature of New Testament eschatology. With such a conception, the delay of the Parousia effectively undermines the credibility of primitive expectations. The reading being set forth here is that the most salient feature of New Testament eschatology is the substantive presence of the new age in the midst of the old. It is existence "between the times," better, existence in the dialectical interpenetration of the times. The task is to grasp the way in which the world and its claims present themselves to awareness when existence is determined by such an interplay. It is to discern how such an awareness impacts our presumptions about the authority of values which are constitutive of the present world order.

5. There is, of course, talk about consequences, consequences of not responding faithfully to the claims of the kingdom of God, consequences of disobedience. Consequences of this sort are quite different, however, from those associated with a calculative estimate of alternative action possibilities. They have to do with the eschatological judgment which hovers before all human activity. A closer analogy to modern consequentialist thought is provided by Paul's admonition to "liberated" Christians at Corinth to consider whether they might cause weaker brothers and sisters to stumble if they should exercise their freedom to eat meat which has been sacrificed to idols (1 Corinthians 8). Even here we do not have a general orientation to the assessment of actions with reference to their probable consequences. We rather have an imaginative exercise aimed at giving concrete meaning to the imperative to act so as to build up persons in the community of faith. In the forefront of attention is the perfecting of persons, and the determination of the requisite communal conditions for such perfection.

6. For a discussion of the ending to Mark, see Willi Marxsen's *Mark the Evangelist: Studies on the Redaction History of the Gospel* (Nashville: Abingdon Press, 1969), esp. 208–16.

7. Cf. Robinson, *Problem of History in Mark*, 128–30.

8. See Gerhard Barth, "Matthew's Understanding of the Law," in Günther Bornkamm, Gerhard Barth, and H. J. Held, *Tradition and Interpretation in Matthew* (Philadelphia: Westminster Press, 1963), 110–11.

9. In this text Jesus is explaining to the disciples why he speaks in parables. The last citation is a commentary on Isa. 6:9–10. For a discussion of this matter, see Barth, "Matthew's Understanding of the Law," 106, 109–10, 112–16.

10. See the helpful discussion of this theme in Peter F. Ellis, *Matthew:*

His Mind and Message (Collegeville, Minn.: Liturgical Press, 1974), 145–50.

11. On Luke's treatment of the new leadership of the true Israel, see Jacob Jervell's essay, "The Twelve on Israel's Thrones: Luke's Understanding of the Apostolate," in *Luke and the People of God: A New Look at Luke-Acts* (Minneapolis: Augsburg Pub. House, 1972), 75–112.

12. See Robinson, *Problem of History in Mark*, 130–33.

13. See Victor Paul Furnish, *The Love Command in the New Testament* (Nashville: Abingdon Press, 1972), 25–30.

14. To these incidents might be added Jesus' exposure of the "Corban" subterfuge (Mark 7:9–13), to which reference has already been made. Mark does not at any point speak of circumcision. He has in view laws and traditions relating to food and Sabbath observance.

15. Robinson, *Problem of History in Mark*, 114.

16. Jervell, *Luke and the People of God*, 42–43.

17. Ibid., 68.

18. Jervell cites in particular Ernst Haenchen, *The Acts of the Apostles*, Eng. trans. B. Noble et al. (Philadelphia: Westminster Press, 1971), 115f., 223; Hans Conzelmann, *Theology of St. Luke*, 147–48, 212; and Gerhard Barth in *Tradition and Interpretation in Matthew*, 63, though the latter largely depends for his judgment on the work of Conzelmann. In Conzelmann's view law belongs to a definite stage in redemption history. In that stage it was strictly observed. In Conzelmann's reading, however, Luke does not believe that the law continues to have binding authority, at least not for gentile Christians. In fact, Conzelmann suggests that the status of law in the Christian life has ceased to be an acute problem by the time of Luke. See especially n. 1, 212.

19. Conzelmann is in agreement with Jervell on this point. See *Theology of St. Luke*, 148. Where Conzelmann and Jervell disagree is over the status of law in the period of gentile Christianity, especially over the meaning and significance of the "apostolic decrees" in Acts 15:20–21, 29. See Jervell, *Luke and the People of God*, 145.

20. It might be noted that these decrees are more unequivocal than Paul's views on the necessity of avoiding food which has been sacrificed to idols. Cf. Acts 15:29 and 1 Corinthians 8.

21. Jervell, *Luke and the People of God*, 144.

22. Ibid., 145–46.

23. Ibid., 143.

24. Cf. Krister Stendahl, *The School of St. Matthew* (Philadelphia: Fortress Press, 1968), xiii.

25. Cf. Luke 16:16–17. Luke's form of this saying presents difficulties for the interpreter since it is preceded by a contrast between the "law and the prophets" and the "good news of the kingdom." The former were "until John"; since then the latter is preached. Following Jervell, however, I have

taken the preaching of the kingdom to refer to the opening up of God's promises to the gentiles, and precisely *as* gentiles. The kingdom does not render the law void; it permits gentile fellowship with Jews without the prior requirement of circumcision.

26. Cf. Barth, "Matthew's Understanding of the Law," 86–90.

27. Jesus says that the sons of God are free to pay the tax, and they are encouraged to do so in order not to give offense.

28. Matt. 24:20 concerns flight on the Sabbath. For a discussion of this curious reference, see Barth, "Matthew's Understanding of the Law," 92.

29. Cf. ibid., 75–76, 94.

30. In Matthew, the saying about adultery is actually addressed to males. It concerns the lustful look at another man's wife. Matthew's patriarchal assumptions are not here the matter of primary interest, however.

31. Compare this dictum with the recurrent theme of the Holiness Code: "You shall be holy; for I the Lord your God am holy"(Lev. 19:2).

32. Cf., e.g., John Rawls's delineation of the formal requisites of moral principles in *A Theory of Justice* (Cambridge, Mass.: Harvard University Press, 1971), 130–36.

33. Cf., e.g., Book I of Aristotle's *Nichomachaean Ethics*.

34. John Howard Yoder, *The Politics of Jesus* (Grand Rapids: Wm. B. Eerdmans, 1972). Yoder's central thesis is stated on 23: "The claims of Jesus are best understood as presenting to men not the avoidance of political options, but one particular social-political-ethical option." I shall comment more fully on Yoder's thesis in my discussion of possessions in Luke-Acts.

35. Hannah Arendt, *The Human Condition* (Chicago: University of Chicago Press, 1958), 197–99.

36. Ibid., 237.

37. See Hannah Arendt's discussion of the American Revolution in her *On Revolution* (New York: Viking Press, 1963), chap. 5, 179–215. The reference is to the motto: *novus ordo seclorum.* Compare this discussion with the account of *natality* in *The Human Condition.* Action initiates something new. It is the self-expression of distinct and unique human actors presenting themselves among equals, 178.

38. Luke T. Johnson, *The Literary Function of Possessions in Luke-Acts* (Missoula, Mont.: Scholars Press, 1977).

39. Johnson, *Literary Function of Possessions in Luke-Acts*, 10, calls attention to the following passages: Luke 11:41, 12:33, 16:9, 18:22, 19:8.

40. According to Luke's chronology, this incident occurs at the beginning of Paul's missionary activity. Luke makes no mention of the offering which Paul speaks about so extensively in his letters. Cf. 1 Cor. 16:1–4; 2 Cor. 8:1–5, 9:1–5; and Rom. 15:26–29 with Acts of the Apostles 20 and 21.

41. Johnson, *Literary Function of Possessions in Luke-Acts*, 177.

42. Ibid., 165–67.

43. Yoder, *Politics of Jesus*, 74, interprets Luke's Jesus as proclaiming the jubilee year. He suggests that Jesus called for the redistribution of capital, 74–77. He acknowledges that the term capital is something of an anachronism. He contends, however, that soil and flocks would be first-century Palestinian equivalents to what we now call capital. In this respect he properly associates the term with "means of production." There are a number of major difficulties with his claims. First, the textual evidence hardly supports his proposal that Jesus is proclaiming the jubilee. Johnson's reading, that we chiefly have to do with almsgiving and with the role of possessions in eschatological existence, is much more strongly grounded in the overall purpose of Luke-Acts. But even if Jesus did intend jubilee, it is far from apparent that the institutional arrangements necessary to make jubilee socially significant were any longer in place. Jubilee presupposes that extended families are fully intact, and that for the most part they maintain their ties with ancestral lands. The poor and the outcast of Luke's Gospel would appear to be wholly landless and without meaningful claims to an ancestral legacy. Moreover, at no point in the New Testament, not even in Luke, do we encounter anything like the distribution or redistribution of capital as such. What we find is the distribution of proceeds from the sale of one's goods, i.e., almsgiving. These goods might include capital, but not necessarily so. They embrace other sorts of holdings as well. No small part of the wealth thus liquidated came from commercial transactions, usury, and the collection of taxes (e.g., Zacchaeus). Distribution at the level of consumption alone falls far short of an economic policy. Yoder is here making claims too strong for his data.

Yoder rightly dramatizes Luke's special interest in the poor, the disabled, and the outcast. He sees correctly that these are the first in the kingdom of God, while the wealthy, the privileged, and the powerful are last. These images are powerful ones. They provide an important stimulus to ethical thinking. Yet their concrete import for contemporary social existence can be worked out only if we pay considerably more attention than Yoder has done to the hermeneutic problem.

5

REVISIONING THE BASES OF HUMAN LIFE: PAUL'S ACCOUNT OF CHRISTIAN FREEDOM

Paul's eschatology is essentially the same as Mark's. His thought is governed by the dawning of the new age in the midst of the old. The effective presence of the new age is marked by the death and resurrection of Jesus Christ. Believers become participants in this occurrence by the power of the Spirit and by the faith it awakens in them. They have their life "in Christ." They walk by the Spirit; they bear the fruits of the Spirit in the kinds of persons they are becoming. Life in Christ binds them to one another: Jew and gentile, male and female, slave and free. They are the body of Christ, the advance and representative embodiment of the power and promise of the coming kingdom. They are summoned to love one another and to build one another up in Christ. They are sent forth into the world to bear witness to Christ and his redemptive presence. They await patiently God's consummation of the work begun among them. It is in the context of these basic notions that Paul's understanding of the moral life appears.

Paul's thought presents considerable difficulties for interpreters. It emerges in the course of his responses to particular problems in the young churches of the gentile mission. The problems reflect the diverse social and cultural backgrounds of the first Christians. They concern significant misunderstandings of what Paul takes to be the gospel message. The difficulty is that we cannot always reconstruct adequately the lines of thinking Paul is seeking to correct. Not only are we apt to miss the force of his polemic; we also lack a suitable context for assessing appropriately the positive images and concepts

135

he puts forward. This difficulty is all the more pressing since the themes Paul treats, and even the vocabulary he uses, are shaped in no small measure by the positions he is criticizing.

To take the most obvious examples, the letter to the Galatians is dominated by Paul's struggle with "Judaizers," while the Corinthian correspondence is apparently determined by his attempts to counter the gnostic tendencies of the "Hellenists." These two groups of opponents present quite different temptations to the young churches. The former resists the eschatological newness of the gospel and seeks to assimilate it once more into traditional Judaism, perhaps its pharisaic strand. The latter hears the gospel as inaugurating a radically new possibility, but loses sight of its concrete social and historical situatedness. In Galatians Paul speaks of the law, God's promise to Abraham, circumcision, justification by faith, the fruits of the Spirit. In Corinthians he speaks of wisdom (and foolishness), the bodily resurrection, spiritual gifts, communal responsibility, the sufferings of apostles.

As the apostle to the gentiles, Paul's task is to lead the churches among diverse impulses which threaten to distort their grasp of the gospel. He is charged with the care of the churches in circumstances analogous to those confronted by ancient Israel as it struggled to maintain covenant faithfulness amid the successive challenges of Baalism and monarchy. At issue is the identity of the eschatological community and its fidelity to Jesus Christ.

Given the occasional nature of Paul's writings, it is important that we resist taking any single theme or image as central to his thought—let us say, justification by faith or the new creation—and interpreting all others on its terms. We must rather take account of what J. Christiaan Beker calls Paul's "hermeneutical versatility," his ability to articulate the gospel in a variety of thought forms and in relation to diverse modes of human understanding.[1] Beker is an especially helpful guide since he manages in his studies to balance the "contingency" and "coherence" of Paul's thought.[2] Paul's writings are contingent on the problems of the churches, especially their uncriticized background assumptions. They also present an essentially coherent set of understandings, governed by the

136

apprehension of the eschatological import of Jesus' death and resurrection.

Drawing upon the work of Gerd Theissen, Beker has outlined Paul's message of salvation around two sets of distinct yet interrelated symbols, one social, the other organic. The primary social symbols speak of liberation, justification, and reconciliation. One is liberated from bondage to the principalities and powers, sin and death, even to the law viewed as an alien power. The positive outcome is freedom. Justification concerns the acquittal of the guilty by a judge whose righteousness transcends the neutrality and objectivity of law. The positive outcome is righteousness. Reconciliation restores the alienated to fellowship with God. The positive outcome is community, life in Christ. The primary organic symbols speak of transformation, resurrection from the dead, and unification. Transformation highlights the fact that we are being changed by God's Spirit into the image and likeness of the Lord, from one degree of glory to another (e.g., 2 Cor. 3:18). Resurrection attests that we who once were dead in our sins, having now died with Jesus Christ, are also alive with God in him (e.g., Rom. 6:5–11). Unification suggests that those who were formerly separated from God and one another are now one in Jesus Christ. The underlying images are the body's assimilation of food, and sexual union between a man and a woman. Unification issues in the metaphor of body to represent the church.[3]

Beker notes a certain pairing of the social and organic symbols: liberation and transformation, justification and resurrection, and reconciliation and unification. The social metaphor in each of these pairs points to the saving activity of God in Jesus Christ; the organic metaphor, to the changes taking place in persons of faith by virtue of their participation in Christ. In no case do these basic symbols indicate closed or self-contained directions of thought. Paul continually weaves them together, moving from one to another, and back again. The center throughout is the lordship of Jesus Christ. Jesus Christ is the crucified and risen one who effects the presence of the new age and prefigures God's final triumph.[4]

In the exposition which follows, I shall focus attention on the central pair in Beker's scheme: justification by faith and resurrection. I shall deal with related symbolic materials chiefly as they interact with these dominant motifs. The first, justification by faith, celebrates the acquittal of the guilty; yet it quickly merges with the announcement of the freedom of persons of faith from forces which have previously tyrannized over them. It highlights what we have come to call the "indicative" of the gospel. It states what is already the case for those who can receive it. The latter motif, resurrection, or dying and rising with Christ, attests the change which the gospel effects in persons of faith. It signals the freedom of human beings to become subject to one another in love. It highlights what we have come to call the "imperative" of the gospel, summoning persons of faith to embody in concrete human existence the life possibilities it offers.

THE PRIMACY OF PROMISE

Promise as Justification by Faith

Paul's concept of justification by faith connects with the ideas introduced by Jeremiah and Ezekiel. These prophets emphasized the anthropological roots of Israel's infidelity. The hope for Israel, they contended, lies in a new heart and a new spirit. Social and cultural challenges to Israel's fidelity were not counted as of no importance, but they were subordinated to a deeper problem, one residing in the human condition as such.

Paul shares this orientation and gives it full development. As he sees it, the fundamental problem is that all human beings, whether they be Jews or gentiles, have sinned and fallen short of the glory of God. Despite their social, ethnic, and cultural differences, they are one in at least this respect: they have violated God's truth and goodness. Gentiles have exchanged the truth about God for a lie; they worship and serve the creature rather than the Creator. Jews claim to honor God and they presume to judge gentile idolatry and immorality; yet they dishonor God by breaking the law which has been given them by God (cf. Rom. 1:18–3:20, esp. 1:25 and 2:1, 23).

Human idolatry and disobedience are not simply acts which bring guilt and shame upon their perpetrators. They also unleash powerful forces in God's created order which dominate and oppress human life. Thus, human beings are not only guilty before God; they are also subject to the power of sin, and to the death to which sin leads. They are at the mercy of forces beyond their control, in no small measure as the penalty for their own wrong doing. Among the gentiles, these forces are epitomized by sexual immorality (cf. Rom. 1:24, 26–27), though they encompass any passions, desires, or feelings which come to dominate human existence (e.g., Rom. 1:28–32). Among the Jews, they show themselves in zealous (compulsive?) regard for the dictates of the law, coupled with violations of its deeper intent. Jews deceive themselves about their righteousness, concealing from themselves the fact that the law itself has become for them a vehicle of sin and death (e.g., Rom. 2:17–24).

Paul's argument does not presuppose Jewish opponents who explicitly contend that salvation is by works of the law. According to Jewish understandings, salvation comes through God's righteous activity on behalf of the people. That activity includes the giving of laws and commandments as constituents of covenant fidelity. Such laws, as I noted earlier, are themselves grace, an offer of life. To love God is, therefore, to keep God's commandments. Regardless of official doctrines, however, Paul is contending that Jewish concern for correct observance of the law, especially food laws and circumcision rites, amounts to a quest for salvation by human performance of the stipulations of the law. Moreover, the more conscientious one is about keeping the law, the more one is forced to deceive oneself about the extent and depth of one's enmity with God. And if one is not self-deceived, one is driven to despair (cf. Rom. 7:13–24). Paul's claim is that human relations with God are not established by the law, but by grace. They depend not upon human accomplishments, but the divine promises. The only appropriate human response is faith.

Paul's gospel is that the righteousness of God has now become manifest in Jesus Christ apart from the law. Jesus Christ is significant not simply with reference to the status of law in the life of the people of God, but also in regard to the underlying problem of human bondage to the power of evil. Jesus Christ is the counterpart of Adam through whom sin came into the world. Just as Adam is the prototype of sinful, disobedient humanity, so Jesus Christ is the prototype of human righteousness and obedience. Just as we became immersed in sin and subject to death by enacting in our own lives the sin of Adam, so now we become participants in the righteousness of God through trust in the abundance of grace given in Jesus Christ (Rom. 5:12–21; cf. 1 Cor. 15:45–50). Jesus Christ means acquittal and life; he establishes peace with God. However, we can claim these gifts only by renouncing our confidence in the law as the basis of our identity and integrity before God.[5]

Does law then have no place whatsoever in the lives of those who place their confidence in the promises of God? Is it always a mark of human estrangement, though perhaps also a protest against that estrangement? Is our choice works of the law or the righteousness of faith?

The Relation of Law and Promise

Paul's basic message is that faith displaces law. Law belongs to childhood (Gal. 4:1–7) and slavery (Gal. 4:21–31). It was added because of transgressions, till the offspring should come to whom the promise has been made (Gal. 3:19). That offspring is Jesus Christ, though Jesus Christ also embraces all who place their trust in him. Pointedly stated, Christ is the end of the law (Rom. 10:4). The term end, *telos,* conveys a sense of fulfillment. That is, insofar as the law is holy and just and good, its intent has been realized in Jesus Christ. Yet the dominant sense is that of annulment. The law has no more significance for those who live by faith in Jesus Christ.

Paul does on occasion speak of the law (*nomos*) of Christ, or of the law of the Spirit of life in Christ (e.g., Rom. 8:2). In such a usage, however, the term *nomos* does not refer to the ordering principles of human life; it is not a functional equivalent to the Mosaic law. It rather designates something akin to an operative principle or a fundamental dynamic. Thus, in Romans 8 the dynamic or operative principle at work in the Spirit of life in Jesus Christ is contrasted with the dynamic or operative principle at work in sin and death. Paul does not envision a new set of regulations, or instructions, derived from the Spirit of life in Christ which can order

140

human life. Nor does he, like Matthew, offer a new interpretation of the law of Moses. We rather have the enunciation of an altogether different basis for securing human life, dignity, worth, and wholeness with God.

What complicates this claim is that Paul appears throughout his letters to give all sorts of lawlike admonitions to individuals and churches. He urges Christians to abstain from immorality, especially sexual immorality (1 Thess. 4:1; 1 Cor. 6:9-11). He commands the Corinthians to discipline one of their members who is openly living with his father's widow (presumably a stepmother, 1 Cor. 5:1-5). When Corinthian ecstatics argue that "all things are lawful" — apparently quoting Paul himself, or at least carrying forward the logic of his gospel — Paul accepts their saying only by adding the qualification, "but not all things are helpful" (1 Cor. 6:12; cf. also 10:23). When the "things" in question refer to sexual practices which Paul judges to be immoral (for example, sexual intercourse with a prostitute), Paul elaborates his point by arguing that "the body is not meant for immorality, but for the Lord, and the Lord for the body" (6:13). When the "things" in question refer to the eating of meat which has been prepared in the context of a pagan cult, he develops his understanding in terms of the community. "Knowledge puffs up," he contends, while love "builds up" (1 Cor. 8:1). Or again: "All things are lawful, but not all things build up." "Let no one seek his own good," he adds, "but the good of his neighbor" (1 Cor. 10:23-24). Therefore, if eating meat is likely to cause a neighbor to fall, then in order to serve the good of that neighbor, to build him or her up in the faith, one should refrain from eating meat.

In more general terms Paul repeatedly calls Christians to be servants of one another (Gal. 5:13), to bear one another's burdens (Gal. 6:5), to do good insofar as possible to all, but especially to the household of faith (Gal. 6:10). He opposes factiousness, quarreling, and strife, especially lawsuits among Christians in pagan courts (1 Cor. 6:1-6). He urges patience and forbearance, even the suffering of wrong, that peace might prevail in the churches. He commends neighbor love, characterizing it as the fulfilling of the law. According to Paul, the commandments — he specifically cites the "second table" of the ten commandments — are summed up in one sentence, "You shall love your neighbor as yourself" (Rom. 13:8–10). (The command to love God is not mentioned, apparently because it has been incorporated into the teaching about faith.)

Paul has a good deal to say about how Christians should conduct themselves toward one another in the churches. He also counsels them on how they should relate to the structures and expectations of institutions belonging to the world which is passing away, especially the state and the household. This counsel contains a good deal of lawlike language. He mocks those who boast about their knowledge and their righteousness, who consequently are arrogant and proud. He admonishes them to be humble, to give God the glory, and to count others better than themselves.

What is noteworthy about these instructions and admonitions is that they encompass the most important relationships in which persons find themselves: relations to body, to fellow human beings, to social institutions, to God. If we were to add discussions of animals and the natural environment, no facet of the moral life would have been omitted from consideration.[6] The function of law is simply to make explicit certain basic rules for ordering the various relationships which figure in human life. If Paul is different from Moses or any other lawmaker, it would appear that he is simply more ad hoc and personal in his approach, claiming charismatic rather than traditional or legal authority. From the standpoint of the law, however, this characteristic would be a deficiency. If Christ is the end of the law, then what is the meaning of all of these instructions and admonitions in Paul's thought?

What Paul is seeking to accomplish is a new way of articulating the nature of the relationships which make up human existence. This new way is required by what he announces as the righteousness of God given in Jesus Christ. It renders passé our previous taken-for-granted assumptions about the bases of human life. Paul's underlying claim is that law is not constitutive of the relationships which form human life. Indeed, where law comes into the picture, these relationships have already been violated, distorted, or broken. In themselves the formative relationships rest not upon law, but promise. Promise is grace. It connotes commitment to the well-being of the one to whom one is related. Ultimately, we have to do with the promise of God, though the divine promise finds expression in other levels of promising as well. Where promise can be trusted and is in fact trusted, law is irrelevant. Participants in the relationships enact readily and without constraint what the law requires, but with a depth and fullness the law by itself is incapable of expressing or bringing about. Where promise breaks down or where confidence in its sustaining power is lost, law cannot restore or compensate for what is lacking. At its best it can place some constraints on the proliferating power of evil, and it can disclose human failure, though without fundamental remedy; at its worst it tempts its advocates to self-deception and even to a subtle, duplicitous promotion of the wrong. The point is not that the law is evil, Paul insists. In itself the law is holy (Rom. 7:12). The point is that sin which has gained dominion over human existence makes use of the commandments of God to deceive human beings and to increase the power of sin in their lives. "The very commandment which promised life proved to be death to me," Paul laments (Rom. 7:10; cf. 7:13). If the relationships which constitute human life are to be restored, law as their ordering principle must be surpassed. Promise must once again become effective as their basis.

Paul interprets Israel's own existence in terms of promise. Israel's identity is not based upon fidelity to the commandments which God offered the people in the covenant at Sinai. It is based upon faith in the promises of God first given to Abraham. The promises of God stem from the righteousness of God, which is bestowed upon human beings apart from the law. (Though, as Paul notes, law and prophets bear witness to it. Cf. Rom. 4:13–24; Gal. 3:15–18.) Thus, Abraham, not Moses, is the central figure in Israelite life. Abraham lived by faith, and his faith was reckoned to him as righteousness.

Law has indeed been prominent in Israel. It is, moreover, good. It contains the oracles of God. Yet its primary function has not been to establish Israel as the covenant people of God. It has been to give knowledge of sin (e.g., Rom. 3:20, 7:7). It came in, Paul argues, because of trespasses. It presupposes the power of sin already at work in human life. "It was ordained by angels," Paul suggests, and it was given "through an intermediary" (Gal. 3:19). We could add that the law is itself intermediate. It lies between parties to a relationship. It calls attention to itself and demands respect for itself in its own right, even though it claims to serve the relationships it regulates. Where law is operative, I do not in the first instance have to do with the other to whom I would relate. I have to do with the law which directs me in relationships. I presume perhaps, though without satisfactory warrant, that the law will protect, enable, and facilitate my relating. A promise, in contrast, is given face to face. It is more direct than law. The reference here is not to the limited promises which form contracts, but to an encompassing commitment to the well-being of the other. Promise in this sense is more fundamental than law and it surpasses law.

If Israel's life stems from promise rather than law, Paul reasons, then Israel's heritage is itself available to the nations independently of the law. Since Abraham's righteousness comes by faith and not by adherence to the law, then any who follow Abraham's example also have access to the promises of God. "We hold," Paul says, "that a person is justified by faith apart from works of law." "Is God the God of Jews only?" he continues. "Is he not the God of gentiles also? Yes, of gentiles also, since God is one; God will justify the circumcized on the grounds of their faith, and the uncircumcized through faith," he concludes (Rom. 3:28–31, au. trans.). Paul is claiming that his analysis of law and promise in the Jewish heritage holds, doubtless in diverse ways, for human beings in all societies and cultures. In this respect his mission to the gentiles is integral to his basic grasp of the gospel. Since human life is founded on the promises of God, then those promises, having been made fully actual in Jesus Christ, are available to the nations. The solidarity of Jew and gentile in sin is matched by a solidarity in grace.

If we are to live by faith in the promises of God, however, we must reside in the relationships they establish. More specifically, we must let our relationships to body, to other human beings, and to institutions be governed by and encompassed in our central relationship to Jesus Christ. We cannot be nourished by this central relation and repeatedly surrender ourselves once more to impulses and involvements which are antithetical to it, indeed, which led to our subjection to sin and death in the first place. What appear

144

to be statements of laws or principles or rules to regulate Christian existence are upon closer examination admonitions to abide in that relationship which is grace and promise, which is freedom and life. "You were called to freedom," Paul tells the Galatians, "only do not use your freedom as an opportunity for the flesh" (Gal. 5:13). "The desires of the flesh are against the Spirit," he continues, "and the desires of the Spirit are against the flesh: for these are opposed to each other, to prevent you from doing what you would" (Gal. 5:17). Paul lists some of the works of the flesh: "fornication, impurity, licentiousness, idolatry, sorcery, enmity, strife, jealousy, anger, selfishness, dissension, party spirit, envy, drunkenness, carousing, and the like" (Gal. 5:19–21). Paul is saying that to yield ourselves to such passions and desires is to fall once more into bondage to sin and death. The various admonitions and instructions noted earlier simply reiterate this point over and over with reference to quite specific questions. The summons is always to live by the Spirit and to bear its fruits. "If you are led by the Spirit," Paul promises, "you are not under the law" (Gal. 5:18).

The originality of Paul's insights into the meaning of the gospel comes forcefully into view when we compare his thought with the treatment of law in Matthew's presentation of the teachings of Jesus. Matthew's Jesus, I noted above, discusses in the language of law what cannot readily be grasped by way of such language: the perfection of the disciple. In lifting up as the essential intent of the law the total involvement of human selves in relationships which make up the fullness of the kingdom of heaven, Matthew stretches legal categories to the breaking point. Paul sets forth analogous understandings, but with a firm sense of the inadequacy of legal categories to express what needs to be said. Matthew's Jesus reinterprets the law of Moses to set forth God's expectations for eschatological community. What the law commands is love of God and love of neighbor. It concerns not merely behavioral correctness, but the total self; not simply purposive resolve, but affections, attitudes, feelings, and desires. It commands a readiness to endure suffering, even unjust suffering, at the hands of others rather than perpetuating the cycle of violence that orders the affairs of a world passing away. In contrast, Paul reinterprets not simply the law of

145

Israel, but the constitutive principles of Israelite existence as the people of God. The formative truth and power of Israel is promise, not law; it is epitomized by Abraham, not Moses; it finds its basis not in the unity of covenant and commandment, but in a righteousness which transcends law and commandment.

Paul's undertaking moves the whole discussion to a more fundamental level. He poses in the most radical terms the issues raised by the proclamation that Jesus is the Christ, the bearer of the new age in the midst of the old. His theme is faith, trust in the promises of God; it is the life of the Spirit which flows from faith to faith.

DYING AND RISING
WITH CHRIST
The Resource for Christian Freedom

In order to drive home his basic understanding, Paul turns from justification language to the language of death and resurrection. The shift is necessitated by a persistent and troublesome question: are we to continue in sin that grace may abound (Rom. 6:1)? The social image of salvation, taken by itself, tends to leave us with a picture of guilty persons being acquitted by an indulgent judge. Such indulgence suggests the end to human accountability. It implies that everything is permitted. To counter this impression, Paul takes up and develops a new image. To live by faith is not simply to be reckoned righteous; it is to participate by faith in Jesus Christ. To participate in Christ is to die and rise with him. In baptism we act out this process. To be baptized in the name of Jesus is to be baptized into his death, to be buried with him, that as Christ was raised from the dead, so we too might walk in newness of life (Rom. 6:2–11).

The dying is a dying to sin. It is the sinful self that is crucified, and the sinful body that is destroyed. If our sinful self has been crucified, dead, and buried, then sin no longer has dominion over us. We are now free of sin, for no tyrant can rule over a dead person. If we have died with Christ, Paul continues, we should also live with him. "You must consider yourselves dead to sin and alive to God in Jesus Christ," he concludes (Rom. 6:11).

At this point Paul's exposition has shifted in mood, from the in-

146

dicative to the imperative: "we should . . ."; "we must . . ." What is going on in this shift? Paul recognizes that the death to sin is not as simple, complete, and final as his language suggests. What he is setting forth is a life possibility which is offered by the gospel. It is a life possibility that we in part claim and that in part escapes us. We slip out of the participatory relation that sustains us in newness of life and lapse once again into bondage to sin and death. Consequently, we must continually be summoned to take up that relation once again. Paul uses the imperative mood to issue the call. "Let not sin therefore reign in your mortal bodies, to make you obey their passions. Do not yield your members to sin as instruments of wickedness, but yield yourselves to God as persons who have been brought from death to life, and your members to God as instruments of righteousness. For sin will have no dominion over you, since you are not under law but under grace" (Rom. 6:12–14, au. trans.).

The imperative mood in Paul's thought does not express a law or commandment. It directs us to the relationship within which life, freedom, righteousness, and peace can be ours, and it does so with some urgency. When sinful passions of one sort or another pull at us, we are not to deal with them by treating them as temptations to violate particular laws or commandments, for example, an impulse to covet something which is our neighbor's. We are to respond by unmasking the bondage and death to which such passions lead. We resist their pull not by striving all the more zealously to maintain particular standards of behavior which may be required of us, but by claiming once again the offer of life which is graciously given in Jesus Christ. We may not be able to control ourselves in particular facets of our lives by determined resolve alone. But we do have the possibility of placing ourselves again and again in that relation within which we can regain our freedom and live out in fullness the righteousness God bestows upon us.

The subtle interplay of indicative and imperative moods in Paul's presentation of the gospel reflects the fact that the eschatological tension which characterizes Christian existence cuts into the believer's own self-experience. It is not limited to the struggle of the church with social institutions and cultural forms belonging to the old age. As a person coming to life in Jesus Christ, I continue to be pulled at, assaulted, and disturbed by the power of my old self, even though that old self has now been consigned to death and is passing away. We could say that Paul has uncovered the interior dimensions of the tensions figuring in eschatological existence.

Thus far, the accent has fallen on the resources given to faith to resist the power of evil at work in our lives. Does life in Christ also offer positive indications of how we are to live our lives? The answer is clearly yes.

The Model for Christian Obedience
In Paul's usage, the death-resurrection motif functions not only to describe the Christian's participation in Christ and his or her resultant freedom from sin, death, and the law. It also functions as a model of Christian self-giving which we are called to imitate. Life in Christ involves both participation by faith in his death and resurrection, and also imitation of his suffering and self-giving in our demeanor and our activity. The summons to imitate Christ, and also to imitate Paul who himself imitates Christ, is never self-contained, an autonomous moral example. It presupposes and rests upon participation. It expresses the imperative dimensions of participation, just as participation expresses the indicative basis of imitation. It is as participants in Christ that we are called to imitate Christ. In this context Christ's dying and rising, particularly his dying, have normative significance for the moral life of the Christian.[7]

Paul's treatment of imitation does not take us back to Jesus' life and public ministry. It focuses on the death and resurrection of Christ, illumined theologically as the saving activity of God. It has a number of strata. Three are crucial: a readiness to suffer for the sake of the gospel; humility and self-abasement before God; and self-giving, even self-subjection, to the neighbor. (The latter is often treated as the mutual self-giving of brothers and sisters in the faith: be subject to one another in love.)

The accent on suffering is reminiscent of Mark's account of eschatological existence. Since life in Christ is life lived for the new age, but amid institutions and social arrangements which belong to the old age, it invariably evokes conflict and leads to suffering.

148

Persons who stake their lives on the power and authority of the old age are threatened by the new movement. They make use of instrumentalities at their disposal to resist, frustrate, and ultimately destroy its challenge to their manner of life. Those who are faithful to the mission generated by the gospel sooner or later become objects of these efforts. As such they are participants in Christ's sufferings.

It is in the Corinthian correspondence that Paul deals most extensively with his own sufferings. As he views the Corinthians, there are those among them who live as though the new age has in some sense already been fully realized, at least for believers. They act as though there are no more stresses or trials to be endured. "Already you are filled! Already you have become rich! Without us you have become kings! And would that you did reign, so that we might share the rule with you" (1 Cor. 4:8). So Paul taunts his critics. He then catalogs the sufferings he has endured for the sake of the gospel (vv. 9–13).

Paul interprets his sufferings in terms of the death and resurrection of Jesus Christ, making clear that the power which enables him to endure and persevere is not his own, but the power of God. "While we live," he states, "we are always being given up to death for Jesus' sake, so that the life of Jesus may be manifested in our mortal flesh" (2 Cor. 4:11). He compares himself to an earthen vessel filled with treasure, "to show that the transcendent power belongs to God and not to us" (2 Cor. 4:7).

What is striking about Paul's account of his sufferings is that he dares to call others to be imitators of his own life. The apostle who imitates Jesus in suffering and death is also to be imitated by others (e.g., 1 Thess. 1:6–7; Phil. 3:17). He bases his authority as an apostle not simply on his call, but also on his participation in Christ's sufferings. By these marks of fidelity he claims a hearing in the churches as one charged with their care.[8] The point is not that Paul has himself become a part of the gospel, completing, as it were, what is lacking in Christ's sufferings. As an apostle Paul remains completely subordinate to the gospel of Christ as the source and norm of his activity. At the same time, the gospel whose power was disclosed in the weakness of Christ's death continues to be manifest in the work of the apostle, and also in the communities for which he bears responsibility. Thus, while Paul's activity rests in the gospel he preaches, it is also evident in his own life and deeds: the power of God made effective in human vulnerability and weakness.[9]

The imitation of Christ is not limited, however, to the readiness to endure suffering. It also indicates a fundamental attitude and demeanor for the believer, one of self-effacement and humility before God, of acknowledging God's power as the power by which the believer lives. This motif appears in virtually all of the accounts of Paul's sufferings cited above. It is thematically central in the Philippian letter. "Whatever gain I had," Paul testifies, "I counted as loss for the sake of Christ. . . . For his sake I have suffered the loss of all things, and count them as refuse, in order that I may gain Christ and be found in him . . . ; that I may know him and the power of his resurrection, and may share his sufferings, becoming like him in his death, that if possible I may attain the resurrection from the dead" (Phil. 3:7, 8, 10).

This same spirit of humility is central to the other-regardingness which for Paul is the essence of neighbor love. Paul draws the connection between humility and the imitation of Christ by reciting what may have been a hymn of the early church. The hymn recounts the self-emptying of Christ, his becoming a servant, his obedience unto death. It then celebrates the exaltation of this humiliated one above all creatures by the power of God (Phil. 2:6–11). Paul sees in this portrait a model for the mind and spirit proper to the people of God in their interactions with one another. "Do nothing from selfishness or conceit, but in humility count others better than yourselves. Let each of you look not only to his [or her] own interests, but also to the interests of others" (Phil. 2:3–4). With this admonition, Paul introduces the hymn itself. Thus, humility, servitude, even humiliation and suffering, mark the stance of the person of faith toward fellow human beings.

Paul's advocacy of this stance is not without problems. It appears to glorify self-hatred and to disparage self-respect. It provides ready material for reinforcing the feelings of those who through various life experiences have come to have a low opinion of themselves. It may also function to rationalize the acquiescence of oppressed persons in lowly positions and limited opportunities. This latter possibility will have to be examined in the context of Paul's explicit treatment of social institutions. The point which needs emphasis here, however, is that Paul sees a paradoxical relation between weakness and power, humility and dignity. Paul is not simply saying that we will eventually be exalted if we are first willing to be humble, or that we will eventually be powerful if we will now consent to weakness. His claim is that a stance which on the surface appears to be weak is in fact strong, and one that appears to be humiliating is to be honored above all. He is undertaking a transvaluation of values based on the Christian's radical freedom in Christ. Insofar as human beings can let go of the drive to self-justification by personal or social accomplishments, trusting rather in the promises of God, they have extraordinary resources for enduring suffering, stress, and humiliation, and for service and self-giving to neighbors in need. They have unshakable confidence and unassailable dignity no matter what may befall them. They have such capacities by the power of God at work in them. Freedom from the dominion of sin and death, and from the accusations of law, is freedom for fidelity to the liberating truth of the gospel, and for loving service to the neighbor.

Thus, the death and resurrection of Jesus disclose for Paul not simply the basis of the Christian life but also its fundamental shape and its substantive content. Life in Christ involves fidelity to the gospel, despite the inevitability of conflict and suffering. It involves humility before God and unqualified confidence in the power of God to sustain and vindicate the believer, to work effectively in and through human weakness. It involves self-giving to the neighbor, in which one grants priority to the neighbor's needs. Indeed, death and resurrection indicate as well the self-discipline the person of faith is to exercise over his or her own body, for the suffering of the Christian is like the training the athlete endures in preparing for the big race (1 Cor. 9:24–27).

To reiterate the central points, justification by faith announces that human life and well-being are founded not on law, but on promise, not on works, but on faith. Jesus Christ is the restoration of promise as the ground of human hope. This restoration both fulfills the inner intent of the law while annulling its continuing authority in human affairs. Dying and rising with Christ highlights the changes taking place in the believer which render law irrelevant as a constraint and guide to life. It also displays Paul's distinctive way of dealing with normative aspects of the Christian life Christian existence is dying and rising with Christ in ways appropriate to the various relationships in which one stands. The final step is to consider some of the ramifications these basic understandings have for social and institutional life.

CULTURAL PLURALISM AND THE UNITY OF FAITH

As in the case of the Synoptic Gospels, the institutional impact of Paul's gospel chiefly concerns traditional religious practices, especially within Judaism, but also in Hellenistic life. His task is to clarify the status of these practices in the emerging eschatological communities. He also gives no small amount of attention to the bearing of the gospel on kinship ties and household relations. These ties and relations lose their foundational significance, giving way to the ordered patterns of the new communities. In comparison with these two interests, political and economic institutions remain marginal to Paul's thought since they belong essentially to the old age which is passing away. Insofar as they continue to enjoy provisional validity, their function is to preserve a modicum of social order as a context for the work of the gospel. Paul's central preoccupation is to devise concrete ways in which Jew and gentile, slave and free, male and female might enact in human community their oneness in Christ.

Whereas Matthew lifts up the motif of forgiveness and Luke that of property in setting forth the formative principles of communal existence, Paul brings to the fore a recognition of the plurality of cultures in interaction with the unifying promises of the gospel. His thesis is that all human cultures are relative to the lordship of Jesus Christ. This thesis is founded on the primacy of promise over law as the constitutive basis of social existence. Law is a category of tradition. It binds us to the past, to the cumulative experiences of a society over time. Law is amenable to innovative interpretations.

152

It can host fresh applications of its seminal impulses to novel social circumstances. However, such interpretations amount to incremental adaptations of an authoritative tradition. They are on the whole resistant to the creation of significantly new cultural forms. Promise in contrast is essentially a category of the future. It points to fundamental commitments and intentions to be carried out in time to come. It leaves unsettled the determination of concrete ways of articulating these commitments. Promise does gain its orientation from the past. It is not without precedents. Nonetheless, its genius is to foster cultural creativity, especially in attempts to negotiate a common life among persons of diverse backgrounds.

The Unity of Jew and Gentile

The theme of cultural relativity shows itself most clearly in Paul's struggles for Jewish and gentile unity within Christian communities. His approach to this problem is subtle and complex. His basic conviction is that Jew and gentile enjoy full equality in the Christian community. I noted that Luke interprets gentile membership in the church on the analogy of the "strangers" who once dwelt among the Jews and adapted themselves in specified ways to Jewish requirements. In Luke's view the foundation of the church is a repentant Israel, which means an Israel obedient in all respects to the dictates of the law. Paul uses images which point in a similar direction. In his letter to the Romans he suggests that gentiles are "shoots" from a wild olive tree which have been grafted onto a cultivated tree in order that they might share its riches. They replace branches which have been broken off (Rom. 11:17–18). "Remember it is not you that support the root," Paul reminds his gentile readers, "but the root that supports you" (Rom. 11:18). Yet the basic thrust of Paul's thought is not that gentiles are simply grafted onto a faithful Israel. Israel too must be reconstituted. Its link with law must be set aside in order to restore its more ancient heritage of promise. It is "root" only as bearer of promise. In the nature of the case promise is as fully open to gentiles as to Jews, and on altogether equal terms. Thus, the metaphor of root and branches indicates at most only the proximate, historical origins of Jew and gentile in the formation of the people of God. In essence both Jew and gentile live by the promises of God, that is, the righteousness of God given apart from the law in Jesus Christ. In sin and grace they are now one people.

In light of this conviction Paul insists that practices which interfere with the full equality of Jew and gentile in the one people of God must either be abrogated or fundamentally modified. For Jewish Christians circumcision and food laws provide the crucial test cases. Against the tradition of a Jewish mission which requires the circumcision of gentile males, Paul insists that circumcision is not necessary for gentiles. To require it is to deny the truth of the gospel. It is to make law rather than promise constitutive for Christian existence (Gal. 2:1–10). Paul is equally clear in asserting that circumcision is no liability for Jews. In itself it does not in any way count against the life of faith (cf. 1 Cor. 7:18). "Neither circumcision counts for anything nor uncircumcision, but keeping the commandments of God" (1 Cor. 7:19). Paul's generalization is that everyone should remain in the state in which he or she was called (1 Cor. 7:20). Thus, the male Jew is a person in Christ as circumcized; the male gentile, as uncircumcized. The practice of circumcision is relativized and subordinated to the promises of God in Jesus Christ. It no longer marks the people of God, though it may continue to mark Jewish males who belong to that people.

The food laws are more problematic since they cannot be left unchanged without disrupting fellowship between Jews and gentiles in the Christian communities. If one is Jewish, one either observes the food laws, and so refuses table fellowship with gentiles, or one grants precedence in the Christian community to table fellowship with gentiles, and so violates the food laws. Paul insists upon the latter course, arguing that a refusal of table fellowship amounts to putting one's trust in the law rather than promise, works rather than faith. Jewish Christians could not continue to observe the food laws, except perhaps in the privacy of their homes. New rituals had to be devised to express the corporate reality of the new communities: baptism, the Lord's supper, and love feasts. These rituals could themselves enjoy importance only insofar as they embodied the gospel promise (cf. Paul's belittling of baptism, 1 Cor. 1:14–17, and his critique of Corinthian desecration of the Lord's Supper, 1 Cor. 11:17–34).

154

The test case for gentiles concerns the eating of meat prepared in a context of pagan sacrifice. On the face of it, Christians would have to avoid such meat, lest they participate in a form of idol worship. In most gentile cities, the avoidance of meat linked to pagan sacrifices would entail giving up meat altogether. Based on his acute sense of Christian freedom, however, Paul draws neither of these conclusions, at least not directly. The relativity of cultural forms is such that all is permitted which is compatible with Christ. Apparently quoting some of the Corinthians, Paul asserts what mature Christians allegedly know well: "An idol has no real existence" and "There is no God but one" (1 Cor. 8:4). Thus, meat prepared in pagan sacrifices could in no way be thereby tainted, nor could its consumption amount to idol worship. Still, Paul recognizes that all do not see through these relative cultural forms. For some, participation in them may connote apostasy, a fundamental compromise to faith in Christ. Such persons must avoid meat lest they lose Christ. Moreover, in light of our obligation to build one another up in faith, all of us, even the mature, indeed, especially the mature, must be ready to give up meat if partaking suggests idolatry to weaker brothers and sisters (1 Cor. 8:10–13).

Paul's generalization about eating meat parallels his observation about circumcision: "Food will not commend us to God. We are no worse off if we do not eat, and no better off if we do" (1 Cor. 8:8). The point is to avoid jeopardizing the community of faith. Just as the Jew must compromise the food laws for the sake of table fellowship with gentiles, so liberated Christians must exercise their freedom in Christ with restraint, sensitive to the growth needs of fellow members in the community.

For Paul, all cultural forms are relative to given social settings, to the experiences of particular peoples. None can as such be requisite to Christian existence. This insight opens the way to community among persons of quite diverse backgrounds. By the same token, the freedom from all determinate social and cultural forms is a freedom to accept all as provisionally valid provided they are subject to the essential conditions of such freedom. That is to say, they must no longer be vehicles for the tyrannical power of evil. Their compulsive dominance in our lives must be broken. We must participate in them as those who have in Christ died to the old self,

155

entering into the liberty of the children of God. Then we have access to all human ways. Indeed, we embrace them for the sake of Christ. "Though I am free from all human ways," Paul states, "I have made myself a slave to all, that I might win the more" (1 Cor. 9:19, au. trans.). He continues:

> To the Jews I became as a Jew, in order to win Jews; to those under the law I became as one under the law — though not being myself under the law — that I might win those under the law. To those outside the law I became as one outside the law — not being without law toward God but under the law [i.e., *nomos*, or principle] of Christ — that I might win those outside the law. To the weak I became weak, that I might win the weak. I have become all things to all people, that I might by all means save some. I do it all for the sake of the gospel, that I may share in its blessings (1 Cor. 9:20–23, au. trans.).

Paul is not saying, "everything is permitted." He is contrasting the relativity of human cultures with the foundational understandings of the gospel. The gospel summons us to celebrate pluralism, to welcome it into the internal life of the community of faith. Paul's position means that a Jewish Christian could remain Jewish, provided he or she appreciated the relativity of Jewish patterns and observed them in a fashion which did not divide, but rather built up and enriched the whole community of faith. On the same terms, a gentile Christian could remain gentile. Paul is pointing toward forms of fellowship which allow for ritual differences among the people of God. He challenges us to see how a social order grounded in promise can entertain and be enriched by a multiform cultural substance.

The outcome of this analysis is startling. On the one hand, Paul negates traditional first-century Jewish understandings as thoroughly as does Mark. He strikes at the heart of the matter: the place of Torah in the makeup of the people of God. He claims continuity with Judaism only by presuming to understand the Israelite legacy better than do its authoritative teachers. He goes behind Moses and the law to Abraham and the concept of promise. In so doing he makes clear that the Christian gospel inaugurates a new religious reality. It cannot be encompassed within well-established Jewish notions. On the other hand, Paul is able to affirm the con-

156

tinuation of Judaism, albeit with modifications, more completely than Luke or Matthew. If the relativity of Jewish practices is clearly perceived, then they can be acknowledged as having ongoing legitimacy. For Luke and Matthew, the only Israel which has legitimacy is the one incorporated into Christian understanding. All else is a negation of the gospel.

Paul's perspective even permits him to grant that Jews who refuse the claims of the gospel may yet have a positive role to play in the divine economy. His view of this matter is not without ambiguity. "A hardening has come upon part of Israel," he notes, "until the full number of Gentiles comes in" (Rom. 11:25). But why a "hardening"? How does Jewish "unbelief" help? Is Paul saying that the gentile mission gained its impetus because some Jews did not accept Jesus as the Christ? Yet "all Israel will be saved," he adds (Rom. 11:25). "As regards the gospel," he continues, "they are enemies of God for your sake; but as regards election they are beloved for the sake of their forefathers. For the gifts and the call of God are irrevocable" (Rom. 11:28–29). Paul does not concede that Jews might have good and substantial reasons to refuse the Christian proclamation. Their refusal is a "hardening." It is "unbelief." Yet he does grant that this hardening may be God's doing though its rationale remains a mystery. If it is God's doing, then it has a place in the divine purpose. It need not imply the ultimate rejection of any part of Israel. Indeed, one can assume Jewish salvation since God's call is "irrevocable."

Paul's insistence upon Israel's secure place in God's redemptive activity blunts any imperative to seek the conversion of Jews to Christianity. It even establishes a frame of reference within which it is possible to affirm the continuing importance of the Jewish people for Christian understanding, and precisely in their Jewishness. This latter possibility goes beyond what Paul himself explicitly states. It suggests that most Jewish people may have had to reject the Christian gospel, not because of their unbelief, or because a hardening had come upon them, but for the sake of their fidelity to their calling and in keeping with their distinctive insight into the human condition. It also suggests that the Christian community has continuing need of a faithful Jewish witness as a summons to fidelity in its own distinctive vocation. Paul never granted so much, though his appreciation of the relativity of all human ways provides a matrix of understanding within which such a view might emerge. Even so, Paul alone among New Testament writers seems to have considered the continuation of Judaism, precisely as Judaism, to be compatible with God's overall purpose. He provided an opening, admittedly small, through which subsequent interpreters of Christian faith might move in establishing models for Jewish-Christian relations other than the deep-seated anti-Semitism of Christian history. It is Paul's insight into cultural relativity which makes this move possible.

As far as social and institutional life is concerned, Paul's greatest contribution is to show how the gospel enables us to honor the diversity and relativity of human cultures. In this accomplishment he brings a new level of understanding to the universal outreach of biblical faith. God's promise to Abraham does not come to the nations solely through their adoption of Israelite and Jewish ways, for example, instruction in Torah or an orientation to Zion. It comes essentially as grace, as unqualified affirmation. It liberates peoples in all the earth from their compulsive attachments to their own norms of social order that they might be free to negotiate a common life with one another. The humiliation and exaltation of Jesus Christ attest the pain and suffering of God under the rigid insistence of human beings that their own laws and customs are the sole way to dignity and worth. They offer an alternative to cultural arrogance, a promise of fellowship based not on law, but on an open-ended commitment of love and service. They model receptivity to fellow human beings in their strangeness and difference in order that new modes of community might be formed.

Paul had firsthand experience in working through the ramifications of his position with respect to Jewish and gentile unity in a community of faith. His reflections provide important materials for the imaginative development of social thought in a modern context of cultural pluralism. They suggest the negotiation and continual renegotiation of patterns of relationship among diverse peoples until arrangements can be devised which allow all to flourish, and flourish in their diversity. The controlling image is that of a common life which embraces and even encourages plurality so long as that plurality does not violate the whole, but rather enriches it and builds it up.

If Paul is to serve as a resource for original social thought in the modern world, it will probably be on the basis of his grasp of the possibilities of community among culturally diverse peoples. His vision goes beyond a social order founded primarily on the formalities of economic and political exchange, where substantive cultural materials are largely relegated to a private sphere in which everything is permitted. It points instead to an engagement between peoples in their differences. It summons them to a stance of mutual recognition and regard instead of a mere tolerance of human oddities. It entails a readiness on the part of all to work out in concrete processes of negotiation a shared world of meaning which nourishes and strengthens them all, which builds them up in love. Such negotiation cannot preserve everything since everything is not compatible with the realization of a more inclusive community. Nor can negotiation consist solely in a selection among admissible cultural resources already somewhere in place. When it is vital, this negotiation issues in new creations appropriate to developing forms of community. The desired outcome is not a more encompassing though highly eclectic culture which simply displaces more discrete traditional cultures. It is rather a community which continues to preserve significant regions of difference, but within a common framework of life. The central challenge Paul brings to modern social thought is to keep more clearly in view the importance of substantive cultural realities, including especially their elemental ritual features, in ordering the relationships of diverse peoples. At issue is a more adequate grasp of cultural pluralism as an informing principle of postindustrial societies.

Marriage and Household Relations

Paul's gospel not only disturbed traditional Jewish and Hellenistic religious patterns. It modified established household arrangements as well. The gathered nature of Christian communities meant that individual members of a household could enter the Christian life without the support or approval of the patriarchal head. Subordinate members of the household in particular took advantage of this opportunity. Thus, women and slaves developed associations in the Christian communities which gave them new social standing, but without the clear sanction of the household. For Paul, as for the Synoptic authors, the community of faith displaces the household as the primary social unit. Household relations by no means disappear, but they lose their foundational significance for human society. They are relativized and subordinated to the communities of faith.

This view entails a recognition of singleness as an acceptable life pattern. More explicitly than the Synoptic Gospels, Paul calls attention to the appropriateness of the single state. The single person is in no way an incomplete human being or a social oddity lacking clear status and position. He or she has standing as a full member of the community of faith. Indeed, singleness has positive advantages. The single person is free, Paul observes, to focus total attention on the promises and imperatives of the gospel and to persevere without equivocation in the face of the hardships accompanying Christian mission. The married person must hold in mind the needs of the partner and other household members. Fitting this obligation with the claims of the gospel can on occasion cause complicating vexations (cf. 1 Cor. 7:25–28). Paul is able to take this position because the Christian community as he perceives it does not maintain itself through the propagation and socialization of offspring. It lives by mission. Its basis is not blood, but faith, and faith comes in response to the preaching of the gospel.

Though Paul considers singleness and celibacy to be preferred ways of living, he turns neither pattern into a principle of Christian existence. He recognizes the legitimacy of marriage, including marriage to unbelievers. He also endorses the desire of the betrothed to enter into marriage. He states his basic position in general terms: "Let everyone lead the life which the Lord has assigned to him [or her]. . . . This is my rule in all the churches" (1 Cor. 7:17; cf. vv. 17–24). "Assigned" (memériken) means "in which you find yourself," except that we are to view our placement in life not as fate or as social and political necessity, but as vocation, calling. The claim is that household arrangements have lost their absolute and binding authority, yet they are not incompatible with Christian existence insofar as their subjection to the lordship of Jesus Christ is fully understood. If the Christian takes part in these relationships in accord with the divine call, they can delineate a proper sphere of Christian existence. The decisive thing, Paul says, is "keeping the commandments of God" (1 Cor. 7:19). (I suspect he might more accurately have said; "abiding in the promises of God.")

Thus, believers should not divorce unbelieving spouses, unless those spouses desire it (1 Cor. 7:12–16). In the latter case, they should for the sake of peace grant the request of the estranged spouse (1 Cor. 7:15). Married couples should remain married, and, except by special agreement for periods of prayer, should continue to relate sexually. Indeed, each is *obliged* to grant to the other his or her conjugal rights (1 Cor. 7:1–11). Paul's reasoning on this particular matter is remarkable. When we marry, he contends, we no longer retain mastery over our own bodies. We surrender our bodies to our spouses, wives to husbands and husbands to wives. Therefore, we may not refuse one another, except perhaps for a season, and then only by mutual agreement. The full reciprocity is noteworthy, but even more so, the unqualified priority of the claims of the spouse. Yet this account is altogether in accord with Paul's general admonition that we be subject to one another in love, on the analogy of Christ's suffering, humiliation, death, and exaltation.

Single persons, including those who are betrothed, are encouraged to remain single that they might give total attention to the work of the Lord. Still, if sexual passion is strong enough to make them vulnerable to the lure of improper sexual outlets, then they do no wrong to marry (1 Cor. 7:8–9, 36–38). What Paul apparently finds wholly unacceptable is sexual activity outside of marriage. Such activity suggests to him an enslavement to the passions which fundamentally contradicts the promise of freedom in Christ.

The sweeping nature of Paul's condemnation of sexual activity apart from marriage is not altogether clear. We can, I suspect, readily concede that our sexual drives, like any other human passions, may so dominate us that we are no longer able to exercise judgments of appropriateness in giving them expression. Then our sexual activity will indeed epitomize our bondage to the flesh (cf.

Rom. 1:28–32, or 1 Cor. 6:9–11). It will contradict our freedom in Christ. However, that sexual activity outside of marriage, perhaps with a partner of the same sex, always and everywhere entails such bondage is not so clear. Paul rightly calls attention to the deep emotional ties which are often forged between persons through sexual union. Sexual union is never merely a physiological process, a release of bodily energy; it is also profoundly interpersonal. What is not clear, however, is why the bodily union of marriage partners is held to be compatible with life in Christ, while a union of partners who are not married is not (Paul cites the case of a prostitute, 1 Cor. 7:4). I would not suggest that no significant moral distinctions can be made between sexual activity within and outside of marriage. The point is that these distinctions remain largely unstated in Paul's extant writings. Consequently, the absolute contrast he draws between the two does not escape a certain arbitrariness.

Paul's thoughts about human sexuality are in no sense complete. He gives us some illuminating commentary on a few selected cases, and some central themes to guide our thinking, for example, the contrast between bondage and freedom, or between "having knowledge" or "having the law" and building up the neighbor. Similarly, we have his emphasis on the Christian's freedom in Christ to give of him- or herself to the neighbor in service and love. If we are to follow Paul's lead, it is with reference to notions such as these that we must articulate a more complete sexual ethic.

Paul gives little attention to the import of his understandings for the relative status of husbands and wives (or of men and women) within the household itself. He does affirm the full equality of women and men within the community of faith. He draws a parallel between Jew-gentile relations, on the one hand, and those of male and female and of slave and free, on the other. The classic text is oft-cited: "There is neither Jew nor Greek, there is neither slave nor free, there is neither male nor female; for you are all one in Christ Jesus" (Gal. 3:28). The passage concludes with a reference to the promises of God as constitutive of existence in faith.

This parallelism, though striking, is not without problems. Jew-gentile relations concern cultural differences and their mediation within a faith community. One could assume that Jewish and gentile Christians might continue to belong respectively to Jewish and gentile households, unless their individual decisions to enter one of the Christian communities seriously alienated them from family members. Relations of slave and free and of male and female concern differences in social status within a common culture, and perhaps within a given household. Paul's letter to Philemon, for example, has to do with a Christian master and his runaway slave, the slave having in the meantime also become a Christian.

Paul's response to social differences is first to assert their nullity in Jesus Christ and then to encourage acceptance of their provisional and continuing validity, to be sure, with appropriate qualifications. Neither circumcision nor uncircumcision amounts to anything, he claims. Neither is necessary; and both are compatible with life in Christ. Analogously, the status assignments of men and women and of slaves and free have no necessity about them, yet all are apparently suitable placements for the life of faith. Paul makes this point explicitly with reference to the circumstances of slaves. Should slaves be offered freedom, he counsels, let them avail themselves of the opportunity. Otherwise, they should content themselves to remain slaves knowing that they are free persons in the Lord (1 Cor. 7:21–22). Christian slaveholders, for example, Philemon, should be cognizant of the changed standing of slaves who are one with them in Jesus Christ. They should receive their slaves as "more than slaves" and as "beloved brothers" in the Lord (v. 16). Apparently, however, they have no specific obligation to release their slaves from further servitude. Thus, Paul accepts household slavery in its historical relativity and cultural specificity, even though within the faith community the status differences it implies no longer have any meaning.

Regarding the ordering of male and female relations in the household, Paul's comments are largely limited to the propriety of marriage, including marriage to unbelievers, and to the mutuality of sexual obligations between spouses. Can we assume that Paul accepted the patriarchal household precisely as he accepted slavery, that is, as having no inherent necessity, but as nonetheless being a social arrangement within which persons in the Lord could live out their calling in Christ? Such seems to be the logic of his thinking. A position of this kind permits openness to a range of family patterns in different societies, and it fosters an adaptability to social change. In itself, however, it provides little impetus to such change.

Did Paul accommodate himself too completely to existing social realities? The intent of the question is not to second-guess Paul, but to set in relief the force of his position. The central point is that Paul grants unqualified primacy to the ordered life of the community of faith over all other social institutions. His eschatological radicalism is chiefly addressed to that community. The household in comparison is quite secondary in importance, and of only relative interest. Thus, it is within the church that we should expect Paul to pursue most vigorously the oneness of all in Christ, whether Jew or gentile, slave or free, male or female. Within the church there must be table fellowship between Jew and gentile, and the slave must be received as more than a slave and as a "beloved brother," and the wife or single woman must be honored as a full companion in the Lord.

In Paul's gospel it is apparent that a person need not first bring about basic social change before finding a place within the institutions of the larger society to live out his or her faith in Christ. The freedom to accommodate oneself to the situation of one's "calling" holds especially for those in subordinate roles in relation to "unbelievers," whether husbands, masters, or fathers. The Christian is always and everywhere free for service provided he or she understands that the institutional form of the service is only relative and provisional—a qualification, it might be noted, which a patriarchal head might find difficult to bear!

What is not so apparent is how a Christian master who has learned to accept his slave as a beloved brother in the Lord could, nonetheless, continue to be a party to the institution of slavery. How, for example, might he subject himself to his slave in the Lord? Similarly, how could a husband who has realized the nullity of maleness and femaleness in Christ continue to function as the master of his wife? It would seem that the emerging patterns of equality within the church, if effective, would erode the hierarchical patterns of households deeply touched by Paul's gospel. Or alternatively, the persistence of hierarchical patterns within the household would eventually impact back upon associations within the church itself, blunting the principle of the oneness of all in Jesus Christ.

When we turn to the deutero-Pauline literature, we see that Paul's grasp of cultural relativity has largely been displaced by a theological sanction for the patriarchal household (Col. 3:18 – 4:1 and Eph. 5:22 – 6:8).[10] The material in Colossians is probably closer to Paul's own views. The address is primarily to subordinate parties in three sets of relationships: wives-husbands, children-fathers, and slaves-masters. Persons in the subordinate positions are admonished to "subject themselves" to their dominant counterparts, and to do so "in the Lord" (Col. 3:18, 20, 22). This stance is consistent with Paul's general charge that we embody the mind of Christ in our dealings with others. The dominant parties are also addressed, but not "in the Lord," a curious note since the text clearly implies readers who are persons of faith. Thus, husbands are called to love their wives; fathers, not to provoke their children; and masters, to treat their slaves justly and fairly. At no point, however, are either the normative content or the motives of these attitudes and actions christologically grounded. It is as though the writer recognizes that the asymmetry in these relations does not fit well with the more characteristic reciprocity of Pauline thought.

The Ephesian text begins with a general commendation of reciprocity: "Be subject to one another out of reverence for Christ" (Eph. 5:21). In the following verses, however, the reciprocity gives way to a pattern of domination and subordination in basic household relations. Where husbands and wives are concerned, the parallel is not Jew-gentile unity in Christ, but the relation of Christ and his church (Eph. 5:22–33). This analogy establishes a clear order of authority and power for the interactions of husband and wife. The remaining two pairs of relations are treated in a fashion similar to Colossians, though with greater elaboration.

These texts indicate that Paul's keen sense of historical relativity is not fully understood (or accepted) by his successors. Whereas Paul treats existing household arrangements as suitable spheres for acting out one's calling in the Lord, these same arrangements are later incorporated into the fundamental structure of the Christian life. Thus, the patriarchal order stands as the normative model for the Christian household. The pastoral epistles and the writings of the early church "fathers" further solidify this direction of development (e.g., Did. 4:9–11; Barn. 19:5–7; and 1 Clem. 21:6–9).

The comparison with Colossians and Ephesians dramatizes the distinctiveness of Paul's insights even if he may not have given as much attention as might be desirable to the implications of his gospel for the internal relations of households. Paul summarizes his overall position in terms of his eschatology: " . . . the appointed time has grown very short; from now on, let those who have wives live as though they had none, and those who mourn as though they were not mourning, and those who rejoice as though they were not rejoicing, and those who buy as though they had no goods, and those who deal with the world as though they had no dealings with it. For the form of this world is passing away" (1 Cor. 7:29–31). Cultural materials and institutional arrangements are provisional and relative. They can be utilized freely in the Lord, but none of them merits ultimate sanction in terms of the gospel itself.

Paul's views of the state and the economic order largely parallel his treatments of the household. Christians are expected to continue working to support themselves and others, despite the nearness of the end (1 Thess. 4:9). Paul continued to pursue his craft even though he believed he was entitled to community support in his activity as an apostle (1 Cor. 9:3–18). Similarly, he urges respectful obedience to governing authorities, including the paying of taxes. He emphasizes the positive contribution of the state to the maintenance of public order (Rom. 13:1–7). He does not explicitly stress the relativity of economic and governmental institutions, but the eschatological orientation which underlies these admonitions is identical with that which pervades his thought as a whole. Christians are being summoned to live for the new age in the midst of the old, accepting structures which continue to embody the old as spheres for their activity on behalf of the new. Thus, these institutional forms lose their ultimacy, but otherwise, they continue to enjoy provisional significance in the ordering of human life.

The Equality of Women

Paul's gospel entails the full equality of women within the household of faith, a thrust which in itself shakes the self-evident status of patriarchal assumptions. This claim needs additional comment since at least two passages in Paul's authentic letters appear to contradict it. The key passages are both in 1 Corinthians (1 Cor. 11:3–16; 14:33b–36). In one, women are commanded to wear veils in the church, though they are permitted, like men, to prophesy. The veil is set forth as a mark of subordination, and subordination is justified in terms of God's created order. "The head of every man is Christ, the head of a woman is her husband, and the head of Christ is God" (1 Cor. 11:3). And further, "a man . . . is the image and glory of God; but woman is the glory of man" (1 Cor. 11:7). Subsequent references to interdependence (1 Cor. 11:11–12) cannot, so far as I can see, mitigate the hierarchical force of these assertions. In a second passage, even more problematic than the first, women are ordered to keep silence in the churches. "If there is anything they desire to know, let them ask their husbands at home. For it is shameful for a woman to speak in church" (1 Cor. 14:35; cf. 1 Tim. 2:11–15). This passage subordinates women to men in both church and household.

It is unlikely that either of these passages is original with Paul. Both are intrusive in their present settings; both utilize categories and forms of argument which are uncharacteristic of Paul; and both contradict Paul's explicit beliefs and apostolic practice. There is strong scholarly opinion for this view with regard to the second of these passages.[11] The status of the former text is more in dispute. Quite a number of scholars accept the passage as Pauline and seek to interpret it in terms of basic Pauline ideas.[12] Yet this text certainly interrupts the flow of thought. The opening verse in the chapter leads quite naturally into the discussion of the Lord's Supper beginning with verse 17. More important, the argument for the veil appeals for grounding to patterns in the created order, whereas Paul normally links crucial points to Jesus Christ and his redemptive activity. Finally, one cannot easily defend the veil as Pauline without in some measure excusing him for his immersion in his own times, that is, without conceding that on this matter at least he may not have fully comprehended the radical logic of his own position.[13] Even if these arguments do not prove wholly convincing, they show that these two texts are problematic, and that we cannot allow them to control our reading of other Pauline materials pertinent to the status of women. The bold declaration of Gal. 3:28 remains fundamental: "There is neither Jew nor Greek, there is neither slave nor free, there is neither male nor female; for you are all one in Christ Jesus."

THE PAULINE CHALLENGE TO
MORAL UNDERSTANDING

Paul shares the eschatological orientation of the Synoptic Gospels, especially Mark. He writes with a sense of the emerging reality of the new age in the midst of the old. He anticipates the coming consummation of the new age. To a degree not found in the Synoptics, however, Paul's eschatology pushes him to a fundamentally different interpretation of the Israelite legacy. The key point is that promise replaces law as the constitutive basis of personal and social existence.

Promise designates God's unconditional commitment to a people, initially Abraham and his descendants, but in Jesus Christ, to a people gathered from all the earth, Jew and gentile, slave and free, male and female. Promise is grace. It calls forth faith. It creates a community of freedom and love. It is more primordial than law and commandment. Rather than being integral to the covenant, as in the preexilic pentateuchal traditions, promise discloses the derivative and secondary status of law. Law is essentially a contingent divine response to the human failure to live in terms of promise. It presupposes the awful reality of human sin, and while it may constrain sin, it is powerless to overcome it. Indeed, law may even function as an incitement to sin! Its primary function is to uncover the pervasive presence of sin in human life. Only the righteousness of God given apart from the law in Jesus Christ can break the power of sin and restore humanity to relationships based in promise. The righteousness of God effective in Jesus Christ brings law to an end as a determinative feature of existence.

Christian existence is not life according to the law, not even as internalized and perfected. It is life in the Spirit where there is no longer any such thing as law. Life in the Spirit and life in Christ are for Paul variant ways of saying the same thing. Life in Christ is life which derives its power from the righteousness of God given in Christ Jesus. It is a participation by faith in the death and resurrection of Christ. It is at the same time life modeled after the self-giving love by which Jesus was obedient unto death, even the death of the cross.

Paul's account of life in Christ is perfectionist in thrust. It points to the promise of human wholeness. Such wholeness is a gift. It stems from faith in the righteousness of God in Jesus Christ. In content it has three principal levels of meaning. It refers to humility before God, which includes total trust in the sufficiency of God and a readiness to obey God in all things. It accents a freedom in faith to endure triumphantly the suffering which is inevitably thrust upon faithful witnesses to the gospel. It specifies the self-giving love Christians are called to have for one another, and, so far as possible, for all human beings. "Be subject to one another in love" is the Pauline watchword.

Paul's perfectionism is never abstracted, however, from community. Throughout, his care is for the churches, and hence, for the corporate life of Christians. He is calling the people to build up a loving community. His theological task is to find ways of expressing community-maintaining and community-building obligations without resorting once more to categories of law and commandment. The notion of promise guides this effort. If we are to speak of deontology in Pauline understanding, we have to have in view a deontology founded on grace and centering in promise.

Promise highlights the immediacy of relationships between persons rather than the ground rules which might be judged requisite to the relationships. It emphasizes concrete dynamics over formal structures. It presumes that the ground rules of human association

169

are not interesting in themselves, but only as devices to protect elemental human relationships. The precise strategies for establishing, maintaining, renewing, and strengthening relationships are not made up of predetermined and universally valid forms; they are historically relative arrangements which are continually in need of negotiation and renegotiation. They have to be worked out step by step in actual interactions among persons and in terms of the concrete meanings they hold for persons. Even Paul's lawlike admonitions function primarily to direct us to the underlying relationships themselves. They are not principles which Paul is surreptitiously reintroducing into a discussion that presumes to have left behind any further reliance on notions of this sort. Paul does sometimes offer specific suggestions of ways of acting which are likely to foster human community, for example, the avoidance of meat which has been offered to idols. Yet he makes clear that the suggestions are altogether conditional: "If eating meat might cause a neighbor to stumble. . . ." On occasion Paul even insists on a quite specific course of action, for example, table fellowship between Jew and gentile. When he is so directly prescriptive, however, it is because of a conviction that only this particular action will in the circumstances in question contribute to the oneness of God's people in Jesus Christ. Every admonition finally rests in promise, in the righteousness of God given apart from the law in Jesus Christ.

Paul's approach to established social institutions fills out his sense of the place of law and commandment in the Christian life. Institutions consist in laws, rules; and regulations. Paul commends their acceptance as provisional constituents of the worldly spheres of our witness and service. Yet the institutional forms are altogether relative. They are transient ways of ordering human life in the age which is passing away. Laws and principles which figure in these institutional forms are, like the institutions themselves, subordinate to the substantive relationships of communities of faith. The social institutions of the old age are relative to given societies and cultures. Where we incorporate them into our constructive thinking, their precise form and content are always matters to be negotiated and worked out. Paul might be able to say, as Matthew's Jesus, that not one iota of the law shall pass till all is accomplished. Yet his gospel would impel him to add: but all has now been accomplished in Jesus Christ; hence, Christ is the end of the law.

With regard to a social ethic, Paul's most creative contribution is to bring into view a deep appreciation for social and cultural relativity. If Luke's emphasis on the social nature of property stimulates our thinking on economic questions; and Matthew's accent on forgiveness, our sense of the preconditions of a distinctively political order; then Paul offers promising resources for our attempts to conceive a human community capable of sustaining and fostering cultural pluralism. Paul's insight into the primacy of both grace and promise sustain his effort. They permit culturally diverse peoples to negotiate community. They enable people to respect and maintain differences as they forge a common life together. However, even Paul's pluralism cannot encompass the diversity of the world's religions without modification. The christocentric nature of his thought inhibits that undertaking, unless his christocentrism were itself to undergo enlargement and transformation in a richer and more complex discourse among the world's peoples. Nonetheless, Paul does put us in touch with resources in the Christian gospel for openness to the plurality of the world.

Finally, Paul's grasp of the relativity of social institutions permits us to accept them and function within them as spheres of our own activity without at the same time bestowing absolute and binding authority upon them. Freedom in Christ is a freedom to adapt to a variety of social arrangements and circumstances, fully recognizing their ambiguous and contingent nature, and also appreciating their provisional significance as forms which establish space for human life. Where Paul has not been so helpful is in indicating how the distinctive understandings of the gospel might themselves become a leaven for change in institutions which are independent of the church but which nonetheless are deeply impacted by persons who make up the church. Even so, the new patterns of life emerging in the church as eschatological community create a matrix of experience within which possibilities of this sort can come into view. In this respect Paul provides a frame of reference which can undergird our own creative involvement in processes of social change.

171

NOTES

1. J. Christiaan Beker, *Paul the Apostle: The Triumph of God in Life and Thought* (Philadelphia: Fortress Press, 1980), 259. Beker is a key resource for my treatment of Paul.

2. Ibid., chap. 3, 23–26.

3. Ibid., 256–59.

4. The interpenetration of diverse symbolic patterns characterizes virtually all of Paul's great summary statements of the gospel of Jesus Christ: 1 Thess. 4:14–18; Gal. 2:14b–16, 19–21; 1 Cor. 2:2–5, 15:3–11; 2 Cor. 5:16–21; Rom. 3:21–26, 5:6–11; Phil. 2:1–11. Doubtless other texts also lay claim to inclusion in this list. I am taking as the genuine Pauline letters 1 Thessalonians, Galatians, 1 and 2 Corinthians, Romans, Philippians, and Philemon.

5. For a good treatment of the Christ-Adam typology, see Robin Scroggs, *The Last Adam: A Study in Pauline Anthropology* (Philadelphia: Fortress Press, 1966).

6. Romans 8 embraces the cosmic order, though not explicitly in the mode of instruction: "For the creation waits with eager longing for the revealing of the sons of God. . . . ; the creation itself will be set free from its bondage to decay and obtain the glorious liberty of the children of God" (vv. 19–21).

7. These connections are skillfully portrayed by Robert Tannehill in *Dying and Rising with Christ* (Berlin: Alfred Töpelmann, 1967). The book is structured in terms of two principal sections. The first is entitled "Dying with Christ as the Basis of the New Life." Romans 6 is central, but attention is given as well to Gal. 2:19–20, 5:24–25, 6:14–15, and 2 Cor. 5:14–17. The second section is entitled "Dying and Rising with Christ as the Structure of the New Life." Subsections deal with ethical action and suffering.

8. This motif has been effectively developed by John Schütz, *Paul and the Anatomy of Apostolic Authority* (New York and Cambridge: Cambridge University Press, 1975). See esp. chap. 8 on the "Rhetoric of Apostolic Authority," 204–48.

9. Cf. ibid., 248.

10. Cf. as well 1 Pet. 2:13–3:7; 1 Tim. 2:8–15, especially vv. 11–15, and 6:1–2; Titus 2:1–10. For a helpful discussion of these "household rules" see James E. Crouch, *The Origin and Intention of the Colossian Haustafel* (Göttingen: Vandenhoeck & Ruprecht, 1972). Crouch argues that these rules, which did not belong to the most primitive Christian teaching, represented a "Christianizing" of Hellenistic Jewish materials in response to specific needs in the early church. Cf. 83, 121–22.

11. See Victor Furnish, *The Moral Teaching of Paul* (Nashville: Abingdon Press, 1979), 91–92, for a discussion of the issues. Furnish surveys the

172

evidence in the authentic Pauline letters of leadership by women: Chloe, Euodia and Syntyche, Prisca, Phoebe, and others, 102–110.

12. Of special interest are studies which in general argue that Paul is a positive resource for feminist treatments of Christian faith. Cf. Robin Scroggs, "Paul and the Eschatological Woman," *Journal of the American Academy of Religion* 40 (1972): 283–303, esp. 297ff. See also Furnish, *Moral Teaching of Paul*, 95–102.

13. See especially Darrell J. Doughty, "Women and Liberation in the Churches of Paul and the Pauline Tradition," *Drew Gateway* 50 (Winter 1979): 7–8. Doughty follows and expands the arguments of William Walker, "I Corinthians 11.2–16 and Paul's Views Regarding Women," *Journal of Biblical Literature* 94 (1975): 94–110.

6

TOWARD COMMON GROUNDS
OF UNDERSTANDING

The subject matter of this study is the use of the Bible in Christian ethics. It is not biblical ethics as such in the sense of a critical re-presentation of moral understandings contained in biblical literature. Nor is it Christian ethics in the sense of a fully articulated constructive treatment of the moral life. It occupies an intermediate position. It is an interpretation of biblical materials which is governed by an interest in moving toward contemporary formulations of moral thought and experience.

The purpose of the study is to open up a dialogue with the biblical texts on the moral life. It is to establish the place of such dialogue in Christian ethics. The dialogue assumes real differences between biblical perspectives and categories and those operative in the consciousness of contemporary thinkers. It does not venture to bypass the hermeneutical problems posed by these differences. It calls attention to them and seeks to work them through critically. The goal of the dialogue is the achievement of a common mind, a "fusion of horizons," between biblical worlds of meaning and those which make up our sense of reality.

The presentation of biblical notions has been guided by a set of preunderstandings of the moral life. These preunderstandings express certain of the taken-for-granted ideas at work in moral thought and experience. They establish a frame of reference which permits us to engage the biblical texts not simply as artifacts of an ancient culture but as utterances possibly saying something true about our own reality. The preunderstandings are strictly preparatory, not definitive or final. They establish a point of contact with an ancient tradition. They initiate a conversation. They cannot control the direction of the conversation nor determine its outcome. Indeed, if fruitful dialogue does occur, the preunderstandings will themselves be placed in question. They will be transformed through the encounter with the texts.

Transformation does not entail total surrender to the texts. It does not require us to give up all independent judgment, all personal responsibility for apprehending and articulating what is true and good. It occurs as a meeting of minds. It consists in the discovery of meanings capable of binding together contemporary interpreter and ancient text. These shared meanings are not simply uncovered in the activity of interpreting, as though they were already present in the text in some obscure or perhaps implicit manner; they are in significant measure generated in a creative act. They are the fruits of the productive imagination of the interpreter. Every successful act of interpretation brings something new into being. It is never a mere re-presentation of something fully intact. The paradox of interpreting is that we are able to say the same thing as the text only by saying something different. The originality of the interpreter is to venture formulations which can contribute to the common mind toward which understanding reaches. The point is to gain a more adequate grasp of the moral life by way of an engagement with biblical materials.

The observations which follow are still only preliminary, suggestions of ways to proceed. They are attempts to identify notions which have come out of the study and which present themselves as possible ingredients in a common set of moral understandings. They are guidelines toward the construction of a biblically informed Christian ethic. They are the initial result of a substantive discourse with selected biblical texts on the nature of the moral life. I shall deal first with the eschatological horizon of moral understanding. I shall conclude by noting the impact of biblical perspectives on our conceptualizations of the basic modalities of moral understanding.

THE ESCHATOLOGICAL HORIZON OF MORAL UNDERSTANDING

Futurist and Dialectical Eschatologies

The primary challenge to Christian ethics is to find suitable ways of articulating the import of the eschatology which figures in the biblical materials. To speak of eschatology is to characterize the larger horizon of meaning which in given traditions displays the signficance and authority of moral notions. This meaning horizon does not directly generate specifically moral notions, but it profoundly qualifies them and substantively informs the manner in which they present themselves to consciousness.

In this study I have highlighted two basic types of eschatology (and subvariants can be identified in each). We can label them futurist (or consistent) and dialectical eschatologies. The futurist eschatologies are most apparent in the exilic and postexilic literature of the Old Testament. Particularly pertinent is Ezra's attempt to reconstitute the Jewish people as a religious community under the dominion of the great world empires. These eschatologies call attention to the alien nature of the existing world, yet refuse to grant ultimacy to that world. They envision and hope for a world which is hospitable to the deepest human yearnings for fulfillment. They presuppose a community oriented to this hoped-for world in spite of the sufferings and hardships of the existing world.

Futurist eschatologies generate ethical perspectives marked by a fundamental duality: an ethic of hope directed to a world which is not yet, and an ethic of patient waiting and faithful enduring in the alien circumstances of the present. The ethic of hope looks to a coming world where human well-being and fulfillment are genuine possibilities. It nurtures understandings and expectations which belong to that world, even though they are out of line with presently existing realities. It refuses to concede the final word to the taken-for-granted dictums of the present age. It is quite able and willing to expose and resist their oppressive features. The ethic of patient waiting and faithful enduring concerns ways of coping with the alien realities of the present. For this ethic, the issue is fidelity to a manner of life capable of sustaining a people in hope in a world which contradicts hope.

177

Both features in the ethic of futurist eschatologies presuppose a faithful community which maintains standards and perceptions different from the dominant society. This community keeps hope alive, and it reinforces the will of the people to persevere in their distinctiveness. It also undergirds and supports its members who must endure difficulties and disabilities because of their refusal to conform to the larger society. The faithful community does not expect to change the world. It lacks the resources for such a bold undertaking. It does not even expect to create protected space within existing societies where its highest hopes can be realized. Its power is its endurance. It commits itself to steadfast allegiance to the constitutive principles of its own peculiar vocation. Its crowning achievement is its fidelity through the most difficult of circumstances.

The variant forms of futurist eschatology stem from diverse readings of the depth and alienness of the present age, and also of the intensity of the enmity of that age toward the faithful community. Different assessments of these matters will lead to different judgments of whether and with what qualifications the faithful may involve themselves in responsibility for the basic institutions of the larger society, especially economic and political institutions. There are also interesting variants in the ways of conceiving how and when the hoped-for world is to become a reality. The primary issue is whether the realization of the coming age depends in some fashion on human initiatives. If the answer is no, patience emerges as a special virtue. If the answer is yes, the central questions concern the nature of appropriate human initiatives, which may range from the most diligent exercise of personal piety to the most rational attempt to organize effectively for armed struggle. Persistent throughout is a strong sense of duality in moral understanding, with one set of expectations governing present life in the faithful community, including the manner of its interface with the larger society, and another delineating the manner of life in the coming world for which the faithful hope. The tensions at play between these two sets of expectations reflect a profound awareness of the hiatus which exists between what now is and what will be.

Dialectical eschatologies reflect most of the features of futurist eschatologies, but with one quite important modification: they hold that the hoped-for age is already becoming a substantive reality in selected spheres of human life despite the general persistence of the present evil age. The coming new age is not yet fully actual, not even in limited regions of experience. It is present only in a proleptic fashion. Thus, the coming reality shows itself in its incompleteness at the same time that it displays its genuine actuality. Dialectical eschatologies are comprised of opposing tendencies in constant interaction. They say at one and the same time: yea and nay, already and not yet.

Like futurist eschatologies, dialectical eschatologies depend for their social reality on faithful communities which stand over against the world even as they are situated within it. It is within discrete communities that the coming age takes form, albeit only in provisional and anticipatory ways. What is distinctive is that these communities attest the newness of the power at work in them to a degree not so clearly manifest in futurist eschatologies. The people are not simply enduring, no matter how faithfully; they are also participating in the transforming power of the age for which they hope. They are not simply preserving an ancient heritage in the face of pressures which threaten to destroy it; they are working out new understandings and new ways of being together which challenge the institutional arrangements of the larger society. They are already an eschatological community.

The ethic of dialectical eschatologies is itself dialectical in form. On the one hand, it seeks appropriate ways of articulating the moral import of the present reality of the new age. We have seen various responses to this challenge: Mark's insistence on the primacy of the moral law; Matthew's reinterpretation of the Mosaic law as the perfection of love; Luke's celebration of the inclusion of the poor, the disabled, and the outcast in a repentant Israel; Paul's treatment of promise as the constitutive basis of personal and social existence. These themes attest the effective operation of something new. Underlying them all is the conviction that communities of persons gathered by faith in Jesus Christ and by a readiness to become his disciples have replaced families and kinship groupings as the foundational units of society. At the same time, a dialectical ethic reflects

179

the incompleteness of the new age. Paul, for example, thematizes this incompleteness in an explicit dialectic between indicative and imperative moods: "consider yourselves dead to sin and alive to God in Christ Jesus"; "let not sin therefore reign in your mortal bodies" (Rom. 6:11, 12). The same dialectic also appears in the Synoptic Gospels. In Mark, the readiness of the disciples to follow Jesus wherever he might go is countered by their persistent lack of understanding, and finally, by betrayal, denial, and abandonment. In Matthew, the commitment of the disciples to do all that Jesus commands is countered by the reminder that they are but persons of "little faith." The new reality is present, but the old reality remains in force, nonetheless.

We can easily overstate the difference between these two eschatologies, especially when we consider the interface between the faithful communities and the institutions of the larger society. The social locus of both eschatologies is a community which stands apart from the larger society, resisting full integration into its life and thought. Such apartness is particularly apparent in the primary religious and moral commitments of the people and in the ritual patterns which give those commitments social form. The faithful communities may concede a good deal of authority to the basic institutions of the society: the household, the economic order, the state. Yet they tend not to be highly interested in the moral substance of these institutions nor in the special concerns of persons who exercise responsibility for them. Even so, the faithful cannot wholly avoid involvement in political and economic processes, and such involvement may in various ways be sanctioned. In the materials examined in this study, there are no direct challenges to the basic institutions of society, but some noteworthy expressions of their positive role in the divine purpose. Within limits, these institutions are recognized as serving a human good. At a minimum they preserve social order, maintaining social space for human life. Paul probably provides the most coherent account of the status of such institutions. They are relative and provisional, not absolute and final; yet in their relativity they are suitable spheres for living out one's call in Jesus Christ.

180

The most salient differences between the two eschatologies concern the ways in which the two communities place themselves in the total movement of history. At issue is the degree of continuity perceived to hold between past and present and between present and future. The futurist eschatologies tend to accent continuity with a sacral tradition. The integrity of the tradition is endangered by existing or emerging social forces. There is need to protect the tradition and the way of life it prescribes. Ethnic and cultural factors figure prominently in the identity of the community, reinforcing its cohesion. The redemption offered by the hoped-for future can be realized only by a qualitative break with present realities, especially the realities of the larger society, but in important respects, those of the faithful community itself. In substantive theological terms, the Messiah has not yet come.

For dialectical eschatologies, a decisive break with the past has already occurred. Sacral traditions are not disregarded or simply sloughed off, but they are significantly modified by new realities coming into being. The readiness to rethink an ancient legacy permits a new kind of openness to the plurality of human cultures and to the formation of community with persons from many nations and races. The orientation of the dialectical eschatologies is to the creation of the new, and the reach of the new is universal, finally involving the whole inhabited earth. In theological terms, the Messiah has indeed come, and the messianic age has been inaugurated, though its consummation remains outstanding.

In institutional terms, the crucial distinctions between the two eschatologies concern the relations of family and household to the makeup of the community of faith. In postexilic Judaism, as in ancient Israel, the family is foundational for the existence of the people. The community of faith is constituted through the joining of families in covenant. In this respect the Jewish community might be called a natural community, that is, a community emerging out of the propagation and socialization of offspring. For Christian understanding, the family is secondary and derivative; the community of faith, primary and fundamental. The community of faith is in its essence a gathered community. It lives and grows by way of an evangelistic witness. This witness is directed not to families, but to individual persons, Jew and gentile, slave and free, male and female.

What complicates the picture is that communities which are formally Christian may function in ways that are essentially identical with characteristics of the Jewish heritage. That is, they base themselves on family units, they display a distinct linkage to particular racial and ethnic groups and to specific social classes, and they concern themselves preeminently with the maintenance of a received tradition. They do not display in their practical everyday affairs a strong sense of the inauguration of the messianic age with the openness to new understandings and associations which that implies. They are conservators of a familiar way of life in the face of social change. Insofar as eschatology continues to figure in their basic understandings, it takes a largely futurist form.

Social Alienation and Communal Commitment

Can contemporary interpreters of Christian faith find common ground with eschatologically determined ethical perspectives? From the standpoint of concrete experience, two things would seem to be crucial: some degree of alienation from the institutional arrangements of the larger society, and deep involvement with a community which is engaged in developing qualitatively distinct alternatives to those arrangements. The alienation and the involvement provide points of contact for comprehending what the biblical texts are saying.

Neither of these characteristics has been especially prominent in recent Christian ethics in America. More common has been a primary identification with the larger society, with its problems and possibilities, and a corresponding measure of alienation from the church, especially as a major locus of moral interest. Ethical perspectives reflecting a strong identification with the larger society derive their moral substance from normative understandings integral to the basic institutions of society. If the interest is political, these understandings may be funded by democratic liberalism, or constitutional law, or perhaps the American civil religion. If the interest is economy, or more broadly, political economy, these understandings may stem from capitalist ideology, for example, its emphasis on enterprise, disciplined work, free choice. In some societies, they may be informed by critiques of capitalism and by attempts to work out socialist alternatives. If the interest is in professional activity, the normative substance of ethical thought is apt to arise from the professional codes and from the larger ethos which authorizes and justifies the codes. Ethical reflection which has some chance of effectively addressing the institutional contexts of economic, political, and professional activity would have to build upon understandings already operative, though perhaps only implicitly, in these contexts.

The relegation of the church to the private sector in advanced industrial society limits its capacity to address the major social questions of the day, though church bodies regularly venture to speak to such matters. The churches may provide support for values in the secular culture which have certain affinities with their own distinctive commitments, but they have little chance of successfully communicating an original angle of vision in a public discourse. Indeed, any distinctive contributions they might make could well be inappropriate given the plurality of religious traditions in an essentially secular society. For the most part, the churches have been among the more conservative units of society, in part because of their strong association with the private sector where change is more apt to be resisted. The primary impetus to morally significant social change has come from movements and organizations operating more or less independently of the churches, though often in association with them, for example, the civil rights movement, opposition to the Vietnam War, the women's movement, the struggle to protect the natural environment, and most recently, a revitalized peace movement concentrating on the call for nuclear freeze. For persons deeply concerned with the major social questions of the day, these factors make the church less interesting as a focus of ethical inquiry. As a result, social ethics tends to be only remotely Christian, if at all, and Christian treatments of ethics tend to deal chiefly with personal morality, with interpersonal relationships (perhaps in a professional context), and with issues of family life.

Ancient texts cannot in themselves alter what we experience, and we can only accept as real what presents itself to us with the accent of reality. Yet ancient texts can be the occasion of a fresh seeing. They can suggest an altered reading of the realities of our world. On the one hand, they can stimulate us to attend with greater care to neglected features of experience. On the other hand, they can awaken in us a disposition to cut through the deceptions and distortions in the conventional understandings of the dominant culture. An engagement with an eschatologically determined ethic will tend to push in both directions.

Unless we believe that the greater American community is itself the bearer of the eschatological impulses of biblical faith,[1] a biblically informed ethic directs our energies in the first instance to the building up of communities of faith oriented to the promised new age and embodying its dawning reality in their own being and activity. Parallel to this focus is a critical distancing from the dominant culture and its institutional forms. Insofar as existing social and cultural forms function to maintain space for human life, they can be provisionally accepted as spheres of Christian existence. They cannot, however, enjoy final or even paramount authority for participants in eschatological community.

In contemporary American thought, maintaining critical distance from the dominant social institutions may have to be in the forefront of attention since the alien nature of these institutions is not self-evident, not even to persons and groups experiencing considerable hardship in the society. In such a context, critique must be fully explicit if we are to disabuse ourselves of the surface attractions of our social order. To be effective, it must also be rendered by means of the analytical tools of modern culture. It requires critical theory. Critical theory displays the sources of human alienation in particular social arrangements and processes. It discloses the fact that these arrangements and processes have no essential or final necessity. It awakens a sense of alternatives for social order. It stirs up a hunger for those alternatives and a readiness to labor for their realization.

Critical theory is itself motivated by experiences of alienation in the everyday life world. Apart from such experiences there would not be sufficient reason to adopt its stance of suspicion, either toward the existing social order or toward theories of society which justify or explain away or minimize the disabilities it imposes. At the same time, critical theory sharpens our perception of alienation. It helps us acknowledge the negative experiences we actually have. It enables us to see more clearly their nature and significance. It is a formative element in a state of awareness akin to the duality of an eschatological ethic: hope for a world which does not yet exist, but which would make human fulfillment possible; and a will to resist pressures to succumb to the alien circumstances of the present.

Critical theory does not in itself constitute the eschatological distancing of Christian ethics. The latter encompasses institutional realities, yet reaches as well to the most elemental questions of human existence, especially those which concern the being of God and God's involvement with human life. Yet Christian ethics is free to utilize critical theory in developing its own critique, even when the theory rests upon convictions and commitments somewhat at variance with its own. This freedom is a contemporary equivalent to the Pauline acknowledgement of the provisional validity of relative social and cultural forms.

Though criticism is quite important, it remains abstract and empty unless it is funded by concrete experiences of social alternatives. An eschatological orientation requires eschatological communities, minimally to sustain hope in what is not yet, optimally to embody in their own life and activity features of the new age which are present possibilities. A Christian ethic attentive to the eschatological horizon of Pauline and Synoptic thought is an ethic closely linked to the church and its ministry. It finds central expression in the practice of ministry.

If Christian ethics is to incorporate the eschatological impulses of the New Testament, it must give far more attention than is presently customary to the life of the church and its ministry. Here the transfer of New Testament themes to contemporary social realities can be strong indeed. To begin with, the church is a fellowship in which the fundamental equality of all people is clearly acknowledged. The equality is rooted in the solidarity of people in both sin and grace. The poor, the disabled, the outcast, the strangers are not only wholly welcome to share in this solidarity. They represent its essential meaning! In this respect they are a

185

primary reference group for the distinctive nature of Christian fellowship. The equality of all people finds expression in forms of social organization which allow distinctions among people only on the basis of their readiness and capacity to take on responsibility for the building up of a people in love and care. For the sake of community vitality, there may be differentials in authority and responsibility; but there can be no fixed hierarchies which imply essential differences in status and power. As the bearer of the new age, the church breaks down and overcomes standard class and status differences.

The church is a fellowship open to the plurality of the world. It reaches out to the world's people, even to the ends of the inhabited earth. It acknowledges and celebrates their diversity. It involves them in negotiating patterns of community which can encompass and also preserve their diversity. Though the church takes concrete form in particular social and cultural contexts, its life is fully compatible with the plurality of human cultures. It is free to be all things to all people that it might win some. The community it fosters has no pregiven structure other than that determined by grace itself. Grace is manifest in self-giving modeled after and empowered by the death and resurrection of Jesus Christ. On the basis of grace, the specific ground rules and ritual patterns of a common life are matters to be negotiated. They emerge, develop, and change over time in terms of insights and understandings generated through the productive interactions of the people in their quest for a common life. The negotiation is open, and its results are ever subject to review. It arrives at stopping points only where resolutions are achieved which are capable of gaining the full consent of the people. And even those stopping points are not final, but way stations in the human pilgrimage.

The church is a fellowship of mutual caring and mutual forbearance. Its people bear one another's burdens. They are responsive to one another's needs. They resolve their conflicts by bringing them into the open and subjecting them to a vision of common good. They continually renew fellowship by concrete acts of mutual forgiveness.

186

Does such a community exist? Not in the dialectic of eschatological existence, at least not in such an unqualified fashion. The dialectic which marks the Christian life resides not simply in the interface between the church and the institutions of the larger society. It is operative in the concrete reality of the church as well. The new age is already a reality, and it is not yet a reality. Language describing the promise of the eschatological community has its place. It expresses the indicative of the gospel. It sets forth some of the substantive content of the new age as it is taking form. Yet the new age is also a task and a demand. It calls for works of ministry which give concrete social reality to its promises. These works reflect the imperative of the gospel. That imperative confronts resistance, certainly in the larger society, but also in the church as it actually exists. Indeed, it cuts through the personal lives of those who would respond to it in acts of ministry.

An eschatologically determined ethic gives primary weight to the issues involved in building up and sustaining eschatological communities, communities bearing authentic alternatives to the cultural norms and institutional arrangements of the larger society. These issues concern not simply the ways of nurturing a loving and inclusive community. They concern as well the disciplines which enable individuals and communities to detach themselves step by step from needs, desires, and gratifications that hinder their full participation in the coming new age. The vision is grand, even breathtaking; but the ministry it calls forth has its tough and realistic dimensions. It is a summons to new life, which includes a readiness to let go of the old with its special securities and gratifications.

The Possibility of a Social Witness

Can an eschatological ethic also concern itself directly with the well-being of the larger society? Paul and the Synoptic authors seem not to have taken up this question, except to remind their readers that the secular state has a provisional role in the divine purpose and hence merits recognition and obedience. Also, Luke contends that the Christian movement is in no way a threat to state authority, and that the disturbances which surround it are invariably instigated by others. Still, there is nothing about the early Christian eschatologies which indicates that the church is inherently a small, marginal community. Its mission reaches to the ends of the earth. Its commission is to make disciples of all nations. The universal outreach suggests the possibility of a community gaining sufficient strength so that it could no longer avoid taking appropriate responsibility for the affairs of the larger world, perhaps even of institutional forms which continue to belong to the age which is passing away.

At this point the possible patterns of social responsibility become as numerous and diverse as the multiplicity of church forms in the long history of the Christian movement. To mention only the leading examples, the church could, first of all, eschew direct involvement in the oversight of the basic economic, political, and cultural structures of the larger society. Its adherents could be, within limits, employees and citizens, but not managers and magistrates. Its direct witness to the larger society would be evangelistic. Otherwise, its social import would be indirect. It would consist in the modeling of alternative social possibilities, but without attempts at advocacy to those who elected to remain outside of the realities they embodied. The radical reformers of the sixteenth century and their successors represent this stance most clearly and consistently.

Second, the church could encourage its members to take responsibility for the whole range of social positions, including such things as soldier and executioner. This model takes Christian freedom to include the freedom to accommodate oneself to the demands of office in the institutional arrangements of the present age even while belonging essentially to the world to come. The dialectic of the "already" and the "not yet" is a dialectic of religious and secular vocations, or of personal life and official duty. The first variant is reflected in the great Thomistic synthesis of the thirteenth century; the second, in the thought of Martin Luther. There is also a popular version of this position which emerges out of American revivalism. It is the notion that the Christian message impacts the society through the conversion of individuals who in turn influence the quality of life wherever they are. For this view, Christian societies are essentially aggregates of Christian individuals. This latter version, unfortunately, is naive about the nature of social institutions, and so tends to lapse into sentimentality.

Third, the church could discern the possibility of encompassing the whole of society in the impulses of the coming new age, venturing a theocratic, or perhaps christocratic, transformation of social existence. Here the society itself takes on the characteristics of an eschatological order. This vision is expressed in John Calvin's reforming activity and in subsequent Calvinist movements: the Geneva Consistory, the seventeenth-century Puritan revolution in England, and the experiment with divine commonwealth in colonial New England.

Fourth, one might find in powerful social and political movements secular equivalents to the eschatological impulses of Christian faith. Persons nurtured in Christian faith exercise their freedom by giving themselves over to these movements, allowing them in various degrees to displace distinctively Christian understandings and practices. This kind of transformation of perspective occurred for many in the American democratic revolution, where liberalism both incorporated and negated crucial elements of the Puritan theocratic vision. It is occurring again in some strands of Latin American liberation theology, where Christian eschatology is transformed into revolutionary struggle for a new social order, informed by Marxist criticism. Thus, New Testament eschatology gives way to secular eschatologies bearing similar formal characteristics.

All of these approaches have some plausibility as contemporary appropriations of biblical eschatology. Virtually any Christian social ethic will take shape as a variant of one or more of these classic possibilities. No account of social ethics suited for present realities can be derived directly from biblical materials; any constructive utilization of biblical materials will involve the productive imagination of the interpreter. It is finally by way of the ongoing discourse of living communities of faith that we generate criteria to assess these and similar possibilities.

I would propose the following. (1) Modern societies are sufficiently alien to the central promises of the Christian gospel that a community faithful to that gospel will in important measure have

189

to be a community apart. (2) The primary task of the leadership of such a community is to equip it for authentic eschatological existence. An associated task is effective criticism of the basic institutions of the larger society lest their alien and oppressive features become obscured in human consciousness. Such criticism, though guided by distinctive Christian understandings, will make appropriate use of pertinent social theory. (3) Christians are free to participate selectively in the basic institutions of modern society insofar as they recognize the provisional and ambiguous nature of these institutions and maintain their primary allegiance to the realities taking form in eschatological community. The participation must, however, be both selective and qualified. A task of Christian ethics is to assist the community of faith in its deliberations on appropriate forms of participation in the life of the larger society. (4) In many societies, though not all, Christians have an opportunity to help shape policy in basic social institutions. Similarly, or alternatively, they may be able to relate actively to movements working to bring about morally significant social change, influencing the determination of goals and objectives, and also decisions about strategy and tactics.

Opportunities of the latter sort present special difficulties for a Christian social ethic, though they may offer the most important challenges as well. The problem is to embody the fundamental dialectic of eschatological existence: on the one hand, accommodating oneself to the setting of one's calling; on the other hand, acting congruently with the promise of Christian freedom. To share responsibility for the activity of a complex organization or a social movement (e.g., a revolutionary movement) is to become subject to its normative understandings and to its established procedures of decision-making and accountability. If we consider such involvement to be appropriate in a particular social context, we cannot at the same time maintain a right to make independent judgments about whether to support or withhold support from individual policies and courses of action which happen to be adopted. In positioning ourselves to influence and shape decision-making, we take upon ourselves general obligations to abide by the outcomes. Of

190

course, no commitment is irrevocable; but also, no commitment should be made or broken casually. The question is: under what circumstances is it legitimate for a Christian to subject him- or herself to norms and procedures which may not be altogether congruent with the primary commitments of eschatological community?

Involvements of the sort described would appear to be legitimate when the organizations and movements in question themselves embody commitments to forms of life analogous to the new realities coming into being in eschatological community. Stated differently, the organizations and movements must themselves display eschatological tendencies. They must bear something of the promise of the new age.

Matters already cited are pertinent. Favored are movements, organizations, and institutions which recognize and promote the fundamental equality of all human beings. Classes of persons normally disadvantaged in the social order present crucial test cases of such commitment. Favored are movements, organizations, and institutions which are open to the plurality of human cultures and life styles, which are ready to negotiate patterns of community inclusive of significant diversity. Favored are movements, organizations, and institutions which incorporate expressions of mutual caring, forbearance, and forgiveness, which celebrate and give concrete social reality to the solidarity of peoples.

On the critical side, to be questioned and challenged are movements, organizations, and institutions which create and maintain fixed hierarchies of power and privilege among human beings, which lead to great disparities in income, wealth, and life chances and which enable some to dominate and control the fortunes of others. To be questioned and challenged are movements, organizations, and institutions which elevate certain cultural forms and social groupings above all others, driving others to subordinate and marginal positions in the social order. Especially to be condemned are social patterns which legitimate cultural arrogance and back up that arrogance with violent force. To be questioned and challenged are movements, organizations, and institutions which isolate

191

people from one another—"every man for himself"—and sanction the social abandonment of oppressed, exploited, and disadvantaged peoples. To be questioned and challenged are movements, organizations, and institutions which routinely handle disputes and conflicts by resorting to physical violence, providing no openings for future reconciliation.

The underlying claim is that a Christian social ethic must proceed not on the basis of explicit New Testament commentary on economic and political institutions, but by analogy to developments within the early Christian communities themselves. It is with reference to the internal relations of these eschatological communities that resources for institutional creativity in the Christian gospel show themselves most clearly. A Christian social ethic which ventures beyond the provisional acceptance of existing institutional forms must be guided by impulses expressed in this creativity. Correspondingly, its social criticism must be informed by insight into social arrangements which frustrate, violate, or contradict this creativity.[2]

THE MODALITY OF MORAL UNDERSTANDING

In the account of preunderstandings of the moral life, I called attention to three types of moral reasoning: consequentialist, deontological, and perfectionist. I associated these three with elemental structures of action and their accompanying moral meanings: the orientation of action to goals and the values which justify action choices; the intersubjective matrix of action and the obligations which constrain and order human interactions; and the self-reference of action and the virtues which delineate the capacities of the actor to function morally. By associating types of moral reasoning with structures of action, we disclose their essential complementarity. We display the importance of incorporating into a more comprehensive ethical theory what have traditionally been competing points of view. Finally, I highlighted the temporal dimension of action, which cuts across the structures already cited. I noted that this dimension helps us grasp the "historialization" of moral experience, in particular, the fact that all concrete moral notions are relative to specific social and cultural contexts. This same dimension also enables us to thematize the question of the meaning of being which hovers before all facets of moral awareness.

The discussion of eschatology represents one way of articulating the question of the meaning of being. I have elaborated some of the ramifications for moral understanding of an eschatological orientation to being. The task now is to unfold the import of biblical faith for aspects of moral experience linked to the basic structures of action. It is to suggest how a biblically informed ethic might properly be placed in relation to classic theoretical options.

Person and Community

I noted that deontological motifs tend to be dominant in preexilic pentateuchal traditions and in the writings of eighth- and seventh-century prophets. The focus is on the makeup of Israel as a covenant people of God. Commandments and ordinances express the fundamental obligations of covenant existence, and the covenant itself is linked to Israel's concrete life as the people of God. Both covenant and commandment have the character of gift, God's gracious offering of life to a people delivered from political bondage and guided through the wilderness into a land of promise. The central crises in Israelite life concern the meaning and import of basic covenantal obligations in changing social and cultural contexts.

In the postexilic period, the traditional laws and commandments tend to be cut loose from concrete historical processes, becoming instead a permanent deposit of divinely revealed moral and religious teaching. Though given to Israel historically through Moses, their source is taken to be the eternal wisdom of God. A secondary sense of the historical does reappear, but it takes the form of ever new interpretations and applications of the original deposit of divine revelation. While this development obscures the constitutive significance of history for moral understanding, the primacy of grace remains. Law is God's good gift to human beings. For those who adhere to it, it is a way of blessing.

In the early period of Israelite life perfectionist motifs are largely assimilated to a deontological orientation. The virtuous person is one who has internalized the laws and commandments and lives in accord with their dictates. The interest, however, is not so much in the virtuous individual as in the realization of a faithful people. It is as a people that Israel stands or falls. In the postexilic period, the individual looms larger, reflecting a loosening of the bonds of social solidarity. New modes of moral reasoning appear which place considerably greater weight on the autonomous judgment of mature individuals. Law is reinterpreted as wisdom, not simply the hidden wisdom of God, but also the practical wisdom available in principle to all prudent human beings. Traditions marked by historicity and the primacy of grace become receptive to understandings inherent in human existence as such. Perfectionist thinking comes into its own as a distinctive mode of moral awareness. The interrelationships of these two modes of understanding do not, however, gain coherent conceptual development in the biblical materials. In this respect, the diversity in the several strands of biblical tradition presents a challenge to constructive thought.

Perfectionist motifs are dominant in the Synoptic Gospels and Paul, reflecting the fact that the eschatological communities are gathered communities, that is, communities coming into being through the faith commitments of individual persons. These persons are by no means called to an isolated or autonomous existence. They are summoned into community. They live by and for community. Yet the community is not already in place. It is in the process of being formed through the collective energies of those who make it up. Moreover, it remains open in principle to the continuing influx of new members through the evangelistic witness of the church.

Perfectionism in the New Testament is understood primarily in relational terms. The Christian life is not realized in the first instance through the habitual practice of virtue, nor is that practice taken to be a consequence of the discipline and modeling of parents and other significant adults (Aristotle). The Christian life is a life of faith. It is enabled by the power of God at work in the believer. In the Synoptics this life is portrayed in terms of discipleship. Discipleship presupposes faith in God and consists in a readiness to follow Jesus. It involves sharing in Jesus' activity and suffering.

Paul's language is especially effective in bringing to the fore the relational nature of Christian existence. The Christian life is life in Christ. Its basis is participation by faith in the death and resurrection of Jesus Christ: dying to the sinful self, receiving the gift of a new righteous self. Its substantive content is an imitation of the model of self-giving presented in the same death and resurrection: humility before God, love and service to the neighbor. A single set of paradigmatic events discloses both the indicative and the imperative of the gospel. The linkage of the two permits Paul to express at one and the same time the primacy of grace and the necessity of discipline and self-control. Thus, habits do come into consideration, but only in the context of the constitutive faith relation. Moreover, since life in Christ is essentially corporate, relationships of faith in Jesus Christ encompass as well relationships of love to the neighbor, especially within the community of faith.

Paul expresses similar understandings in the phrase "life in the Spirit." This phrase is closely associated with personal qualities generated in the believer through his or her relation to God. Life in the Spirit is contrasted with life according to the flesh. Life according to the flesh is life under the power of sin, life which exalts the creature rather than the Creator. Both phrases are relational. The issue is the identification of the controlling relation out of which a person lives. One leads to life and freedom; the other, to death and bondage. In connection with these contrasting modes of life, Paul offers his lists of virtues and vices: the fruits of the spirit, and the works of the flesh (cf., e.g., Gal. 5:19–24). Both characterize the lives of concrete human actors, yet neither is set forth preeminently in terms of habits or of perfections and defects in human powers. Both grant primacy to constitutive relations in which human beings stand, noting only secondarily the resulting habitualities. Here too the perfection of the self has indicative and imperative dimensions. Life in the Spirit expresses the indicative, the faith relation which bears fruit as love, joy, peace, patience, kindness, goodness, faithfulness, gentleness, self-control. Yet it also involves the imperative of self-discipline in which the person of faith strives to embody the life which has been offered.

In considerable measure Luke and Matthew elucidate the content of discipleship in terms of obedience to law, though both, like Mark before them, speak of faith and obedient following. In this respect, the perfectionism of Luke and Matthew is in continuity with classic Israelite and Jewish traditions. For Luke in particular the disciple is one who obeys the law given through Moses. Insofar as Luke bestows a distinctive nuance upon such obedience, it is by way of special emphases: with respect to human interactions, the law commands regard for the poor, the disabled, the outcast; where Jew-gentile relations are concerned, the law has from the beginning provided special stipulations for gentiles living in association with a faithful Israel. The decision of the Apostolic Council to exempt gentiles from circumcision and from certain Jewish dietary practices is, therefore, wholly in accord with the Mosaic law. The faithful disciples, including Paul, fully observe what the law requires, whether they be Jew or gentile.

Matthew is more explicit than Luke in defining the perfection of the disciples as the obedient fulfillment of law. In elaborating this conviction, however, he offers a thoroughgoing reinterpretation of the law. First, law is to be so completely internalized that it embraces fundamental feelings and attitudes, not merely correct outward behavior. Matthew expresses by way of legal categories what perhaps belongs more properly to the language of virtues: the temperate person, the pious person, the truthful person, the loving and patient person. Second, law is to be interpreted as essentially commanding love. Its individual details, though strictly binding in every respect, finally amount to one thing, the obligation to love God and the neighbor. It is the disciple's responsibility, guided by the teaching of law and prophets, to discover how best to fulfill this one obligation in every concrete situation.

Given the sweeping nature of this principle of interpretation, it is difficult to comprehend why Matthew is so insistent on the binding claims of the precise details of Israel's legal traditions. The details would appear to be more heuristic or perhaps pedagogical than constitutive. The appropriate interpretation of the law would in any case seem to require discernment, discretion, and judgment on the part of the disciple. It calls for something akin to Aristotelian prudence. Matthew does not develop these implications of his account of law in discipleship. A constructive appropriation of his insights would, however, require us to think them through more systematically. Finally, when the claims of the law are interpreted as the perfection of love, they are extended virtually without limit. Guided by the model of Jesus' patience, forbearance, and compassion, law is no longer confined to the reasonable expectations of human mutuality and reciprocity. It obligates the disciple to go to any length for the sake of a fellow human being: to love the enemy; to bless the persecutor; to forgive the one who has injured; to give freely, more than is required, to the one who makes oppressive demands. With stipulations such as these, law no longer functions simply to sustain community, to maintain the minimal requisites of social order; it functions to extend and enlarge community and to renew it when it breaks down. Its thrust is to turn enmity and hatred into mercy and mutual forbearance.

There are important advantages to expressing the excellencies of moral actors in terms of a disposition to obey in the totality of one's being what the law requires. Such language dramatizes the link between the perfection of the moral actor and the requirements of communal life. Matthew and Luke alert us to this link. Yet law does not provide a language sufficient for perfectionist themes. It cannot adequately set forth the place of feelings and attitudes in moral actions, nor can it do justice to the discernment and judgment required in applying the moral law to particular situations. For these purposes we have need of some variant of the language of virtues. Crucial for a Christian ethic is to capture the relational basis of the excellencies of the moral actor, not in order to dispense with the cultivation of habits capable of perfecting human powers, but in order to place such habits in contexts created by relationships of faith and love. On this matter Paul is more helpful than the Synoptic authors. The remaining challenge to Christian ethics is to explicate the place of insights drawn from ancient wisdom in relational understandings. Wisdom traditions are important not simply because of their appearance within the Hebrew canon. They are also important for the openings they provide for developing the possible contributions of Greek and Hellenistic thought to Christian ethical perspectives.

In the New Testament deontological interests often accompany perfectionist themes, reflecting the fact that Christian existence is communal existence. The primary concern is to clarify the expectations belonging to life in the community of faith, though relations with the larger world are not neglected. In Matthew and Luke, explicit treatments of the Mosaic law function chiefly to specify the perfection of the disciples. Yet lawlike language also appears when the obligations of the disciples to one another are in question. The Mosaic legacy may underlie these discussions, but not necessarily so. At such points the category of law takes a deontological turn, but usually without losing the more dominant perfectionist associations. A good example of this turn is Matthew's treatment of forgiveness. In general, the disciple is one who is always ready to forgive, indeed, as many as seventy times seven. One's perfection as a disciple encompasses the obligation to forgive, and to forgive from the heart. Yet forgiveness is also a moral requisite of community order. One who has been wronged within the community is obliged to seek reconciliation; and the one who has done the injury is obliged to respond penitently. These obligations are backed by sanctions, by the threat of expulsion from the community (Matt. 18:15–20). At this point processes of community maintenance and renewal are in the forefront of attention.

In Luke-Acts, especially in Acts, the deontological interest in law is stronger and more frequent. A striking example is the radical condemnation — indeed, the divine execution! — of Ananias and Sapphira for violating the covenant of shared property in the Jerusalem community (Acts 5:1–11). Freedom from property, and hence, freedom to place one's property at the disposal of the neighbor, defines the perfection of the disciple. However, when a community makes a collective decision to institutionalize such freedom by sharing all property in common, membership in the community entails a strict obligation to place all that one has at the disposal of the community. To violate that obligation is to violate the community; it is to threaten its very life. Thus, a central perfectionist theme of Luke's Gospel takes on explicit deontological significance. In a similar vein, the Apostolic decrees (Acts 15:19–21) not only clarify the ways in which the Mosaic law figures in the perfection of Jewish and gentile disciples; it also specifies the terms of Jew-gentile relations within the community of faith. Other examples could be cited. What is most interesting about deontological treatments of law in Matthew and Luke is that the perfectionist interest is never far removed. This interest permeates the practical concerns of communal order.

It has been my claim that the language of law is most at home in explicating the fundamental ground rules of communal and social order. Such ground rules presuppose persons having the disposition and the capacity to observe them, but the focus of attention is on the requisites of corporate existence. For Matthew and Luke the weight tends to fall in the other direction, creating a strong possibility that we will miss the force of what they are saying. For them, the focus is on the perfection of the disciples, with an accompanying interest in the welfare of communities of faith.

Law and Promise

Paul ventures to deal with deontological themes without benefit of the category of law. In this respect he makes a major break with Israelite and Jewish legacies. This break is integral to his conceptions of law and gospel. Law belongs to the age which is passing away. It expresses God's will in the only way it can be heard in a world which has violated the divine sovereignty. The new age is based on the righteousness of God given apart from the law in Jesus Christ. Here law has been set aside as a constituent in the life of faith, both for the perfection of individuals and for the building up of the community. In place of law is the notion of promise. Promise stresses an open-ended commitment to concrete relationships rather than general regard for the ground rules which protect and govern social order. These relationships are not without form, but their precise forms are to be negotiated in concrete interactions. An active process of negotiation displaces an ongoing interest in the interpretation and application of traditional moral norms. In this respect the notion of promise is future-oriented, while law is rooted in the cumulative experiences of a people over time.

Promise is fully in accord with Paul's dialectical eschatology. It expresses the moral creativity and imagination elicited by the presence of the new age.

The challenge facing Paul is to find ways of expressing the imperatives of communal order without resorting once more to legal categories. As I have noted, he does not shrink from lawlike admonitions. In fact, such admonitions are characteristic of the parenetic sections of his letters. Yet the force of the admonitions is always to direct attention once more to the fundamental relationships which comprise the communities of faith. They amount to one thing: build one another up in love. Paul does on one occasion cite the second table of the law in relation to the command to love the neighbor (Rom. 13:8–10). Yet he deals with concrete communal problems not by appeals to the law or to interpretations of the law. He rather refers in each instance to fundamental gospel themes and to their meaning for the negotiation of a common life among peoples of many backgrounds and races.

Paul does take account of a functional equivalent of law in describing the placement of persons of faith in the institutional settings of the larger world. In counseling Christians to remain in the state in which they are called, he is telling them to acknowledge and abide by the obligations which belong to their various social contexts. We can presume that these obligations were articulated in specific laws and regulations. As I have noted, the institutional settings, and hence also the laws and regulations which make them up, are relativized and rendered provisional by the eschatological orientation of the Christian message. They lose all claims to absoluteness and finality. Yet with these qualifications they are capable of making binding claims upon the lives of persons of faith.

Within social contexts belonging to the age which is passing away, persons of faith remain subject to the law in a provisional and qualified sense. Here at least the law continues to exercise its restraining and pedagogical functions. Within the communities of faith, law has given way to promise. There the concrete negotiation of relationships marked by freedom and love holds sway.

The crucial question for Pauline thought is whether even eschatological communities can over time order their affairs exclusively in terms of the continual negotiation of concrete relationships. Even here, some fairly stable ground rules would seem to be necessary, not simply to take account of our continuing entrapment in the powers of the old age, but to enable us to solidify and build upon understandings already negotiated. Communities can only grow and develop if they are always open in all of their facets to a new accomplishment of life together. Some matters have to be settled and taken for granted in order that new considerations might come into play. Nothing previously established need be taken as permanently fixed. Yet the greater part of our shared understandings and expectations need to be at least provisionally determined in order that we might be free to attend to the most crucial of the open questions before us. To represent matters which have been more or less settled in a negotiation process, and to keep those matters before the community, the language of law reappears as an essential vehicle of moral understanding.

On this matter, I suspect, Paul's thought needs qualification not so much by way of the Synoptic authors as by way of the preexilic legal traditions of ancient Israel. It is in the preexilic legal traditions and in some of their prophetic interpretations that the community-constitutive significance of law and commandment comes most fully to expression. Law in ancient Israel is directly linked to the concrete reality of a people taking form in the world. It does not presume in its origins to determine and regulate all aspects of human activity. Its primary function is to create space within which a living community can flourish and grow. Its thrust is chiefly negative, to exclude community-destroying possibilities. It identifies the basics of covenant existence. Within the frame of reference created by the fundamental commandments, the people are free to negotiate the precise terms of their life together, always in reference to their calling to be a people of God. The judicial processes which took place "in the gate" served as a focal point for such negotiation, building up a fund of tradition over time upon which the people could rely. The problems begin only when these developing understandings are themselves taken to be absolute and final, and hence, closed to analogously open-ended future negotiations.

Paul's conception of the status of the institutional arrangements in the larger society can itself provide a guide for specifying the status of law in both eschatological community and in the social contexts of the world which is passing away. Law is provisional and relative; yet once its provisional status is recognized and appreciated, it has genuine authority to regulate human activity. Still, the provisional and relative standing of law cannot itself become a fixed principle, or it would effectively block out the negotiation of new possibilities in the community of faith. Law can serve only to express what is relatively settled, what is for the present to be taken for granted. It permits the concentration of the moral imagination on issues in eschatological existence which are most in need of attention at a given moment. Yet even previously settled matters remain open in principle to renegotiation. They can once more become objects of special attention, to be worked out anew with full sensitivity to the concrete understandings and meanings at play within the community.

This account subjects law to promise, shaking loose its connection with the weight of the past. Yet it also permits the eschatological community to profit from past learnings, to build where appropriate on the cumulative experiences of the past. Law and promise are then dialectically related. Law articulates promise, and promise is the underlying basis of law. Promise finds provisional and relative expression in law. In fact, it can scarcely take on concrete reality at all if it does not at least tacitly utilize something akin to law or basic principle. Yet law ever remains subject to testing in light of promise. It is for the sake of promise that it comes into being. By way of promise, it is ever being revised, reworked, reformulated, as the occasion demands. Insofar as this dialectic captures the moral structure of eschatological community, it can also be a guide for attempts, governed by eschatological understandings, to take appropriate responsibility for the institutions of the larger society. It expresses the form of deontological language appropriate to eschatological existence.

A dialectical conception of law and promise would seem to modify slightly Paul's explicitly stated views, though I believe it to be congruent with his basic accomplishment. This conception does challenge biblical materials which treat law as a historically revealed deposit of the eternal wisdom of God, even if such wisdom is construed as continuous with the wisdom and insight derived from natural human endowments. Thus, Luke's insistence on total obedience to the Mosaic law, both by the redeemed Israel and by gentiles associated with them, has the effect of freezing the history of the people of God. Luke does remind us of the centrality of the Jewish legacy for the life of the Christian community. He also stresses the continuity of social experience. Yet his view of the law causes us to lose sight of the social and cultural openness which is implied in the universal outreach of the gospel. Similarly, Matthew's demand that every detail of the law be observed is finally incompatible with his insight into the foundational significance of the commands to love God and the neighbor. Given their full sway, these commands relativize and render provisional the various details of the law quite as fully as the Pauline notion of promise. The laws, we could say, articulate more concretely what the love commands ask of us; at the same time, the laws are ever subject to testing, modification, and revision—not simply reinterpretation!—in light of these two commands. What remains is an appreciation of the role law plays in expressing the settled understandings of the community of faith, and in noting the personal excellencies required for their full observance. In the same vein, Mark's celebration of the primacy of the moral law over the ceremonial law, though classic in its sympathies, appears not to have reached to the heart of the matter. Moral understandings, stated as law and commandment, must themselves be open to fresh interpretation, even continual renegotiation, in the ongoing life of the people of God; and ceremonies and rituals, though perhaps subordinate to moral concerns, are themselves constituents of communal life in provisional and historically relative ways.

Interestingly enough, it is the preexilic legal tradition and its prophetic interpretation which comes closest to the law-promise dialectic I have been describing. Law and commandment are treated not as autonomous and self-contained moral notions, but as integral features in the concrete existence of the people of God. While law and commandment develop and grow over time, incorporating the cumulative experiences of the people, they remain open to modification and adaptation. They take shape as the life of the people takes shape in response to changing social and cultural situations. The more ancient traditions, quite understandably, are not marked so deeply as the thought of Paul by an appreciation of cultural pluralism, or for the building of community capable of embracing the plurality of the world's peoples. Yet they share Paul's strong historical sense. In both cases the concreteness of the historical pilgrimage is an essential characteristic of moral understanding.

I have not offered much comment on the virtual absence of consequentialist thinking in the biblical materials. If consequentialist thought does stem, as I have argued, from the orientation of action to value-laden goals, can it properly be omitted from constructive thought? In my initial discussion of consequentialist thought, I noted its link with the distinctive experiences of modern societies. Consequentialism is a mode of inquiry and reflection which can come into its own only when the people of a society have considerable confidence in their ability to predict and shape the future course of world events. Insofar as it has gained a position of dominance in nineteenth- and twentieth-century thought, it is because of its special congruence with high-technology civilization. If anything, modern society has exaggerated the human capacity to manage the course of events, at least from the standpoint of its utopian projections if not in its actual practice. What implications do these experiences and attitudes have for contemporary attempts to appropriate biblical faith into constructive ethical thought?

Modern societies can no longer function effectively without a good deal of "rational" direction and control based on considerable technical knowledge of geographic, ecological, economic, social, and political processes. Even when this knowledge is distorted by ideological biases and is inadequate to the complexities of the actual world, it provides critical reference points without which large-scale social policies could scarcely be conceived, let alone implemented. Contemporary social ethics must address these realities in some fashion, which means it must come to grips with consequentialist thinking.

If this judgment is sound, then a biblically informed ethic must find suitable ways to develop the possible import of biblical understandings for a world which requires the assessment of policies and courses of action in terms of values likely to be promoted by their probable outcomes. Drawing upon central themes in biblical faith, we have need of a fully articulated account of values which can guide our analyses of policy options. Such an account will have to attend to many factors which scarcely appear as matters of moral concern to the biblical authors: global scarcity, population pressures, ecological vulnerability, the monetary system, international trade and corporate development, urban planning. At a minimum it will have the burden of challenging the tendency of consequentialist thought to reduce the values pertinent to decision-making to economic and political factors.

What a Christian ethic must surely 'resist is the impulse to translate all moral understandings into consequentialist terms. We must be concerned about consequences, but our assessment of probable consequences and their associated values must at every point be constrained and ordered by perfectionist and deontological considerations. Before giving ourselves enthusiastically to grand designs which may or may not eventually be realized, we have need to attend carefully to the basic requisites of communal and social existence as we understand them, and to keep in view the conditions pertinent to moral and spiritual growth. The full explication of these suggestions must, however, await a systematic treatment of Christian ethics.

NOTES

1. This is a position with serious and thoughtful advocates, e.g., James Sellers, *Public Ethics: American Morals and Manners* (New York: Harper & Row, 1970) and Gibson Winter, *Elements for a Social Ethic: Scientific and Ethical Perspectives on Social Process* (New York: Macmillan Co., 1966). There is in addition the considerable body of literature extolling the American civil religion. America is, so Abraham Lincoln suggested in his Gettysburg address, an "almost chosen people." Or alternatively, we are a nation "with the Soul of a Church" (G. K. Chesterton). Cf. Raymond T. Bond, ed., *The Man Who Was Chesterton* (Garden City, N.Y.: Doubleday & Co., Anchor Books, 1960), 131. Also, as I noted earlier, spokespersons for the American Revolution understood themselves to be involved in nothing less than the founding of a "new order of the world."

2. This line of argument bears considerable similarity to Karl Barth's tentative explorations of a possible political ethic. See his "The Christian Community and the Civil Community," in *Community, State and Church: Three Essays* (Garden City, N.Y.: Doubleday & Co., 1960). This essay was initially published in *Theologische Studien* 20 (Zollikon-Zurich: Evangelischer Verlag, 1946).

SELECTED BIBLIOGRAPHY

CLASSICAL TREATMENTS OF ETHICAL THEORY

Aristotle. *Nichomachaean Ethics.* In *Introduction to Aristotle*, ed. Richard McKeon. New York: Modern Library, 1947.

Kant, Immanuel. *Critique of Practical Reason.* Eng. trans. Lewis White Beck. New York: Bobbs-Merrill, 1956.

———. *Fundamental Principles of the Metaphysics of Morals.* Eng. trans. Thomas K. Abbott. New York: Bobbs-Merrill, 1949.

Mill, John Stuart. "Utilitarianism." In *The Philosophy of John Stuart Mill*, ed. Marshall Cohen. New York: Modern Library, 1961.

Niebuhr, H. Richard. *The Responsible Self: An Essay in Christian Moral Philosophy.* New York: Harper & Row, 1963.

Rawls, John. *A Theory of Justice.* Cambridge, Mass.: Harvard University Press, 1971.

Scheler, Max. *Formalism in Ethics and Non-Formal Ethics of Value: A New Attempt toward the Foundation of an Ethical Personalism.* Eng. trans. Manfred S. Frings and Roger L. Funk. Evanston, Ill.: Northwestern University Press, 1973.

Troeltsch, Ernst. "Ethics and Philosophy of History." In *Christian Thought: Its History and Application*, ed. Baron R. von Hügel. New York: Meridian Books, 1957.

HERMENEUTICAL THEORY

Gadamer, Hans-Georg. *Truth and Method.* Eng. trans. Garrett Barden and John Cumming. New York: Seabury Press, 1975.

Ricoeur, Paul. *Freud and Philosophy: An Essay on Interpretation.* Eng. trans. Denis Savage. New Haven, Conn.: Yale University Press, 1970.

———. *Interpretation Theory: Discourse and the Surplus of Meaning.* Fort Worth, Tex.: Texas Christian University Press, 1976.

PHENOMENOLOGICAL RESOURCES FOR
ETHICAL THEORY

Habermas, Jürgen. *Communication and the Evolution of Society.* Eng. trans. Thomas McCarthy. Boston: Beacon Press, 1979.
————. *Knowledge and Human Interests.* Eng. trans. Jeremy Shapiro. Boston: Beacon Press, 1971.
————. *Theory and Practice.* Eng. trans. John Viertel. Boston: Beacon Press, 1973.
Heidegger, Martin. *Being and Time.* Eng. trans. John Macquarrie and Edward Robinson. London: SCM Press, 1962.
————. *On Time and Being.* Eng. trans. Joan Stambaugh. New York: Harper & Row, 1972.
Husserl, Edmund. *Cartesian Meditations: An Introduction to Phenomenology.* Eng. trans. Dorion Cairns. The Hague: Martinus Nijhoff, 1960.
————. *The Crisis of European Sciences and Transcendental Phenomenology: An Introduction to Phenomenological Philosophy.* Eng. trans. David Carr. Evanston, Ill.: Northwestern University Press, 1970.
Ricoeur, Paul. *Freedom and Nature: The Voluntary and the Involuntary.* Evanston, Ill.: Northwestern University Press, 1966.

BIBLICAL THEOLOGY AS A RESOURCE
FOR ETHICAL UNDERSTANDING

Old Testament

Crenshaw, James L. *Studies in Ancient Israelite Wisdom.* New York: KTAV, 1975.
Gottwald, Norman K. *The Tribes of Yahweh: A Sociology of the Religion of Liberated Israel 1250–1050 B.C.E.* Maryknoll, N.Y.: Orbis Books, 1979.
Knight, Douglas A., ed. *Tradition and Theology in the Old Testament.* Philadelphia: Fortress Press, 1977.
Noth, Martin. *The Laws in the Pentateuch and Other Studies.* Eng. trans. D. R. Ap-Thomas. Philadelphia: Fortress Press, 1966.
von Rad, Gerhard. *Old Testament Theology.* Vol. 1, *The Theology of Israel's Historical Traditions.* Eng. trans. D. M. G. Stalker. New York: Harper & Row, 1962.
————. *Old Testament Theology.* Vol. 2, *The Theology of Israel's Prophetic Traditions.* Eng. trans. D. M. G. Stalker. New York: Harper & Row, 1965.
————. *The Problem of the Hexateuch and Other Essays.* Eng. trans. E. W. Trueman Dicken. New York: McGraw-Hill, 1966.
————. *Wisdom in Israel.* Eng. trans. James D. Martin. Nashville: Abingdon Press, 1972.

New Testament

Beker, J. Christiaan. *Paul the Apostle: The Triumph of God in Life and Thought.* Philadelphia: Fortress Press, 1980.

Bornkamm, Gunther, Gerhard Barth, and Heinz Held. *Tradition and Interpretation in Matthew.* Eng. trans. Percy Scott. Philadelphia: Westminster Press, 1963.

Conzelmann, Hans. *The Theology of St. Luke.* Eng. trans. G. Buswell. Philadelphia: Fortress Press, 1982.

Jervell, Jacob. *Luke and the People of God: A New Look at Luke-Acts.* Minneapolis: Augsburg Pub. House, 1972.

Johnson, Luke T. *The Literary Function of Possessions in Luke-Acts.* Society of Biblical Literature Dissertation Series 39. Missoula, Mont.: Scholars Press, 1977.

Keck, Leander. "On the Ethos of Early Christians." *Journal of the American Academy of Religion* 42 (September 1974): 435–52.

Marxsen, Willi. *Mark The Evangelist: Studies on the Redaction History of the Gospel.* Eng. trans. James Boyce et al. Nashville: Abingdon Press, 1969.

Perrin, Norman. *The Kingdom of God in the Teaching of Jesus.* London: SCM Press, 1963.

———. *What Is Redaction Criticism?* Philadelphia: Fortress Press, 1969.

Robinson, James M. *The Problem of History in Mark and Other Marcan Studies.* Philadelphia: Fortress Press, 1982.

STUDIES OF BIBLICAL ETHICS

Crenshaw, James L., and John T. Willis, eds. *Essays in Old Testament Ethics.* New York: KTAV, 1974.

Dodd, C. H. "The Ethics of the New Testament." In *Moral Principles of Action*, ed. Ruth Nanda Anshen, 543–558. New York: Harper & Row, 1952.

———. *Gospel and Law.* New York: Columbia University Press, 1951.

Furnish, Victor Paul. *The Love Command in the New Testament.* Nashville: Abingdon Press, 1972.

———. *The Moral Teaching of Paul: Selected Issues.* Nashville: Abingdon Press, 1979.

———. *Theology and Ethics in Paul.* Nashville: Abingdon Press, 1968.

Gerhardsson, Birger. *The Ethos of the Bible.* Eng. trans. Stephen Westerholm. Philadelphia: Fortress Press, 1981.

Harrelson, Walter. *The Ten Commandments and Human Rights.* Overtures to Biblical Theology 8. Philadelphia: Fortress Press, 1980.

Hempel, J. "Ethics in the Old Testament." In *Interpreter's Dictionary of the Bible*, 2:153–61. Nashville: Abingdon Press, 1962.

Houlden, J. L. *Ethics and the New Testament.* Baltimore: Penguin Books, 1973.

Knox, John. *The Ethics of Jesus in the Teaching of the Church.* Nashville: Abingdon Press, 1961.

Manson, T. W. *Ethics and the Gospel.* New York: Charles Scribner's Sons, 1960.

Minear, Paul S. *Commands of Christ: Authority and Implications.* Nashville: Abingdon Press, 1972.

Muilenburg, James. *The Way of Israel: Biblical Faith and Ethics.* New York: Harper & Row, 1961.

Osborn, Eric. *Ethical Patterns in Early Church Thought.* New York and Cambridge: Cambridge University Press, 1976.

Sanders, Jack T. *Ethics in the New Testament: Change and Development.* Philadelphia: Fortress Press, 1975.

Schnackenburg, Rudolf. *The Moral Teaching of the New Testament.* Eng. trans. J. Holland-Smith and W. J. O'Hara. New York: Herder and Herder, 1965.

White, R. E. O. *Biblical Ethics.* Atlanta: John Knox Press, 1979.

Wilder, Amos N. *Kerygma, Eschatology, and Social Ethics.* Philadelphia: Fortress Press, 1966.

METHODOLOGICAL STUDIES ON THE USE OF THE BIBLE IN CHRISTIAN ETHICS

Birch, Bruce C., and Larry L. Rasmussen. *Bible and Ethics in the Christian Life.* Minneapolis: Augsburg Pub. House, 1976.

Childress, James F. "Scripture and Christian Ethics: Some Reflections on the Role of Scripture in Moral Deliberation and Justification." *Interpretation* 34 (October 1980): 371–80.

Curran, Charles E. "Dialogue with the Scriptures: The Role and Function of the Scriptures in Moral Theology." In *Catholic Moral Theology In Dialogue,* 24–64. Notre Dame, Ind.: Fides Publishers, 1972.

Gustafson, James. "The Place of Scripture in Christian Ethics: A Methodological Study" and "The Relation of the Gospels to the Moral Life." In *Theology and Christian Ethics,* ed. Charles Swezey, 121–45 and 147–59. Philadelphia: United Church Press, 1974.

Hauerwas, Stanley. "The Moral Authority of Scripture." *Interpretation* 34 (October 1980): 356–70.

Kelsey, David H. *The Uses of Scripture in Recent Theology.* Philadelphia: Fortress Press, 1975.

Kimpel, Benjamin Franklin. *Moral Principles in the Bible: A Study of the Contribution of the Bible to a Moral Philosophy.* New York: Philosophical Library, 1956.

Kraemer, Hendrik. *The Bible and Social Ethics*. Philadelphia: Fortress Press, 1965.

Lehmann, Paul. "The Commandments and the Common Life." *Interpretation* 34 (October 1980): 341–55.

Long, Edward LeRoy, Jr. "The Use of the Bible in Christian Ethics: A Look at Basic Options." *Interpretation* 19 (April 1965): 149–62.

Miranda, José P. *Marx and the Bible*. Eng. trans. John Eagleson. Maryknoll, N.Y.: Orbis Books, 1974.

Mouw, Richard J. *Politics and the Biblical Drama*. Grand Rapids: Wm. B. Eerdmans, 1976.

Outka, Gene. "On Harming Others." *Interpretation* 34 (October 1980): 381–93.

Ramsey, Paul. "The Biblical Norm of Righteousness." *Interpretation* 24 (October 1970): 419–29.

Sleeper, C. Freeman. "Ethics as a Context for Biblical Interpretation." *Interpretation* 22 (October 1968): 443–60.

Verhey, Allen. "The Use of Scripture in Ethics." *Religious Studies Review* 4 (January 1978): 28–39.

———. "The Use of Scripture in Moral Discourse: A Case Study of Walter Rauschenbuch." Ph.D. diss., Yale University, 1975.

Via, Dan Otto, Jr. "The Right Strawy Epistle Reconsidered: A Study in Biblical Ethics and Hermeneutic." *Journal of Religion* 49 (July 1969): 253–67.

A SELECTION OF BIBLICALLY GROUNDED TREATMENTS OF CHRISTIAN ETHICS IN RECENT THOUGHT

Barth, Karl. *Church Dogmatics: The Doctrine of God* II:2. Eng. trans. and ed. G. W. Bromiley et al. Edinburgh: T. & T. Clark, 1957.

———. *Church Dogmatics: The Doctrine of Creation* III:4. Eng. trans. and ed. G. W. Bromiley. Edinburgh: T. & T. Clark, 1960.

———. *Church Dogmatics: The Doctrine of Reconciliation* IV:4 (Fragments). Eng. trans. and ed. G. W. Bromiley. Edinburgh: T. & T. Clark, 1981.

———. *Ethics*. Eng. trans. G. W. Bromiley. New York: Seabury Press, 1981.

Bonhoeffer, Dietrich. *The Cost of Discipleship*. Eng. trans. R. H. Fuller. New York: Macmillan Co., 1957.

———. *Ethics*, ed. E. Bethge. New York: Macmillan Co., 1955.

Brunner, Emil. *The Divine Imperative*. Eng. trans. Olive Wyon. Philadelphia: Westminster Press, 1947.

Gustafson, James M. *Ethics from a Theocentric Perspective*. Vol. 1 of *Theology and Ethics*. Chicago: University of Chicago Press, 1981.

BIBLIOGRAPHY

Hauerwas, Stanley. *A Community of Character: Toward a Constructive Christian Social Ethic*. Notre Dame, Ind.: University of Notre Dame Press, 1981.

————. *Truthfulness and Tragedy: Further Investigations in Christian Ethics*. Notre Dame, Ind.: University of Notre Dame Press, 1966.

Lehmann, Paul. *Ethics in a Christian Context*. New York: Harper & Row, 1963.

Mott, Stephen Charles. *Biblical Ethics and Social Change*. New York and London: Oxford University Press, 1982.

Ramsey, Paul. *Basic Christian Ethics*. New York: Charles Scribner's Sons, 1950.

Thielicke, Helmut. *Theological Ethics*. Vol. 1 of *Foundations*, ed. William H. Lazareth. Philadelphia: Fortress Press, 1966.

Yoder, John H. *The Politics of Jesus*. Grand Rapids: Wm. B. Eerdmans, 1972.

INDEX

SUBJECT INDEX

Bold notations refer to key blocks of text

Abraham, 71, 136, 143-44, 146, 168
Action: goal-oriented, 18-22, 23, 24, 43n.15, 192; intentional structure of, **18-20**, 34
Actor, moral, 18, **28-34**, 195, 197. *See also* Character; Self
Administrative agencies, 27
Adultery, 98, 105, 110, 133n.30
Almsgiving, **123-24**
America: Christian ethics in, 182-84; civil religion in, 17, 182, 205n.1; as eschatological community, 184
American revolution, 189
Anger, 110
Apocalyptic thought, 71, 76
Apodictic commands, 53-54
Apostolic decrees, 101, 132n.20, 198

Baal, cult of, 60, 65
Baalism, 60-61, 64, 71
Beneficence, 23, 31
Bible: as literature, 10; as Sacred Scripture, 8, 9 (*See also* Scripture principle); unity and diversity of, 11
Biblical authority, 1
Biblical texts, canonical shaping of, 8-9
Blessing, 49
Body, 19, 30, 144
Book of the Covenant, 53, 66-67

Canaan, 49, 52, 71
Canaanite culture, 59-61
Care, 72-73, 90, 190

Casuistic regulations, 53-54
Character, 31, 34. *See also* Actor; Self
Christ: and Adam, 139-40; dying and rising with, 90, 137, 138, 146-52, 172n.7, 195; imitation of, **148-51**, 195; life in, 135, 137, 140, 147, 169, 195
Church, 11, 33, 40, 89, 102, 113, 115, 141, 142, 153, 160, 164, 171, **183-86**. *See also* Community, eschatological; Community, of faith
Churches, care of, 136, 169
Circumcision, 101, 154
Clans, Israelite, 49, 71. *See also* Tribal confederation
Classical, 2
Common ground of understanding, 2, 3, 47, **175-205**
Communities, Christian, 118-19, 128
Community, 51, 80; eschatological, 89, 91, 116-19, 120, 136, 145, 152, 171, **178-80**, 185, 189-91, 194, 200-201, 202; of faith, 88, 90, 92, 113, 120, 160, 163, 178, 179, 181-82, 195; gathered, 90, 91, 115, 121, 122, 126, 128-29, 159, 194; of goods, 119, 123, 124-25, 129, 198; and perfectionism, 90, 198; personal, 26, 43n.20; restoration, 75
Comprehensibility, 25
Conflict, 89, 97, 113, 127
Consequentialist ethical thought, 4, 16, 18, 20-22, 23, 24, 26, 31, 48, 91, 192, 204-5

213

Courage, 30
Covenant, 11, 49-53, 65-66, 193
Covenantal obligations, 49-53, 69, 73, 79, 193. *See also* Decalogue; Deuteronomic Code; Holiness Code; Law; Priestly Code
Covenant failure, 65-69, 73
Covenant fidelity, 58-64, 73, 104
Critical theory, 37-38, 184-85
Cult and social injustice, 69
Cultic and social regulations, 54-55, 73. *See also* Law, moral and ceremonial
Culture, 35-37
Cursing, 49

David, 63, 66, 69, 83n.20, 84n.22, 98
David-Zion traditions, 62-63, 66
Decalogue, 52, 53, 66-67, 78, 83n.7. *See also* Covenantal obligations; Law
Deciding, 19-20, 21, 34, 190
Deeds, 19, 23, 29, 41n.7
Democratic socialism, 126
Deontology, 4, 16, 24-28, 31, 47, 48, 76, 79, 90, 91, 114, 169, 192-93, 198, 199; and virtue, 31
Deuteronomic Code, 53. *See also* Covenantal obligations; Law
Diaspora, 74
Dignity, 23, 24, 28
Discipleship, 90, 91, 92-97, 105, 129, 145, 194, 196-97
Discourse, 25-26, 27. *See also* Interactions, communicative; Negotiation
Divorce, 98, 103, 160-61
Duty, 24, 31, 32, 34, 35, 47, 90

Economic life, 7, 10, 21, 55, 59-60, 92, 116, 117, 118, 119, 125-27, 129-30, 134n.43, 152, 166, 178, 192
Economics, 22
Egypt, 49, 50, 52, 59
Embodiment, 18, 30, 34, 41n.6
Enlightenment, 17, 71
Equality, 154-57, 167-68
Eschatological existence, 92, 148, 202
Eschatology, 11, 69-71, 73, 87, 88, 89, 90, 91, 122, 127, 193; dialectical and futurist, 70, 79, 89, 147-48, **177-82**, **185-92**, 202-3; secular versions of, 189
Ethical theory, 4, 12, 34, 89, 192
Eucharist, 97, 104, 154
Evil, anthropological dimensions of, 71-72, 81. *See also* Sin
Exclusiveness, 57-58, 65, 72
Exile, 70, 74
Exodus, 52, 63

Fairness, 23, 73
Faith, 95, 111, 114, 137, 140, 144, 146-51, 169, 194-95, 197
Family, 33, 55-56, 61, 93-95, 179, 181-82
Feelings, 31, 110, **112-14**, 145, 197
"Female power," 61
Food laws, 98, 105, 154
Forgiveness, 92, **119-21**, 129, 152, 190, 198
Form criticism, 6, 8, 10
Freedom, 73-74, 144, 146, 147, 171, 190, 195
"Fusion of horizons," 3, 4, 12, 47, 175

"Gate," 83n.6, 201
Good, 39
Goods, 20, 31, 32
Grace, 38, 39, 51, 76, 114, 145, 146-47, 193-94, 195

Habit, 30-31, 34, 194-95, 197
Heart, 70, 71, 81
Hellenists, 91, 136
Hermeneutics, 1-7, 11, 175. *See also* Interpretation
Hexateuch, 51
Historical contextualism, 5, 17, 18, 34-41, 47, 58, 87
Historical situatedness, 2, 35-36
Historicity, 2, 5, 17, 35-38, 79-80, 192
Holiness Code, 51, 53, 56, 133n.31. *See also* Covenantal obligations; Law
Holy, 39
Hope, 38, 177
Household, 91, 159-67, 163-66; rules, 165-67, 172n.10. *See also* Family
Human origins, 50-51, 71
Humility, 150, 151, 195

Identity, 29, 30–31, 39, 58, 63, 73, 78, 136, 143; and integrity, 58–59, 84 n.24
Ideology, 7, 183, 205
Inclusiveness, 59, 65, 72, 158–59, 190
Individualism, 27, 33, 193
Institutional creativity, 116–19, 128, 192
Institutional settings, 7, 34, 81, 89, 90, 91, 129, 142, 144, 147, 152, 158–59, 164, 170–71, 181–82, 190, 192, 199, 201–2
Integrity, 58–59, 84 n.24. See also Identity
Intentionality, 18–19, 23, 26, 34
Interactions: communicative, 24, 25, 43 n.15; human, 23–28, 35. See also Discourse; Negotiation
Interpretation, 1–6, 12, 41 n.3, 176; as discourse with texts, 2, 4, 7, 15; as questioning, 2–4, 15. See also Hermeneutics
Intersubjectivity, 18, 23–24, 26, 42 n.14, 192. See also Interactions

Jerusalem, 63, 70
Jesus, public ministry of, 87, 88, 92
Jesus Christ, death and resurrection of, 87, 135, 137, 148
Jubilee year, 134 n.43
Judaism, 91, 97, 98, 99, 100–101, 115, 116, 128, 153–54, 156–58, 168, 196, 199, 203
Judaizers, 136
Judicial, 68
Justice, 23, 59, 66, 68–69, 72, 80, 85 n.30, 106
Justification by faith, 114, 137–38, 144, 146, 151

Kingdom of God (heaven), 88, 92–94, 99, 127, 129, 131 n.5, 132–33 n.25, 135, 145

Law: in the Christian life, 90, 91–92, 97–115, 132 n.18, 139, 140–46, 152–53, 168–69, 196–97, 199–204; courts of, 27, 55, 67, 68; in Israel, 53–58, 64–67, 72, 74–76, 77, 201; moral and ceremonial, 54–55, 69, 97–98, 101, 104, 106, 128, 203; and negotiation, 203–4; and promise, 140–46, 199–205

Life situations, 6
Life world, 4, 5, 7, 18, 29, 34, 36
Literary criticism, 10, 14 n.13, 87
Love commandments, 95, 97, 102–3, 108, 110, 112, 114, 119, 123, 128, 141–42, 145, 150, 196, 203

Maccabees, 74
Marxism, 126, 189
Maxims, 24–25
Meaning of being, 38–41, 193
Meat offered to idols, 155
Meliorism, 16, 22
Military, 48, 81, 84 n.27
Mission, 72, 88, 91, 115
Monarchy, 48, 61–64, 65, 67, 71, 81
Moral discernment, 29, 32, 44 n.28, 78, 196–97
Moral experience, 1, 5, 15, 18, 22, 193
Moral law, 24–28, 31, 97
Moral life: consequences in the, 131 n.5; monologic conceptions of, 25; preunderstandings of, 3, 4, 5, 15–46, 47, 175–76, 192; relational views of, 194–95, 197; and religious beliefs, 7, 41 n.1
Moral principles, 25, 26, 31
Moral requisites, of social life, 26, 28, 47–48, 76, 90, 197, 198–99
Moses, 49, 53, 63, 75, 76, 101, 102, 103, 142, 143, 145–46, 193, 196
Mt. Sinai, 49, 52, 59

Narrative, 51–52, 75, 82 n.4
Negotiation, 170, 191, 199–201
New covenant, 70

Obligation, 23, 25, 26–27, 28–29, 34, 38–39, 40, 47, 94, 110, 190, 192, 198. See also Covenantal obligations; Duty
Oppressed, 73–74, 80, 192
Oppression, 7, 33, 56, 66, 67–69
Other(s), 23–24, 25, 150–51

Patriarchal order, 56, 60, 81, 83 n.10, 163–67
Patriarchal traditions, 50
Paul: imitation of, 149; lawlike admonitions in, 141–43, 198, 200
Pentateuchal source criticism: "Elohist" of, 52; "Yahwist" of, 52, 82 n.4

Perfectionist ethical theory, 4, 16, 17, 28, 31-34, 90, 192, 193
Perfectionist motifs, in the Bible, 48, 76-79, 90, 111-12, 114, 128, 145, 169, 193-95, 198
Phenomenology, 4, 17, 18
Pluralism, cultural, 16, 152-68, 171, 190, 204
Political processes, 10, 21, 40, 49-50, 59-60, 61-64, 81, 92, 116-17, 119, 121-22, 129-30, 152, 178, 192. See also Monarchy; Public policy; State
Political science, 22
Poor, 56, 68-69, 96, 104, 117, 122, 126, 128, 196
Possessions, 119, 122-27, 129. See also Community, of goods; Property
Post-exilic traditions, 74-79
Practical wisdom, 32, 78, 196. See also Prudence
Pragmatism, 16, 22
Priestly code, 53. See also Covenantal obligations; Law
Project(s), 19, 23, 29, 34
Promise, 138-46, 168-70, 199-204
Property, 92, 119, 129, 198. See also Community, of goods; Possessions
Prophetic judgment, 64-69, 81
Prudence, 32. See also Practical wisdom
Psychology, 33
Public policy, 21, 22, 190, 205. See also Political processes

Radical monotheism, 39
Radical reformation, 188
Reason, autonomous, 17-18, 35, 50-51
Redaction criticism, 6, 87
Relationships, 25, 33, 111, 142-43, 144-45, 147, 169, 199, 200
Relativism, 36-37
Relativity, 12, 25, 32, 35, 153-59, 165, 170, 171, 192-93, 202, 203
Respect, 23, 31, 72
Revivalism, 188
Revolutionary, 37, 190
Righteousness, 51, 68, 72, 77, 84-85 n.30, 137, 139, 142, 144, 147, 169
Rules for social cooperation, 25, 49-50, 56, 77, 169-70, 199

Sabbath, 97-98, 103, 105, 133 n.28
Sages, 76
Salvation history, 88
Scripture principle, 9. See also Biblical authority
Self, 18, 28-34. See also Actor; Character
Self-consciousness, 29
Semiotics, 10
Sexual activity, 60, 161-62
Sin, 138-40, 144, 146-47, 195. See also Evil, anthropological dimensions of
Singleness, 160-61
Skepticism, 37
Slaves, 160, 163, 164-65. See also Equality
Sociality, 26, 34, 80-81
Social processes, 6, 7, 13 n.8
Social psychology, 33
Sociology, 28
Spirit: age of the, 88, 89, 95; fruits of the, 88, 145, 195; life in the, 135, 144, 146, 169, 195
State, 63-64, 81, 91, 116-17, 118, 129, 166. See also Political processes
Structuralism, 10, 14 n.14
Suffering, 52, 69, 70, 72, 90, 92, 141, 145, 148-50, 169, 194
Survival, ethics of, 39, 70, 79, 89

Temperance, 30
Temple, 62
Temporality, 17, 18, 30-31, 34-41, 45 n.35, 192
Texts, autonomy of, 2, 12 n.2
Theocracy, 189
Theophany, at Mt. Sinai, 49, 52
Thomist social thought, 188
Torah, 74, 76
Traditio-historical school, 7, 8
Tradition criticism, 6, 7, 8, 10
Tradition history, 6, 8
Tragic vision, 38
Tribal confederation, 59-61, 75, 81

Unconscious, 29
Universality, 29, 59, 72-74, 80, 115
Universalizability, 17, 24, 25, 57
Universal pragmatics, 42 n.17, 19
Utilitarianism, 16, 21, 31
Utility, principle of, 22, 23

Value realm, 21–22, 35, 39, 42 n.10
Values, 19–20, 21, 28–29, 31, 34, 35, 38–39, 40, 48, 78, 192; general theory of, 21–22, 26, 48
Violence, 107–8, 119, 127, 145, 191, 192
Virtue, theories of, 28, 31
Virtues, 32, 34, 35, 38, 40, 77, 192, 193, 194–95, 197
Voluntary associations, 33, 35, 37

Vulnerable, 55–57, 67, 73, 80
Vulnerability, 31, 39, 44 n.27, 108
Welfare, 22
Wilderness, 70
Wisdom, 76, 85 n.33, 197
Women, equality of, 160, 162–64, 167–68; leadership by, 172–73 n.11

Yahweh, 48, 49, 57–58, 59–61, 65–67, 69–71, 72–74, 94

SCRIPTURE INDEX

OLD TESTAMENT

Genesis
1–11–50, 71
11:31–71
12–50–50

Exodus
3–50
12:1-20–53
12:43-49–53
19–24–82 n.2
20:23–23:19–53, 54
22:21-23–56
24–49, 53
34–53

Leviticus
1–7–53
11–15–53
11:7–83 n.14
16–53
17–18–101
17–26–53
18–60
19–51
19:1-4–53
19:11-18–53
19:33-34–56
25:42–56
25:44-46–56

Numbers
28–29–53
28:9-10–107

Deuteronomy
5–53
6:4-9–77

12–16–53
14:8–83 n.14

Judges
9:8-21–83 n.20

1 Samuel
8:11-17–83 n.20

2 Samuel
2:4–84 n.20
5:3–84 n.20
6:1-19–84 n.20
7–84 n.22

1 Kings
12:3-19–84
18:40–60
21–67, 83 n.17

2 Kings
9–60
16:10-18–62
21:4-9–62
23:4-7–62

Psalms
1–77
19–76
19:7-14–77
110–84 n.22
119–76, 77
132–84 n.22

Proverbs
1–9–76, 85 n.33
8–76
22:20-24–78

Isaiah
1:10-20–84 n.28
1:17–67
1:26–66
2:1-4–72
3:1-8–68
3:14-15–67
5:8-10–68
5:23–67
6:9-10–131
7:4–66
8:11-15–66
8:12–66
10:1-2–67
10:12-19–66
10:20–66
11–68
11:1-8–64
11:1-9–66
29:1-8–64
29:13–105
40–55–65
42:5-9–72
53:10-11–72
56–66–65
58:6-14–73
61–96
61:1-4–73

Jeremiah
7:9-10–67
7:21, 23–53
31:31-34–70

Ezekiel
11:14-21–70

Hosea
2:8–65

2:16–23 – 69
4:2 – 67
6:6 – 107
7:8 – 66
8:4 – 66, 83 n.20
8:14 – 66
9:10–11 – 65
10:13 – 66
11:1–4 – 64
12:7 – 67
12:13 – 64
13:4–5 – 64
13:10 – 66
13:11 – 83 n.20

Amos
2:7 – 67
2:9–10 – 64
3:2 – 72
5:10–12 – 67
5:15 – 65
5:18 – 65
5:21–24 – 84 n.28
7:7–9 – 65
8:1–3 – 65

Micah
2:2–9 – 68
3:2 – 67
3:9–12 – 64
5:1–2 – 64
6:6–8 – 84 n.28
6:11–12 – 67

THE APOCRYPHA

Sirach
1 – 76
24 – 76

NEW TESTAMENT

Matthew
5:17–48 – 108
5:18–19 – 105
5:21, 43 – 105
5:23–24 – 105, 110
5:38–42 – 108
5:43–48 – 103, 108
5:48 – 110
6:1–7:12 – 108
6:14–15 – 120
6:30 – 95

6:33 – 111
7:12 – 103, 108
7:21 – 105
8:26 – 95
12:1 – 107
12:1–14 – 105
12:5 – 107
12:7–8 – 107
12:9–14 – 107
12:11 – 105
12:11–12 – 107
12:46–50 – 94
13:11 – 95
13:16–17 – 95
13:24–30 – 113
14:31 – 95
15:1–2, 10–20 – 105
15:3–9 – 105
15:19 – 105
16:8 – 95
17:20 – 95
17:24–27 – 105
18:3–7 – 103
18:15–20 – 113, 120, 198
18:17 – 113
18:18 – 113
18:22 – 120
18:32–33 – 120
18:35 – 120
19:27–30 – 94
22:36 – 102
22:37 – 111
22:40 – 103
23:23 – 103, 105
23:36–40 – 106
24:20 – 105
28:19 – 94

Mark
2:23–28 – 98
2:27 – 103
2:27–28 – 98
3:13–19 – 92
3:31, 35 – 94
4:10 – 92
5:18–19 – 92
6:34–44 – 97
7:1–13 – 105
7:1–23 – 98, 103
7:3–4 – 97
7:8 – 103
7:9–13 – 94, 132 n.14
7:21–22 – 98, 105

8:1–9, 14–21 – 97
10:1–12 – 103
10:2–9 – 94, 98
10:29–30 – 94
10:35–45 – 97
10:42 – 99
12:1–11 – 99
12:28 – 102
12:33 – 103
12:33, 34 – 97
13:9, 12 – 93
13:28, 30–31 – 88
13:32–37 – 88
14:22–25 – 97
16:8 – 93

Luke
4:18–19 – 96
6:1–5, 6–11 – 103
6:24 – 96
7:22 – 96
8:2–3 – 124
8:9–20 – 94
9:3 – 124
9:10–17 – 125
10:4–8 – 124
10:16 – 103
10:25–28 – 102
10:29–37 – 123
11:37–41 – 103
11:41 – 133 n.39
11:42 – 103
12:33 – 123, 133 n.39
12:42 – 125
13:10–17 – 103
13:15 – 103
14:16 – 103
16:9 – 133 n.39
16:14 – 123
16:15 – 123
16:16–17 – 132 n.25
16:18 – 103
18:18–30 – 123
18:22 – 133 n.39
18:28–30 – 94
19:1–10 – 123
19:8 – 133 n.39
22:24–27 – 126
22:36 – 124
24:41 – 100

Acts
1:8 – 88

2:41 – 100
2:44-45 – 124
3:25 – 100
4:4 – 100
4:32 – 124
4:35 – 124
5:1–11 – 125, 198
5:14 – 100
6:1 – 125
6:1, 7 – 100
6:2–6 – 125
6:11, 13, 14 – 102
6:14 – 103
9:42 – 100
10:14–16 – 103
10:43 – 100
11:3, 8 – 103
11:27–30 – 124
12:24 – 100
13:38–39 – 100
13:43 – 100
13:47 – 100
14:1 – 100
14:47 – 102
15:13–21 – 100
15:19–21 – 128, 198
15:20 – 101
15:20–21, 29 – 132 n.19
15:29 – 132 n.20
17:10–12 – 100
18:1–4, 21–24 – 125
18:13 – 102
20 – 133 n.40
21 – 133 n.40
21:20 – 100
21:21 – 103
21:21, 28 – 102
25:8 – 102
28:17 – 102, 103
28:30 – 125
28:31 – 89

Romans
1:18 – 3:20 – 138
1:24, 26–27 – 139
1:25 – 138
1:28–32 – 139, 162
2:1, 23 – 138
2:17–24 – 139
3:20 – 143
3:21–26 – 172 n.4
3:28–31 – 144
4:13–24 – 143

5:6–11 – 172 n.4
5:12–21 – 140
6 – 172 n.7
6:1 – 146
6:2–11 – 146
6:5–11 – 137
6:11 – 146
6:11, 12 – 180
6:12–14 – 147
7:7 – 143
7:10 – 143
7:12 – 143
7:13 – 143
7:13–24 – 139
8 – 140
8:2 – 140
8:19–21 – 172 n.6
10:4 – 140
11:17–18 – 153
11:18 – 153
11:25 – 157
11:28–29 – 157
13:1–7 – 166
13:8–10 – 142, 200
15:26–29 – 133 n.40

1 Corinthians
1:14–17 – 154
2:2–5 – 172 n.4
4:8 – 149
4:9–13 – 149
5:1–5 – 141
6:1–6 – 141
6:9–11 – 141, 162
6:12 – 141
7:1–11 – 161
7:4 – 162
7:8–9 – 161
7:12–16 – 161
7:15 – 161
7:16 – 163
7:17 – 160
7:18 – 154
7:19 – 154, 161
7:20 – 154
7:21–22 – 163
7:25–28 – 160
7:29–31 – 166
7:36–38 – 161
8 – 132 n.20
8:1 – 141
8:4 – 155
8:8 – 155

8:10–13 – 155
9:3–18 – 166
9:19 – 156
9:20–23 – 156
9:24–27 – 151
10:23 – 141
10:23–24 – 141
11:3 – 167
11:3–16 – 167
11:7 – 167
11:11–12 – 167
11:17–34 – 154
14:17 – 167
14:33b–36 – 167
14:35 – 167
15:3–11 – 172 n.4
15:24–28 – 88
15:45–50 – 140
16:1–4 – 133 n.40
17:17–24 – 160

2 Corinthians
3:18 – 137
4:7 – 149
4:11 – 149
5:14–17 – 172 n.7
5:16–21 – 172 n.4
8:1–5 – 133 n.40
9:1–5 – 133 n.40

Galatians
2:1–10 – 154
2:14b–16, 19–21 – 172 n.4
2:19–20 – 172 n.7
3:15–18 – 143
3:19 – 140, 143
3:28 – 162, 168
4:1–7 – 140
4:21–31 – 140
5:13 – 141, 145
5:17 – 145
5:18 – 145
5:19–21 – 145
5:19–24 – 195
5:24–25 – 172 n.7
6:5 – 141
6:10 – 141
6:14–15 – 172 n.7

Ephesians
5:21 – 165
5:22–33 – 165
5:22 – 6:8 – 165

Philippians
2:1–11 – 172 n.4
2:3–4 – 150
2:6–11 – 150
3:7, 8, 10 – 150
3:17 – 149

Colossians
3:18, 20, 22 – 165
3:18 – 4:1 – 165

1 Thessalonians
1:6–7 – 149

4:1 – 141
4:9 – 166
4:14–18 – 172 n.4

1 Timothy
2:8–15 – 172 n.10
2:11–15 – 167, 172 n.10
6:1–2 – 172 n.10

Titus
2:1–10 – 172 n.10

1 Peter
2:13 – 3:7 – 172 n.10

APOSTOLIC
WRITINGS

Didache
4:9–11 – 166

Barnabas
19:5–7 – 166

1 Clement
21:6–9 – 166